Modern International Law

An Introduction to the Law of Nations

James H. Wolfe

Department of Political Science
University of Southern Mississippi

Prentice Hall

Upper Saddle River, New Jersey 07458

Library of Congress Cataloging-in-Publication Data

Wolfe, James Hastings.
    Modern international law: an introduction to the law of nations / by James H. Wolfe.
      p. cm.
    Includes index.
    ISBN 0-13-017043-7
      1. International law. I. Title.

    KZ 3195.W65 A36 2002
    341—dc21

    2001021860

VP, Editorial Director: Laura Pearson
Senior Editor: Heather Shelstad
Editorial Assistant: Carmen Garcia-Prieta
Assistant Editor: Brian Prybella
Executive Managing Editor: Ann Marie McCarthy
Production Editor: Terry Routley/
   Carlisle Communications, Ltd.

Production Liaison: Frances Russello
Prepress and Manufacturing Buyer: Ben Smith
AVP, Director of Marketing: Beth Gillett Mejia
Art Director: Jayne Conte
Cover Designer: Bruce Kensclaar

This book was set in 10/12 Times Ten by Carlisle Communications, Ltd.
and printed and bound by Courier Companies, Inc.
The cover was printed by Phoenix Color Corp.

 © 2002 by Pearson Education, Inc.
Upper Saddle River, New Jersey 07458

Printed in the United States of America

10 9 8 7 6 5 4 3 2 1

ISBN 0-13-017043-7

Pearson Education LTD., London
Pearson Education Australia PTY, Limited, Sydney
Pearson Education Singapore, Ltd.
Pearson Education North Asia Ltd., Hong Kong
Pearson Education Canada, Ltd., Toronto
Pearson Education de Mexico, S.A. de C.V.
Pearson Education Japan, Tokyo
Pearson Education Malaysia, Pte. Ltd.
Pearson Education, Upper Saddle River, New Jersey

Contents

Preface

In the fall of 1998 an acquaintance with Prentice-Hall visited and inquired about my writing schedule. As we talked, the idea evolved that I might write a textbook in my primary field of interest—public international law. In over two decades of teaching the subject at two universities I had often wondered why I did not write a textbook. Colleagues have been kind enough to encourage me, and students offered their support. I soon found, however, that the project was like climbing a mountain. What began as a relatively straightforward endeavor soon proved to be a most demanding task. Now one understands why there are comparatively few textbooks in the field; the material is sometimes overwhelming. I have responded by trying to identify themes and developing these against a background of historical and legal examples. International law reflects the emergence of a post-Westphalian system based less on realpolitik and the balance of power and more on collaborative efforts to cope with such problems as political violence, environmental decay, and transnational criminality which threaten the existence of a world order. The discussion begins in the traditional mode with the international legal theories of John Marshall and John Austin and evolves into an analysis of an interdependent international system based on law and organization. Transition to a new style of international politics is the theme.

James Wolfe
Hattiesburg, Mississippi

Abbreviations

Diplomatic Correspondence

B.F.S.P.: *British Foreign and State Papers* (1806–).
F.R.U.S.: *Foreign Relations of the United States* (1861–).

Treaties and Statutes

Bevans' *Treaties: Treaties and Other International Agreements of the United States of America, 1776–1949,* ed. Charles I. Bevans (1968).
Grenville: *The Major International Treaties, 1914–1945,* ed. J.A.S. Grenville (1987).
Israel: *Major Peace Treaties of Modern History, 1648–1967,* ed. Fred L. Israel (1967).
Parry: *Consolidated Treaty Series,* ed. Clive Parry (1969).
Hurst: *Key Treaties for the Great Powers, 1814–1914,* ed. Michael Hurst (1972).
L.N.T.S.: *League of Nations Treaty Series* (1920–).
Malloy's *Treaties: Treaties, Conventions, International Acts, Protocols and Agreements between the United States of America and Other Powers, 1776–1909,* ed. William M. Malloy (1910) with a supplementary volume covering 1910–1923, ed. C.F. Redmond (1923).
Stat.: *United States Statutes at Large* (1789–).
U.N.R.I.A.A.: *United Nations Reports of International Arbitral Awards* (1948–).
U.N.T.S.: *United Nations Treaty Series* (1947–).
U.S.T.: *United States Treaties and Other International Agreements* (1950–) with the *Treaties and Other International Acts* (T.I.A.S.) series.

U.S. Department of State Digests

Hackworth: *Digest of International Law,* ed. Green Haywood Hackworth (1940).
Moore: *International Law Digest,* ed. John Bassett Moore (1906).
Nash: *Digest of United States Practice in International Law* (1974–1986) and *Cumulative Digest of United States Practice in International Law* (1981–1988), ed. Marian Nash (Leich) (1974–1995).
Whiteman: *Digest of United States Practice in International Law,* ed. Marjorie M. Whiteman (1963–1973).

Documents

Brownlie, *Documents: Basic Documents in International Law,* ed. Ian Brownlie, 3rd ed. (1983).
I.L.M.: *International Legal Materials,* American Society of International Law (1962–).
U.S. Foreign Policy: *Contemporary U.S. Foreign Policy: Documents and Commentary,* ed. Elmer Plischke (1991).

Reports of Judicial Proceedings

Fd 3rd: *Federal Reporter,* 3rd series (U.S. Circuit Courts).

F. Supp.: *Federal Supplement* (U.S. District Courts).

I.C.J. *Reports:* International Court of Justice, *Reports of Judgments, Advisory Opinions and Orders* (1949–).

I.L.R. *Reports: International Law Reports,* ed. E. Lauterpacht and C. J. Greenwood (New York: Oxford University Press, 1950–).

P.C.I.J. *Opinions: Collection of Advisory Opinions,* Series B: Permanent Court of International Justice, League of Nations (1920–1940).

P.C.I.J. *Reports: Annual Reports,* Series E: ibid. (1920–1940).

U.S.: *United States Reports: Official Reports of the Supreme Court* (1790–).

Casebooks

Bishop: *International Law: Cases and Materials,* comp. William W. Bishop, Jr., 3rd ed. (Boston: Little, Brown and Co., 1962).

Briggs: *The Law of Nations: Cases Documents, and Notes,* comp. Herbert W. Briggs, 2nd ed. (New York: Appleton-Century-Crofts, 1952).

Collins: *International Law in a Changing World: Cases, Documents, and Readings,* ed. Edward Collins, Jr. (1970).

Oliver: *Cases and Materials on the International Legal System,* comp. Covey T. Oliver et al. (Westbury, NY: Foundation Press, 1995).

Scott: *Cases on International Law,* ed. James Brown Scott and Walter H. E. Jaeger (1937).

Books and Monographs

Brierly, J. L.: *The Law of Nations,* revised by Humphrey Waldock, 6th ed. (1963).

Brownlie, Ian: *Principles of Public International Law,* 5th ed. (1998).

Fenwick, Charles G.: *International Law* (1934).

Green, N. A. Maryan: *International Law,* 3rd ed. (1987).

Hall, William Edward: *A Treatise on International Law,* 8th ed. (1924).

Hyde, Charles Cheney: *International Law Chiefly as Interpreted and Applied by the United States* (1922, 1983).

Kelsen, Hans: *Principles of International Law,* revised by Robert W. Tucker, 2nd ed. (1966).

Lauterpacht's Oppenheim: *Oppenheim's International Law: A Treatise,* 6th ed., revised by H. Lauterpacht (1947).

Malanczuk's Akehurst: *Akehurst's Modern Introduction to International Law,* 7th ed., revised by Peter Malanczuk (London: Routledge, 1997).

Nussbaum, Arthur: *A Concise History of the Law of Nations* (New York: Macmillan Co., 1954).

Shaw, Malcolm N.: *International Law,* 4th ed. (1997).

Slomanson, William R.: *Fundamental Perspectives on International Law,* 3rd ed. (2000).

Van Dervort, Thomas R.: *International Law and Organization* (1998).

Von Glahn, Gerhard: *Law among Nations: An Introduction to Public International Law,* 7th ed. (1996).

CHAPTER 1

Law of Nations

International law is not true law. Whenever a treaty is arbitrarily denounced or a diplomat held hostage, one invariably hears this assertion. Absent a world government, the environment of international politics is that of a loose anarchy. Observance of the law is voluntary, for no superior political authority exists to compel obedience. The counterargument is that interdependence increasingly characterizes the society of nations (*société des nations*), whose members recognize that now more than ever they need rules to regulate relations with each other. Without such rules, the diplomacy on which international politics depends could not take place. The lesson of necessity is age-old. For example, as early as 1269 B.C., Ramses II of Egypt concluded the first known treaty of friendship and cooperation with King Hattusili III of the Hittites.[1] The treaty highlighted the principle of reciprocity, which is the basis of modern international law.

SCHOOLS OF THOUGHT

Two contending schools of thought express the debate over the reality of international law: the naturalists and the positivists. A British jurist, Sir Henry Maine (1822–1888), argued that the Roman doctrine of *jus gentium,* a "law of nations" encompassing principles of law purportedly common to all peoples, provided a basis for the development of international law.[2] The *jus gentium* was the legal underpinning of the Roman peace— three centuries of enforced stability beginning with the Emperor Augustus (ruled 29 B.C. to A.D. 14). Complementing the *jus gentium* was the Roman doctrine of *jus naturale* (the law of nature), which recognized certain human rights, such as a right to life, as inherent. The naturalist school stands on two pillars: universally held principles of law and a philosophical commitment to human rights.

John Austin (1790–1859) represented the opposing school known as positivism.[3] Austin recognized the significance of positive morality as derived from the consent of those governed rather than imposed by those who govern, and he placed international law in the category of positive morality. True law, he continued, requires the enforcement of obedience by political authority. The legislative, executive, and judicial organs of state power must craft, enforce, and interpret statutes before a system of law can be

---

[1]United Nations, General Assembly, 25th Session, 1849th Meeting, 24 September 1970, *Official Records* (A/PV.1848), p. 17. Also see Baron S. A. Korff, "An Introduction to the History of International Law," *American Journal of International Law* 18 (April 1924): 249.

[2]Sir Henry Maine, *International Law* (London: John Murray, 1890), pp. 26–35. Also see his, *Ancient Law: Its Connection with Early History of Society, and Its Relation to Modern Ideas,* 4th ed. (London: John Murray, 1870), pp. 8–14 and 49–53.

[3]John Austin, *The Province of Jurisprudence Determined and the Uses of the Study of Jurisprudence* (London: John Murray, 1832; reprint ed., New York: Noonday Press, 1954), pp. 4–12 and 127. Also see W. Jethro Brown, *The Austinian Theory of Law* (London: John Murray, 1906), pp. 50–53.

said to exist. A system of law must have as its foundation a sense of political obligation capable of imbuing in individual citizens a respect for constitutional norms. Positive law is, therefore, a set of rules designed by political superiors for the management of society. Accordingly, the rules will evolve to meet the requirements of changing social conditions. To the positivist, the notion of enduring rights as manifested in the law of nature merits polite respect, but plays little role in the making of public policy.

POWER POLITICS AND THE LAW OF NATIONS

Classics often help to focus one's thinking on the essential questions of politics, and the chronicle of the Peloponnesian War (331–304 B.C.) by the Greek historian Thucydides is a premier example. In the epic struggle between the maritime empire of Athens and the autocratic land power of Sparta, the question of whether a government should determine policy on the basis of expediency or principle was in the forefront. Shortly before the outbreak of the war, diplomats from the rival states of Corcyra and Corinth debated before the Athenian assembly. The Corcyreans sought a military alliance with Athens and justified their case in geopolitical terms. Their argument was that Athens should break its treaty commitment to neutrality for the sake of expediency. The Corinthian rebuttal began with an appeal to justice backed by a reminder that Athens was obligated by treaty to remain aloof from the impending conflict. The Corinthians concluded that neutrality is "what Hellenic law entitles us to demand as a right."[4] Advocates of the thesis that legal norms count for little in the anarchy of international politics will point to the futility of the Corinthian argument and the subsequent intervention of Athens on the side of Corcyra.

The universality of the question of expediency or principle is demonstrated in the political writings of ancient India. In the fourth century B.C., the Hindu statesman Chanakya served his emperor during the invasion of India by Alexander of Macedon (321 B.C.) and later inspired wrote a classic manual on the organization of government. Using the pen name Kautilya ("suppleness of mind"), Chanakya drew upon a lifetime in politics to compile an encyclopedic study of statecraft entitled the *Science of Polity* (*Arthasastra*) in which he advanced the thesis that a successful foreign policy depends upon good government at home. Kautilya developed a mathematical model of the international system based on a core power known as the conqueror, who was confronted by four principal kings—the enemy state, the ally, the mediatory power, and the neutral state.[5] The mediatory power possessed the capability of overcoming both the conqueror and his enemy as compared with the neutral, who was too weak to intervene. The system maintained itself through a process of action and reaction within the framework of a balance of power, and Kautilya recognized the existence of rules governing state behavior. Today we would view these rules as international law.

---

[4]Thucydides, *The Peloponnesian War,* trans. John H. Finley, Jr. (New York: The Modern Library, 1951), p. 26.
[5]R. Shama Sastry (ed. and trans.), *Kautilya's Arthasastra* (Mysore: Mysore Printing and Publishing House, 1915 *et seq.*), books six and seven. For a discussion of international law in the Indian state system, see C. J. Chacko, "International Law in India: Ancient India," *The Indian Journal of International Law* 2 (January 1962); 48–64, Hiralal Chatterjee, *International Law and Inter-State Relations in Ancient India* (Calcutta: Firma K.L. Mukhopadhyay, 1958), and S. V. Viswanatha, *International Law in Ancient India* (Calcutta and London: Longmans, Green & Co., 1925).

The nature of sovereignty (legal personality), the sanctity of treaties, title to territory, alliance obligations, and permissible stratagems of war lent themselves to the formation of normative standards of state action in the Kautilyan system. Hindu statecraft recognized the interrelationship between international law and the governing principles of the international system. In Europe this awareness came centuries later with the creation of the balance-of-power system.

In view of the contributions of Thucydides and Kautilya, it is not surprising that the most widely held theory of international politics is realpolitik, which refers to a policy based on realistic calculations of state power. In the European tradition, the work of the Florentine Niccolò Machiavelli established the four premises of realism.[6] First, a flawed human nature responds to force and not reason. Politics is a struggle for dominance, and power is the arbiter. Second, the twin influences of geography and history endow each state with an overriding goal—a national interest—to which all else is subordinate. Third, diplomacy requires compromise and must not be limited by ties to such universal principles as natural rights. Fourth, society depends upon the survival of the state, and the state may do whatever is necessary to achieve that end. The doctrine of reason of state or *raison d'état* creates a moral imperative for those in power to do whatever is necessary to ensure the security of the state. In essence, the struggle for power creates its own morality. The Austinian notion of law as a code of positive morality set by the state has its roots in realpolitik. Is the existence of a legal norm dependent upon individual states? Positivist thought would seem to lead to such a conclusion, but the proposition is misleading. Whenever a new state comes into existence, it assumes, as a condition of statehood, the full range of rights and duties under international law. In practice, a government will tacitly recognize the principles of international law, although modern constitutions often make an explicit commitment to the rule of law.[7] For example, a government may announce that it is not bound by a specific rule, such as the twelve-mile limit of the territorial sea. Barring such a pronouncement, the presumption is that the standard limit applies.

Legal positivism and its concomitant of realpolitik stress the diversity of legal cultures. By comparison, the law of nature focuses on the unity of legal codes and leads to a body of thought which we may characterize as idealpolitik—the formulation of policy choices based on an idealistic view of world politics. The thrust of realist theory from Machiavelli to the present rejects such idealism as impractical and indeed delusionary. As propounded by Woodrow Wilson (1856–1924), idealism links democratic development at home with the establishment of world order abroad. Adherence to international law is the guarantor of representative government. Wilson identified three principles, which are the essence of idealism: (a) the right of every people to determine who shall govern them, (b) the sovereign equality of all states, great or small, with particular regard to their territorial integrity, and (c) an international order based on collective

---

[6]Niccolò Machiavelli, *The Prince,* trans. George Bull (New York: Penguin Books, 1961 *et seq.*). For a comparison of Machiavelli and Austin, see Anthony D'Amato, "The Relevance of Machiavelli to Contemporary World Politics," in *The Political Calculus: Essays on Machiavelli's Philosophy,* ed. Anthony Parel (Toronto: University of Toronto Press, 1972), pp. 217–224.

[7]Hans Kelsen, *Principles of International Law,* 2nd ed., revised by Robert W. Tucker (New York: Holt, Rinehart and Winston, 1966), pp. 576–578.

security against aggressors.[8] Idealpolitik presumes a linkage between domestic and international politics and assigns to international law an overarching mission of maintaining a world order conducive to the survival of constitutional and representative forms of government. Natural rights based on a universal *jus naturale* are the heart of Wilsonian idealism.

THE ECLECTIC APPROACH

Although seemingly irreconcilable, the positivism of realpolitik and the naturalism of idealpolitik do have a point of congruence, in that both schools of thought recognize the utility of international law in providing for the reciprocity so necessary for the orderly relations of states. In the modern period the founder of the eclectic movement was Huig de Groot (1583–1645), whose name is better known by its latinized version of Hugo Grotius. Published in 1625, the *Law of War and Peace* (*De jure belli ac pacis*) represents the full range of Grotius's thought, the key to which is his combination of the law of nature with the positive law of state sovereignty. Grotius began with the assumption that humankind constitutes a single great society bound together by a code of natural rights. Writing during the Thirty Years' War (1618–1648), Grotius understandably linked the law of nature to the use of force and devoted his attention to the theory of a just war. Only a sovereign may lawfully wage war and then in a just cause. Justice will lie with only one side, and not all wars are just.[9]

Grotius witnessed the breakup of the Christian commonwealth (*res publica christiana*) in Europe and its replacement by a patchwork of sovereign territorial states, whose governments steadfastly opposed the institutionalization of international law within a confederation of states. The thrust of Grotius's argument was that in their pursuit of realpolitik, heads of government ought to be constrained by their normative heritage in a law of nature.[10] To this extent Grotius reflected the transformation of international politics from the medieval to the modern period. In its emphasis on the pursuit of power in terms of the national interest, realpolitik stressed the centrality of the French doctrine of *raison d'état* (reason of state), which endowed with legitimacy those political actions undertaken in the interest of the state and for the good of the community. Thus the morality of state action would be measured against the test of survival through the acquisition of power at the expense of others. Grotius sought to counteract the notion of *raison d'état* by asserting that the exercise of reason leads to the conclusion that expediency as a guide for policy is a delusion, for even the most powerful of states requires the protection of treaties of alliance.[11] For Grotius, the law of nations derives its inspiration from the workings of the balance of power as well as the

---

[8]Woodrow Wilson, "Address before the League to Enforce Peace, May 27, 1916," in *Selected Literary and Political Papers and Addresses of Woodrow Wilson*, 3 vols. (New York: Grosset & Dunlap, 1926–27), 2:169–174.

[9]Hedley Bull, "The Importance of Grotius in the Study of International Relations," in *Hugo Grotius and International Relations*, ed. Hedley Bull et al. (Oxford: Clarendon Press, 1990), pp. 84–87.

[10]Richard Falk, "The Grotian Quest," in *International Law: A Contemporary Perspective*, ed. Richard Falk et al. (Boulder: Westview Press, 1985), pp. 37–39.

[11]Hugo Grotius, *Prolegomena to the Law of War and Peace*, trans. Francis W. Kelsey (Indianapolis: Bobbs-Merrill, 1957), par. 22 at p. 16. For the full text of the *Law of War and Peace* (1625), see Hugo Grotius, *De jure belli ac pacis*, in *Classics of International Law*, ed. James Brown Scott, no. 3 (Washington: Carnegie Institution, 1913).

tradition of the law of nature. The combination of political necessity and normative thought is the hallmark of the eclectic school.

Emmerich de Vattel (1714–1767), a diplomat and jurist of Swiss background, published his *Law of Nations (Le Droit des Gens)* in 1758. The work enjoyed the reputation of an authoritative text, as indicated by the fact that some seven editions were published in Philadelphia alone. Vattel built on Grotian theory by advancing the thesis that political society results from an acceptance of the law of nature, and that the "universal society of the human race" rests upon a mutual and reciprocal respect for individual rights.[12] Every government is obligated to contribute all that it lawfully can to the happiness of others, but this duty does not require a government to do an injury to itself in the defense of the law of nature. Therefore, a government may remain passive in the face of acts worthy of condemnation. Moreover, like individuals, states are equals, and each is enjoined to respect the liberty of others.

At this point Vattel introduced an essential distinction between the primary *natural* law of nations, which he categorized as "mere theory," and the secondary *positive* law of nations consisting of either custom or lawmaking treaties.[13] The distinction remains central to the contemporary study of international law. Customary law depends upon voluntary state practice creating an obligation on governments. The historical development of the law of the sea serves as an example. Positive law rests upon the conclusion of specific agreements establishing legal rights and obligations. The present-day codification of international law owes its origin to Vattel's classification of primary and secondary rules of law.[14] A note of caution: Vattel was not a positivist in the strict sense of the word, but his writing provided a basis for modern positivist thought and its concomitant of realpolitik. The framers of the U.S. Constitution drew heavily on Vattel's theory and made it the basis of the American approach to international law.

In his *The Concept of Law* (1961), H.L.A. Hart maintained Vattel's distinction between primary and secondary rules governing human behavior.[15] He began by acknowledging the existence of law in communities lacking well-differentiated structures for the administration of justice. A majority of the community accepts as binding the rule of custom, which is simply a way of doing things. Individuals have rights, but the social protection of these is uncertain. The aggrieved party is left to his or her own resources to defend these rights. Moreover, the definition of these rights is invariably vague and often so rooted in the past that it may no longer serve the needs of the society in question. Alternatively, those exercising social power may invent new rules by resorting to the practice of creating "instant" custom to bolster their control. The problems of law in developing societies parallel the weaknesses of customary law in international relations.

The solution Hart proposes is the elaboration of the primary rules of political obligation through the development of secondary rules, which create an authoritative basis for the administration of law. The secondary rules establish standards for recognizing

---

[12]Emmerich de Vattel, *The Law of Nations; or Principles of the Law of Nature Applied to the Conduct of Affairs of Nations and Sovereigns,* trans. Joseph Chitty, 7th ed. (Philadelphia: T. & J. W. Johnson, 1849), Preliminaries, sec. 10–13, pp. 50–51.

[13]Ibid., Preliminaries, sec. 21, pp. 53–54, note 7.

[14]Leo Gross, "The Peace of Westphalia, 1648–1948," in *International Law: Classic and Contemporary Readings,* ed. Charlotte Ku and Paul F. Diehl (Boulder: Lynne Riemer, 1998), pp. 67–68.

[15]H.L.A. Hart, *The Concept of Law* (New York: Oxford University Press, 1961), pp. 89–93.

breaches in the law and for the imposition of remedies. Especially important for the positivist tradition is the creation of structures capable of updating the law within a scientific paradigm designed to cope with the pressures of social change. In the setting of world politics, positive law represents the secondary rules needed to maintain the state system. The law of nature provides a starting point, but only positivism answers the question of subject status, sanctions, and source.[16] Modern international law has made significant advances in the identification of true subjects, the proportionate imposition of sanctions, and the development of rule-making bodies in the form of international organizations.

THE CONSTITUTION AND INTERNATIONAL LAW

The foregoing discussion of primary and secondary rules provides useful points of reference, but a meaningful clarification requires an historic case study of international law and the entry of a new state into the world system. By the Treaty of Paris (1783), Great Britain recognized the independence of the United States. Recognition of statehood meant that the United States had become a subject of international law and thereby acquired the rights and duties of a sovereign entity. A constitution was needed to answer the question of how international law would become a part of the legal system of the "New Republic". The delegates to the constitutional convention of 1787 recognized the need to establish a government capable of formulating and implementing an effective foreign policy, and the legal rights and duties of the young republic played a role in their deliberations. As a student of law, James Madison underlined the contribution of international law to American security, when he wrote in 1788 that the new government must make treaties, send and receive ambassadors, regulate foreign commerce, suppress piracy, and enforce the law of nations at sea.[17] Madison continued that the constitutional provision terminating the slave trade by 1808 was a victory for humanity although he wished that this prohibition had taken effect immediately. The appeal to the conscience of humankind to end the "unnatural traffic" which relegates individuals to the status of chattels was a precursor of the modern demand for the international protection of human rights.

The constitutional convention of 1787 opened with a consideration of rival plans advanced by New Jersey and Virginia. As different as these designs for a new government were, both recognized the role of the law of nations with reference to the negotiation and implementation of treaties. The conclusion was foregone that the power of foreign policy would be exclusive to the new federal government. The defense of the Republic's rights and the fulfillment of its obligations under international law would devolve upon the United States rather than the constituent states. The Constitution delegated to Congress the power

> To define and punish piracies and felonies committed on the high seas, and offences against the law of nations.[18]

---

[16]Nicholas G. Onuf, "Global Law-making and Legal Thought," in *Law-making in the Global Community,* ed. Nicholas G. Onuf (Durham: Carolina Academic Press, 1982), pp. 6–9.
[17]James Madison, "No. 42," in *The Federalist* (New York: Random House, 1937 *et seq.*), pp. 270–278.
[18]U.S. Constitution, art. 1, sec. 8, cl. 10.

The language of the international law clause is awkward. The reason lies in a last-minute editorial change made by the Committee on Style in the original text. As drafted by Madison, the clause initially read

> To define and punish piracies and felonies on the high seas, and punish offences against the law of nations.[19]

Gouverneur Morris of the Pennsylvania delegation called for the deletion of the second usage of the word *punish,* and the motion passed by a margin of one vote. James Wilson, also a delegate from Pennsylvania, objected that the amended wording would place Congress in the position of *defining* as well as *punishing* offenses against the law of nations. Such an arrogation of power would make the new republican government appear presumptuous in the eyes of the world. Presumably governments of civilized nations had through state practice succeeded in defining the law of nations. Morris responded by describing the law of nations as ". . . being often too vague and deficient to be a rule."[20] The exchange between Wilson and Morris was illustrative of the contending interpretations of international law. Implicit in Wilson's argument was a belief in principles of law common to all peoples—the *jus gentium.* These principles bound governments a priori, from the beginning of their existence. The doctrine of the law of nature is a premier example. Morris's position presaged the Austinian doctrine that the state must create law, and without state action one has only positive morality. International law, therefore, is a posteriori to the positive act of state. An editorial change shifted the meaning of the international law clause from naturalism to positivism, but the debate between the two schools of thought continued to mark the development of American constitutional thought.

Throughout the nineteenth century, the U.S. Supreme Court rendered pathbreaking decisions based on the principles of customary international law. The mastery of customary law requires a scholarly aptitude embracing the study of languages, history, and political theory as well as law. Following the constitutional convention, the separate states convened their individual conventions for the purpose of ratification. In the Virginia convention, James Madison played a key role and he again emphasized the criticality of the law of nations. He spoke of the necessity of a central government capable of upholding treaty commitments as the law of the land under the supremacy clause of Article VI. Pointing out that the word *piracy,* as it appears in the international law clause, is "a technical term of the law of nations," he insisted that an appeal to international law was preferable to relying upon precedents derived from the rulings of British courts.[21]

FOREIGN POLICY AND INTERNATIONAL LAW

As abstract as the debate between the naturalist and positivist schools may appear, diplomats seeking legitimization for their governments' policies frequently draw upon both arguments. The eclectic tradition of Grotius remains a fact of international political

---

[19]For the minutes covering this change, see Max Farrand, *The Records of the Federal Convention of 1787,* 4 vols. (New Haven: Yale University Press, 1937), 2:595, 610–615.

[20]James Madison, *Notes of Debates in the Federal Convention of 1787,* ed. Adrienne Koch (Athens: Ohio University Press, 1966), p. 637.

[21]*The Documentary History of the Ratification of the Constitution,* ed. John P. Kaminski and Gaspare J. Saladino, vol. 10, *Virginia* (Madison: State Historical Society of Wisconsin, 1993), pt. 3:1412–1413.

life. The foreign policy of the United States at its founding is illustrative. The French Revolution of 1789 signaled the beginning of a series of European wars pitting the French Republic against a coalition of powers led in the Atlantic and the Caribbean by England and Spain. Naval warfare in the seas adjacent to the United States threatened to ruin American seaborne commerce, and the administration of President George Washington responded by issuing a proclamation of neutrality on April 22, 1793.[22] Notably, the proclamation made a specific reference to the *law of nations* as its justification, thereby setting a precedent for small maritime states.

The following month Secretary of State Thomas Jefferson lodged a protest with the French ambassador over the seizure of the British ship *Grange* by a French warship patrolling within the waters of Delaware Bay.[23] Jefferson appealed to the law of nations and to immutable justice in support of his argument that the capture of the *Grange* within American territorial waters violated international law. Belligerent governments needed, however, to know the breadth of the Republic's territorial sea in order to define neutral waters within the scope of Washington's proclamation. Drawing upon customary international law, namely the effective range of a cannon ball, Jefferson informed the representatives of the powers that the authority of the president extends three nautical miles seaward from the coast.[24]

Jefferson's advisory letter based the policy of his government on the cannon-shot rule of Cornelius Van Bynkershoek, who published his authoritative work *Sovereignty over the Sea* (*De dominio maris*) in 1744 in Holland.[25] Edmund Randolph, the attorney general, added support by providing a legal opinion which ostensibly assessed the issues involved in the seizure of the *Grange,* but went far beyond to discuss the rights and duties of neutrals.[26] In his written opinion, Randolph made a specific reference to "the *necessary* or *natural* law of nations" and in doing so acknowledged the reality of what Hart would later regard as the primary rules on the basis of which international society exists. To buttress his argument, Randolph made references to the writings of Grotius and Vattel and thereby aligned himself with the eclectic tradition and its reliance upon the law of nature as well as positive law. Jefferson and Randolph demonstrated that the language of diplomacy presumed a role for international law in managing the relations of states.

The protection of neutral rights is critical for small states whose economy is dependent upon overseas trade. In its early years, the Republic had to cope with pirates and privateers, the latter being a form of legalized piracy carried on by private individuals commissioned by a belligerent power to raid enemy shipping in time of war. During the War of 1812, the U.S. Supreme Court ruled on several cases in which the issue

---

[22]Proclamation of Neutrality, 22 April 1793. *American State Papers: Foreign Relations* 1:148.

[23]Jefferson to Ternant, 15 May 1793, ibid., 2:147.

[24]Jefferson to Genet, 8 November 1793, ibid., 1:183. A similar note was sent to the British minister. See Henry G. Crocker, *The Extent of the Marginal Sea: Documents* (Washington: Government Printing Office, 1919), p. 636.

[25]Crocker, 14–15. See also Cornelius van Bynkershoek, *Quaestionum juris publici,*1737 (Questions of public law), trans Tenney Frank in *Classics of International Law,* ed. James Brown Scott (Oxford: Clarendon Press, 1930), chap. 8.

[26]*Official Opinions of the Attorneys General of the United States: 1789–1974,* 42 vols., vol. 1: *1789–1825* (Washington: Robert Farnham, 1852), pp. 32–38.

was a claim to real or alleged enemy goods seized on the high seas. In these instances the Court appealed to principles of customary international law as the basis for its decisions.

Two cases involving the rights of neutrals in the Anglo-American naval war (1812–1815) illustrate the importance of the law of nations. The first dealt with a shipment of sugar which a Danish citizen had consigned to a British vessel. An American privateer seized the British merchantman on the high seas and claimed the cargo as a lawful prize of war. Writing for the Court, Chief Justice John Marshall restored the sugar to its original owner on the grounds that Denmark was a neutral, and the property of its citizens was immune to seizure. Marshall also took the opportunity to advance the following maxim:

> The law of nations is the great source from which we derive those rules respecting belligerent and neutral rights, which are recognized by all civilized and commercial states throughout Europe and America.[27]

In a parallel decision, Marshall upheld the rule of protecting neutral property even though the carrier was a vessel of a belligerent state. A British ship on route from London to Buenos Aires was taken by an American privateer and its cargo condemned. A Spanish citizen whose goods were on board appealed to the Court for restitution, which was granted. Again, the chief justice took the occasion to articulate the principle that ". . . the Court is bound by the law of nations which is a part of the law of the land."[28] Notably Marshall referred to Vattel as an authority. In doing so he acknowledged the existence of international law, whose rules courts of the United States were constitutionally obligated to enforce. At this point the law of nations ceased to be an abstraction in American jurisprudence and became a source of public policy.

The Constitution identified piracy as an international crime, and Congress enacted statutes in 1790 and 1819 defining the offense of piracy and setting the penalty for its commission.[29] In 1820, the Supreme Court rendered four decisions on cases of piracy.[30] In each instance the Court found it necessary to go beyond the text of the statute (black letter law) and to invoke principles of customary international law.[31] Justice Joseph Story authored the opinion in one of the three cases (*U.S. v. Smith*) and wrote that ". . . the pirate is the common enemy of all."[32] In advancing this argument, Story laid the basis for the prosecution of war criminals and others who have committed crimes against humanity. If the pirate is an international felon against whom all civilized governments should unite, then so is the dictator who relies upon terror as a means of keeping himself in power. Story developed his thesis in an extensive

---

[27]*Thirty Hogsheads of Sugar (Bentzon) v. Boyle,* 13 U.S. (9 Cranch) 191, 197 (1815). See also Gerhard von Glahn, *Law Among Nations: An Introduction to Public International Law,* 7th ed. (Boston: Allyn and Bacon, 1996), p. 19.

[28]*The Nereide,* 13 U.S. (9 Cranch) 388, 423 (1815).

[29]*Statutes at Large* 1 (1845): 112–113, and ibid., 3 (1846): 510.

[30]*U.S. v. Klintlock,* 18 U.S. (5 Wheaton) 144 (1820), *U.S. v. Smith,* ibid., 153 (1820), *U.S. v. Furlong et al.* (Pirates) ibid., 184, (1820), *U.S. v. Holmes,* ibid., 412 (1820).

[31]For a discussion of the relationship of international law to the pirate cases, see Thomas Langdon Bell, "The War Powers Resolution of 1973: National Legislation as International Law," *California Western International Law Journal* 15 (Winter 1985): 96–97.

[32]Story quotes the Roman jurist Cicero in *U.S. v. Smith,* 18 U.S. (5 Wheaton) note 4.

discourse on the duties of governments everywhere to pursue and prosecute those who commit offenses against the law of nations. To support his position he drew upon a broad range of sources including historic examples of state practice as well as the writings of such authorities as Grotius and Vattel.

The legal definition of piracy became in 1841 a key issue in a Supreme Court case involving the slave trade. West Africans forced into slavery had seized control of the Spanish ship *Amistad* on which they were being transported to the Caribbean. Being unfamiliar with navigation, they were unable to set a course homeward and eventually landed on Long Island, New York. The owners of the ship brought a charge of piracy against the enslaved Africans, and the Supreme Court heard the case on appeal. Writing for the Court, Justice Story concluded that the Africans were not pirates ". . . in the sense of the law of nations."[33] Reliance upon the law of nations secured the return to freedom of those who had been abducted into slavery. The case of the *Amistad* foretold the coming contribution of international law to the protection of human rights.

State practice had long condemned piracy as a felony, and the Supreme Court's activist response to this public delict was both expected and appropriate. A related issue under the law of nations is the legal effect of treaties in the Republic. Treaty law presents a complex constitutional issue because the interpretation of international agreements affects the boundaries between the Court and the political branches of government. In 1803, the United States acquired the province of Louisiana from France, and sixteen years afterward Spain relinquished claim to East and West Florida, the latter included the ports of Mobile and Pensacola. Individual titles to land were often clouded by imprecise grants from colonial governors, and Congress assigned the responsibility of ruling on the resultant disputes to the Supreme Court.[34]

In 1829, the Court issue a precedential decision on the validity of colonial land titles, and Chief Justice Marshall took the opportunity to write an extended opinion on the role of treaties under the Constitution.[35] The decision established two principles. First, a treaty is a contract between nations and therefore represents a binding commitment between two sovereign states. Second, although the Constitution recognizes a treaty as the law of the land and the equivalent of a legislative act, certain treaties require acts of Congress to implement them.[36] Nevertheless, the need for supplementary legislation does not weaken the constitutional position of an individual treaty. Through the treaty power, the federal government can incorporate into U.S. law the principles of the law of nations.

As the decision in *Foster v. Neilson* enhanced the role of international law in American jurisprudence, so, too, did the requirements of the maritime strategy to which the founders of the Republic were committed.[37] Writing in 1826, James Kent, a former chief judge of the Supreme Court of the State of New York, addressed the question of jurisdiction over waters adjacent to the coast of the Republic. He accepted the cannon-shot rule advocated by Jefferson for the exercise of maritime sovereignty, but he went a step further and argued that for purposes of customs and defense the United States

---

[33]*U.S. v. The Amistad*, 40 U.S. (15 Peters) 518, 594 (1841).
[34]As late as 1998, federal courts confronted a suit arising out of a 1781 Spanish land grant in West Florida. See *U.S. v. Beggerly*, 524 U.S. 38 (1998).
[35]*Foster v. Neilson*, 27 U.S. (2 Peters) 253 (1829).
[36]U.S. Constitution, art. 6, par. 2.
[37]Alexander Hamilton, "No. 11," in *The Federalist* (New York: Random House, 1937 *et seq.*), pp. 62–69.

should have a broad zone of jurisdiction over coastal seas. For example, he proposed drawing a line from Key West, Florida, to the Mississippi delta, within which U.S. law would serve to secure the Gulf coast, especially in time of war. In this regard the English "hovering" acts (1736), whereby agents of the crown could board and seize a ship deemed to be a threat in the narrow seas around Great Britain, provided a useful precedent.[38] As with preceding constitutional theorists, Kent followed the eclectic approach of Vattel combining a belief in the law of nature with an understanding of the need for positive law.

Henry Wheaton (1785–1848), an American diplomat and a contemporary of Kent, wrote an influential commentary on international law, first published in 1836. In the tradition of Vattel, Wheaton began with the concept of a law of nature, which he defined as those rules of justice recognized as necessary for the governance of human conduct. Based on either state practice (i.e., custom) or lawmaking treaties, positive law served to protect natural rights. While the law of nature is a given, positive law is voluntary and may be adapted to meet changing conditions.[39] As a U.S. representative in European capitals, Wheaton regarded the notion that his government could distance itself from the international legal community as unthinkable. Necessity was the most persuasive argument for acceptance of the law of nations.

Adhering to the principle of necessity, Francis Lieber, a professor of law at Columbia University, developed in 1868 a theory of interdependence, which he defined as an "all-pervading law" essential to the formation of national and international society.[40] For Lieber, membership in the "commonwealth of nations" required a positive commitment to upholding international law. A qualified acceptance of international legal norms was untenable.

Throughout the formative years of the Republic, jurists, writing in both a public and private capacity, creatively interpreted the Constitution against a background of international law. Melville Fuller (1833–1910) served as chief justice during the Spanish-American War (1898) and established a reputation as an arbiter of international law disputes, his services being called upon by France (1905) and Great Britain (1899).[41] In 1900, the Supreme Court was again called upon to render a decision based on principles of international law evolved from state practice. Justice Horace Grey wrote the opinion for the majority, in which he concluded that in time of war fishing vessels were immune from seizure by belligerent navies. Despite dissent, Grey's dictum summarizes the historic position of the role of international law in American jurisprudence:

> International law is part of our law, and must be ascertained and administered by the courts of justice.[42]

---

[38]James Kent, *Commentaries on American Law,* 4 vols. (New York: William Kent, 1848), 1:29–30. Also see Charles Cheney Hyde, *International Law Chiefly as Interpreted by the United States,* 2 Littleton, Co.: Fred B. Rothman, 1983), 1:417–418.

[39]Henry Wheaton, *Elements of International Law* (1836), no. 19 in *Classics of International Law,* ed. James Brown Scott (Oxford: The Clarendon Press, 1936), pp. 2–13.

[40]Francis Lieber, *Nationalism and Internationalism* (New York: Charles Scribner & Co., 1868), pp. 20–23. For a modern interpretation of interdependence, see Robert O. Keohane, Jr. and Joseph S. Nye, *Power and Interdependence,* 2nd. ed. (Reading, MA.: Addison-Wesley Educational Publ., 1989).

[41]George G. Wilson, *Hague Arbitration Cases* (Boston: Ginn and Co., 1915; reprint ed. Littleton, CO.: Fred B. Rothman, 1990), pp. 64–67.

[42]*The Paquette Habana, The Lola,* 175 U.S. 677, 700.

TURNABOUT?

The framers of the Constitution cited the works of Grotius and Vattel as evidence that membership in the international community required adherence to the laws of nations. Leading justices of the Supreme Court presumed the mandatory character of international law and rendered decisions consistent with it. Publicists such as Kent, Wheaton, and Lieber argued the case for international law in their commentaries. The record is clear and unbroken.

In 1984, Nicaragua turned to the International Court of Justice and instituted a suit alleging that its territorial integrity had been violated by a secret war waged on behalf of the United States.[43] After extended litigation, during which the United States contested the jurisdiction of the Court, a judgment was rendered in favor of Nicaragua. By direction of the president, Secretary of State George Shultz then notified the secretary general of the United Nations that the United States had withdrawn its 1946 commitment to accept the compulsory jurisdiction of the Court.[44] Hereinafter the United States would agree to litigate cases before the Court only on the basis of reciprocity, that is, a mutual acceptance of the same rules and obligations. Essentially, U.S. participation would be limited to commercial or boundary disputes. By comparison, the tradition of Madison and Marshall was one compliance with the law of nations as a matter both of justice and necessity. Over the long run such adherence would enhance the prestige of the Republic and secure its place in the international community. The decision to limit the role of the International Court of Justice placed expediency before principle, thereby mitigating an established American constitutional doctrine.

Topics for Discussion

1. Naturalist and positivist interpretations of international law differ in their emphasis on the role of the state. For what reason do they differ? What is the relationship of the individual to the state under each theory?
2. Why does a newly recognized state proclaim its allegiance to international law? Lacking influence in world politics, will an emergent state link its diplomacy to international law?
3. Despite the absence of a common authority capable of enforcing international law, most governments adhere to it in the administration of their foreign policy. Why? What short- or long-term motives support such adherence?
4. American jurisprudence emphasizes the interdependence of constitutional democracy and international law. Are authoritarian regimes just as likely or are they less likely to uphold the principles of international law?

---

[43]*Case Concerning Military and Paramilitary Activities in and Against Nicaragua (Nicaragua v. United States of America)*, International Court of Justice, 1984, (1984) *I.C.J. Reports* 392.
[44]U.S. Department of State, "U.S. Terminates Acceptance of ICJ Compulsory Jurisdiction: Secretary's Letter to U.N. Secretary General, Oct. 7, 1985," *Bulletin* 86 (January 1986): 67.

CHAPTER 2

Law and the International System

Jeremy Bentham (1748–1832), an English political theorist, is credited with the introduction of the phrase *international law* in place of *law of nations*.[1] The revised wording was more than a matter of style, for the transition signaled a new phase in the role of law in world politics. Hitherto, the law of nations meant those rules established by sovereigns to regulate their relations with one another. Over time, state practice created the customary law needed to facilitate orderly relations between governments jealous of their independence. By contrast, Bentham's use of international law added a normative dimension and made the sovereign personally culpable for violations of the law. The resort to war, for example, was limited by the principle of the "least possible evil" in relation to the good which might result. Law should ensure the greatest happiness to all. Sovereigns who violated that rule would be held accountable, and Bentham did not hesitate to describe their conduct as "criminal." Proponents of a permanent international criminal court may well borrow from his text.

MONISM AND DUALISM

If international law does act directly on the individual, it must be part of a universal system. The doctrine that principles of law—whether national or international—constitute a single body of rules is monism. In discussing the law of nature, Vattel emphasized the centrality of those rights inherent in the individual prior to entering into political society. In return for obedience, the state has the duty to uphold these rights, and a failure to do so severs the bond of political obligation. The Declaration of Independence is eloquent on this point. The monist concludes that natural rights require a holistic approach to legal obligations, which must be considered in their totality and not reduced to component parts. The concept of natural right embedded in universal law is the basis of monist theory.

The logic of monism rests on the assumption that the human desire for order requires a fusion of international and national legal codes, the latter being termed municipal law. For example, the United Nations Convention against Torture (1984) codified the law proscribing the resort to physical and mental duress as a matter of state policy. Monists insist that the ban on torture must be universal, for international law

---

[1] Jeremy Bentham, "Principles of International Law," in *The Works of Jeremy Bentham,* ed. John Bowring (New York: Russell and Russell, 1962), 2:535–560. See also Thomas Barclay, "International Law" in *The Encyclopedia Britannica,* 13th ed. (1926), 14:694–701.

cannot condemn an activity which then might be permitted under municipal law. The conviction that general international law functions as a constitution governing the community of states is the foundation of monism.[2]

The opposing point of view is dualism. Dualistic theory postulates that international and municipal law are two interrelated, but separate legal codes. Only municipal law acts upon the individual, and the effectiveness of international law depends exclusively on enforcement by a sovereign state. Specifically, the Convention against Torture as cited will only take effect in a given state when its government enacts enabling legislation and demonstrates a willingness to enforce the same. Otherwise the ban on torture is limited to a moral imperative.

Dualists highlight three points in support of their argument. First, they stress that the source of municipal law derives from statutes enacted by national legislatures, while international law reflects inchoate custom and state practice. Second, municipal law is hierarchical in its governance of relations among persons, and international law regulates the ties between sovereign and equal states comprising the international community. Third, municipal law possesses a broad scope as manifested in the power of the state, yet international law applies to a relatively narrow range of transactions among states.[3] For these reasons, dualists insist that municipal law and international law, while they are related, serve different purposes and should not be considered as part of the same system.

FILARTIGA AND PINOCHET

As abstract as the issues surrounding monism and dualism may appear, two proceedings illustrate the practical importance of the debate for the administration of justice. In 1979, Dolly Filartiga, a citizen of Paraguay living in the United States under a grant of political asylum, instituted a suit in a federal court against Americo Norberto Peña-Irala, a Paraguayan temporarily residing in Brooklyn, New York. The plaintiff claimed damages and charged that the defendant had, as a police official in Asunción, Paraguay, been responsible for the death by torture of her seventeen-year-old brother, Joel. Since both parties to the suit were citizens of Paraguay and the offense had been committed there, the issue was one of whether the courts of the United States possessed jurisdiction. The district court ruled that it lacked a statutory basis for hearing the case, but the court of appeals reversed that decision.[4] The reasoning for the reversal is central to understanding the relationship of municipal to international law.

As a basis for his ruling, the circuit judge revisited the opinions of Justices Marshall and Story in the cases involving both the questions of neutral rights and piracy. These

---

[2]A leading advocate of the monist school is Hans Kelsen, especially in his earlier writings. See the first edition of *Principles of International Law* (New York: Rinehart and Co., 1952), pp. 303–305, 404. Arthur Nussbaum has interpreted Kelsen's theory of law as that of a hierarchy with international law at the top and administrative law at the base in his *A Concise History of the Law of Nations,* rev. ed. (New York: Macmillan Co., 1954), p. 280.

[3]Lassa Oppenheim, *International Law: A Treatise,* vol. 1, *Peace,* 6th ed., ed. Hersh Lauterpacht (London: Longmans, Green and Co., 1947), pp. 34–37. Also Malcolm N. Shaw, *International Law,* 4th ed. (Cambridge: At the University Press, 1997), pp. 100–101.

[4]*Dolly M.E. Filartiga et al. v. Americo Norberto Peña-Irala,* Second Circuit Court of Appeals, 630 F. 2nd, 876 (1980).

decisions set a precedent to the effect that even when Congress had not enacted a relevant statute, federal courts were obligated under the Constitution to punish offenses against the law of nations.

Like piracy and the slave trade, the use of torture had become an offense against the law of nations. State practice reinforced by such resolutions of the United Nations General Assembly as the Universal Declaration of Human Rights (1948) condemned torture and governments everywhere incurred an obligation to punish those who employed it, irrespective of whether the perpetrators held official positions. Accordingly, Peña-Irala could be sued under the broad terms of the Alien Tort Statute (1948).[5]

Filartiga demonstrated a commitment to uphold the law of nations even in the absence of a statutory definition of torture as an international offense.[6] Beginning with the Judiciary Act (1789), Congress had sought to incorporate the standards of customary international law into the administration of justice by federal courts.[7] The *Pinochet* case involved an extradition hearing in Great Britain. British jurisprudence requires a grant of authority—usually an act of parliament—before an offense against international law becomes justiciable. Courts will take cognizance of international law only when empowered to do so by municipal law. Municipal and international law must be mutually supporting, which is the essence of dualism. The verdict in *Filartiga* proclaimed the universality of international law and implied an acceptance of monism.

For seventeen years starting in 1973, General Augusto Pinochet exercised dictatorial power over Chile. In the course of consolidating its control, his regime employed torture and execution in what is sometimes referred to as a "dirty" war. After having retired from politics, Pinochet visited London in October 1998 only to find himself detained by the British police acting in response to a request for extradition. A Spanish investigative magistrate, Baltasar Garzòn, had amassed evidence to the effect that many of the victims of state terror in Chile were Spaniards. Accordingly, he initiated proceedings to secure the extradition of Pinochet to Spain, where he would be placed on trial for crimes against humanity.[8] In London, Pinochet's counsel argued that the defendant as a former chief of state and member of the Chilean Senate possessed sovereign immunity. The case progressed through British courts until it reached the House of Lords. After two sequential hearings before separate panels, seven law lords ruled on March 24, 1999, that Pinochet could not claim immunity and was therefore liable for extradition. The home secretary determined, however, that Pinochet's health was so fragile that he could not stand trial, and on March 2, 2000, Pinochet returned to Chile.

The ruling by the law lords stipulated that the putative extradition could only be based on charges that violated both British and Spanish law. On September 29, 1988, a new criminal justice act, revised to encompass Great Britain's adherence to the Convention against Torture, took effect. Allegations of the use of torture prior to that date were not covered by British law and consequently were not extraditable. In sum,

---

[5]The statute does not mention damages resulting from torture at the hands of an official. The use of the general term *tort* could refer only to a liability for injury. See 62 Stat.: 934

[6]Notably, the Convention against Torture and Other Cruel, Inhuman or Degrading Treatment or Punishment (1984) *entered into force* in the United States on November 20, 1994, fourteen years after the decision in *Filartiga*.

[7]An Act to establish the Judicial Courts of the United States (September 24, 1789), 1 Stat. 73, 77.

[8]The governments of France and Switzerland also indicated that they would apply for extradition because of crimes committed against their citizens.

dualism requires that municipal law give force to international legal norms. In *Filartiga,* the appellate court relied upon customary international law (often referred to as federal common law), thereby implicitly endorsing monism.

WORLD ORDER

Beginning with the Age of the Enlightenment, political theorists have advanced plans for international conciliation to limit the resort to war as an instrument of policy. William Penn, a Quaker leader and founder of Pennsylvania, proposed in 1692 the formation of a European confederation whose parliament would impose compulsory arbitration on disputing governments.[9] Basing his grand design on the triumph of reason over aggressive behavior, Penn advocated a democratic solution to the problem of anarchy and its concomitant war. In this respect he foresaw the formation of today's European Union, among whose members war is no longer an option. Peace has become a matter of necessity rather than a far-fetched utopian vision.

The contemporary world order school builds both upon Bentham's belief in rational decisions formulated to maximize benefits and minimize costs for all and upon Penn's approach to structural engineering as a means of solving problems. Accepting these premises counters the notion that only power matters in world politics. Philosophical as well as pragmatic considerations serve to modify an absolute reliance upon power politics. Norms represent a commitment to standards of right reason and to concomitant rules of behavior. For example, the right to life is a norm, and the governing rule is the ban on torture.

Norms and rules encourage predictability in decision making and contribute to the formation of international society.[10] The addition of institutions to norms and rules creates a legal regime.[11] The growth of regimes imposes restraints on the actions of states and compels a revision of the belief that politics is a primordial struggle for power.

The same desire for order which leads individuals to form civil society manifests itself in the creation of international regimes. The list of universal problems is impressive, including as it does arms control, environmental protection, public health, resource allocation, and terrorism. To cope with these challenges governments must establish a pattern of stable relationships which constitute a system comprising both structure and process. Necessity requires policymakers to accept constraints on their action.[12] Such constraints limit the competition for power to the extent that even advocates of realpolitik acknowledge the value of cooperation, for without it the system would produce less than satisfactory outcomes for its members. With cooperation, the collectivity may indeed respond effectively to global needs.[13]

---

[9]William Penn, *Essay towards the Present and Future Peace of Europe,* Library of American Civilization (Boston: Old South Leaflets, 1912), microfiche, 3:5–6.

[10]Friedrich V. Kratochwil, *Rules, Norms, and Decisions: On the Conditions of Practical Legal Reasoning in International Relations and Domestic Affairs* (New York: Cambridge University Press, 1989), pp. 7–13.

[11]See Stephan Haggard and Beth A. Simmons, "Theories of International Regimes," *International Organization* 41 (Summer 1987): 491, 493.

[12]Robert O. Keohane, "The Demand for International Regimes," in *International Regimes,* ed. Stephen D. Krasner, *International Organization* (special issue) 36 (Spring 1982): 325, 327.

[13]Baldev Raj Nayar, "Regimes, Power, and International Aviation," *International Organization* 49 (Winter 1995): 139, 143.

A COMPARATIVE NOTE

The antipodal concepts of monism and dualism may be matched with those of naturalism and positivism. A comparison of concepts may be too general, but it does help to place them in perspective. Four combinations exist:

  a. Naturalism and monism. The philosophical tradition of international law conforms to this pairing. Following the Declaration of Independence, individuals are endowed with natural and therefore inalienable rights. Universal law exists to protect these rights, and these norms take precedence over whatever guarantees may exist in national codes of municipal law.

  b. Naturalism and dualism. In this instance natural rights receive recognition only to the extent that they are defined in municipal law and upheld in the courts of the country in question. The dualist may respect the ideal of natural law but will apply it solely within the context of statutes enacted by a sovereign authority. Municipal law remains coordinate with and not subordinate to international law.

  c. Positivism and monism. The aforementioned observation of Gouverneur Morris at the Constitutional Convention (1787) applies. Morris categorized universal norms as too vague to be a basis for state action, hence the constitutional requirement that Congress define and punish offenses against the law of nations. The legislative branch has incumbent upon it the duty of upholding world law. Justices Marshall and Story took the argument one step further and assigned to the judicial branch the responsibility for implementing international legal norms even if the necessary statutes had not been enacted. The decision in *Filartiga* is illustrative of the point.

  d. Positivism and dualism. This combination is widely accepted in contemporary world law because it appears to reinforce the freedom of action of the sovereign state. Positivism implies a notion of realism, which rejects a transcendent notion of world justice in favor of legal engineering by the state. Dualism gives municipal law priority over the normative standards of customary international law, which may condemn torture, but the condemnation lacks legal force until a specific statute is in effect. The decision of the House of Lords in the *Pinochet* case reflects this point of view.

CASE LAW IN PERSPECTIVE

Judicial outcomes often clarify abstract principles and serve to give meaning to broad concepts of international law. In 1796, the U.S. Supreme Court invoked the principles of international law to decide an appeal for debt relief in the case of *Ware v. Hylton*. The issue was that of state practice regarding the sanctity of treaties. The Anglo-American Treaty of Paris (1783) ended the Revolution and recognized the independence of the United States. As the effective government of the new republic, the Continental Congress approved the treaty in accordance with its procedure of consensus among delegations from the confederated states. Article 4 committed the treaty partners to a policy of reciprocity, whereby neither would interfere with the collection of debts owed by the citizens of one signatory to those of the other. The indebtedness of an American to a British creditor could not be forgiven, whatever the laws of a state, in this case Virginia, may say to the contrary. In his opinion, Justice

James Wilson described a treaty as a "... supreme law, which overrules state laws on the subject." His basic premise is noteworthy:

> When the United States declared their independence, they were bound to receive the law of nations, in its modern state of purity and refinement.[14]

Nineteen years later in his decision in *The Nereide* case, Chief Justice Marshall affirmed this opinion, when he asserted that "... the court is bound by the law of nations, which is part of the law of the land."[15] Neither Justices Wilson nor Marshall hesitated to rely upon international law as a basis for judicial decisions even in the absence of an enabling law enacted by Congress. Their view of international law was monist, and adherence to this interpretation enabled the Court to render precedential decisions in its early years.

A decision rendered by the Scottish Court of Session in 1906 was predicated on the dualist approach and illustrates the difference in legal reasoning which separates monism from dualism. Scottish authorities had arrested Emmanuel Mortensen, a citizen of Denmark and the captain of a fishing vessel registered in Norway, for an illegal method of trawling within the territorial waters of the Moray Firth—a large bay on the North Sea coast. The charge against Mortensen was that he had violated, among others, the Herring Fishery (Scotland) Act of 1889 as well as implementing regulations. Having been convicted in the Sheriff Court of the first instance, Mortensen appealed the verdict of a fine or imprisonment not exceeding sixty days. A full bench of thirteen justices heard the appeal.

Two questions framed the case. First, was Mortensen liable under Scottish law? Second, did Scottish authorities possess jurisdiction in the area of the sea in which Mortensen was trawling? The first question answers itself, in that a citizen and a foreign national alike are bound by the laws of the state, in this case Great Britain. The second question is the more difficult, for international law and state practice regarding maritime boundaries vary. Great Britain and Denmark, but not Norway, were parties to the North Sea Fisheries Convention (1882), under which trawlers of the coastal states were guaranteed equal access to fishing grounds outside of territorial waters (i.e., a belt of the sea adjacent to the coast). A bay like the Moray Firth could be enclosed within territorial waters by drawing a closing line no greater than ten miles in length from headland to headland. The legal principle was known as territorial waters *intra fauces terrae* (the sea between the extensions of land forming a harbor or bay), but the Herring Fishery Act extended the jurisdiction of local authorities over a greater expanse of the sea. Counsel for Mortensen argued that the unilateral extension of jurisdiction over coastal waters violated international custom and the defendant's rights as a Danish citizen under the North Sea Fisheries Convention.

The court, however, upheld the earlier conviction with the argument that Scottish law had established regulations governing the fishing industry. These regulations did not bar fishing vessels from other states, but rather banned practices which would impose a hardship on the local economy. While the concept of environmental protection had yet to be introduced, the judgment of the court reflected this concern. The issue was not Mortensen's treaty right to fish, but the unlawfulness of his indiscriminate method

---

[14]*Ware (Jones) v. Hylton,* 3 U.S. (3 Dallas) 199, 281–282 (1796).
[15]*The Nereide,* 13 U.S. (9 Cranch) 423 (1815).

of trawling. Scottish authorities possessed the right, indeed the duty, to institute measures to protect fishing grounds. The principle was of such significance that the case was heard by a full bench in order to underline the importance of the precedent.

The historic doctrine of freedom of the seas posed an apparent problem for the court. Was the claim of regulating the fishing industry beyond the accepted standard of the cannon-shot rule of three miles in violation of customary international law? Lord Dunedin, lord president of the court, responded as follows:

> It is a trite observation that there is no such thing as a standard of international law extraneous to the domestic law of a kingdom, to which appeal may be made. International law, so far as this Court is concerned, is the body of doctrine regarding rights and duties of states which has been adopted and made part of the law of Scotland.[16]

The statement is a clear-cut exposition of dualism. International law exists, but only when it is defined within the framework of municipal law. The argument made by Marshall in *The Nereide* and Wilson in *Ware* to the effect that courts of the United States are obligated, even in the absence of enabling legislation, to punish offenses against the law of nations stands in sharp contrast to the decision in *Mortensen* whereby a court could act only on the basis of statutory authorization.

In a more contemporary vein, the dualist position undergirds the decision of the Court of Appeals in Great Britain in the *Post Office v. Estuary Radio, Ltd.* (1967 case). As in the case of *Mortensen,* the issue was one of the extent of the government's jurisdiction over marginal seas. The defendants operated an unlicensed radio station situated on an outcropping off the North Sea coast of England. The licensing authority (the post office) argued successfully that the site of the radio transmitter was within the territorial sea, specifically that a series of low tide elevations (i.e., dry land above water except at high tide) provided a basis for extending the legal limits of the coast seaward to encompass the site of Estuary Radio.

The court delivered its ruling based on the terms of the Geneva Convention on the Territorial Sea and the Contiguous Zone (1958) as implemented by the Territorial Waters Order in Council (1964). The Order in Council provided the statutory authority for the decision, and the text of the order took precedence whenever it differed from that of the Geneva Convention. Writing for the court, Lord Diplock stated regarding the Order in Council:

> If its meaning is clear we must give effect to it even if it is different from that of the Convention, for the Crown *may* have changed its mind in the period which elapsed between its ratification of the Convention on Mar. 14, 1960, and the promulgation of the Order in Council, and the Crown has a sovereign right, which the court cannot question, to change its policy even if this involves breaking an international convention to which it is a party and which has come into force so recently as fifteen days before.[17]

Under dualism, municipal law is the dominant authority, and the court must defer to it even at the risk of violating an international commitment.

---

[16]*Mortensen v. Peters,* 8 Court of Sessions (S.C.) 93, 101 (1906).

[17]*Post Office v. Estuary Radio, Ltd.,* 3 The All England Law Reports 663, 682 (1967).

CONVERGENCE

While the American tradition enables courts to act independently and draw upon international custom and state practice, British courts apply municipal law even if it appears to vary from the conventional standards of international law. In the modern period, however, the two systems appear to converge. In the case of the *Hartford Fire Insurance Co. et al. v. California et al.* (1993), the U.S. Supreme Court addressed the issue of extraterritorial jurisdiction. Specifically the Court had to decide if the Sherman Antitrust Act (1890), which prohibited a conspiracy to restrain trade, could be applied to four American insurance companies and the actions of their British associates. Answering the question in the affirmative, the Court based its decision upon the statute without allowing itself to be influenced by such broad issues as the presumed immunity of the British companies, whose counsel contended that their conduct was lawful in Great Britain. The Court observed that "... it is well established by now that the Sherman Act applies to foreign conduct that was meant to produce and did in fact produce some substantial effect in the United States."[18]

The importance of the decision derives not only from its substance but also from its legal reasoning. The argument of inherent powers of a sovereign state was implied throughout the opinion, but the precise conclusion was reached on the basis of what is often called black letter law, (a closely reasoned textual interpretation of the statute). With the rise of the administrative state, the practice of relying on custom, usually as interpreted by noted scholars, is receding. Following the positivist school of scientific jurisprudence, detailed codes of law have developed, and these govern judicial decisions in both municipal and international law. The growth of international law through the conclusion of rule-making treaties to which governments adhere has produced an effect similar to the development of administrative law within a state. As bench-made law becomes less pervasive, one may ask whether in today's world decisions like *Filartiga,* which are based on the normative values of natural law, are an anachronism.

SOURCES OF INTERNATIONAL LAW

Throughout the nineteenth century, American and British jurists rendered decisions on the law of nations as reflected primarily in custom and in the writings of such scholarly commentators as Grotius and Vattel.[19] In 1945, the Statute of the International Court of Justice (ICJ) expanded the list to include the following in order of priority:[20]

   a. international conventions (multilateral lawmaking treaties),
   b. international custom,
   c. general principles of law, and
   d. judicial decisions complemented by writings of publicists.

---

[18] *Hartford Fire Insurance Co. et al. v. California et al.,* 509 U.S. 764, 796 (1993).
[19] The word sometimes used to describe the authors of classical commentaries is *publicists,* which refers particularly to specialists in international law and relations.
[20] United Nations, Statute of the International Court of Justice (New York: Office of Public Information, 1945), Art. 38.

To the foregoing should be added the contribution to international law made by the administrative decisions of intergovernmental international organizations (IGOs). In the performance of their functions, IGOs often elaborate and apply the tenets of international law as listed. Sometimes referred to as soft international law, the rules developed by IGOs often have an authoritative influence on state policy.[21]

The premier position held among sources of international law is that of lawmaking treaties, usually described as conventions or protocols. Starting with the Congress of Vienna (1815), governments have taken advantage of the forum of an international conference to negotiate conventions whose purpose is to convert custom to the cold print of a treaty commitment. The process reduces the often ambiguous principles associated with state practice to a unified and coherent set of rules contributing to the stability of the international system. Landmark conferences were those of the Hague (1899, 1907) and Paris (1919). Since the San Francisco Conference (1945) and the founding of the United Nations, the development of conventional law has proceeded at an accelerated pace. International conventions on human rights, diplomatic privileges and immunities, treaty law, governance of the oceans and outer space, and the humanitarian law of war offer examples of a major trend since 1945 to substitute order for anarchy in world politics.

Conventional law represents a codification of customary law, which constitutes not only state practice but also an acknowledgment that this practice is a fulfillment of a legal obligation. Customary international law must encompass both elements: policy and adherence to legal precepts. Traditional state action alone does not suffice. Moreover, a diversity of legal cultures means that customary law is not always universal, and a government's tacit consent to a legal standard lacks binding force. Nevertheless, customary law made possible the development of modern diplomacy and with it the concept that treaties must be observed. The law of the sea has its foundation in custom starting with the *Consolato del Mare* (1370), a set of regulations formulated by the merchants of Barcelona to facilitate seaborne commerce by establishing, for example, the institution of mercantile consuls.[22] The regulations also spelled out the rules for prize law, that is, the seizure on the high seas of enemy merchant ships or cargo during wartime. Justice Marshall's decision on *The Nereide* reflected the influence of the customary law embodied in the *Consolato del Mare.*

Customary international law remains a basis for modern judicial decisions. In the *Moçambique* case (1893), the House of Lords ruled that it lacked jurisdiction over acts of trespass which occurred abroad.[23] In deciding the *Hesperides* case (1977), the British Court of Appeals applied the *Moçambique* doctrine to an area of the Republic of Cyprus under Turkish military control. The plaintiffs, Greek Cypriots, were denied access to their property by virtue of the military situation on the island republic, and they instituted proceedings against the Turkish Cypriot representative in London. While the

---

[21]Steven R. Ratner, "International Law: The Trials of Global Norms," *Foreign Policy* 110 (Spring 1998): 65–67.

[22]Arthur Nussbaum, *A Concise History of the Law of Nations,* rev. ed. (New York: Macmillan Co., 1954), pp. 30, 58.

[23]*British South Africa Co. v. Companhia de Moçambique and others,* 1891–1894, All England Law Reports 640, 648 (1893).

House of Lords sympathized with the plight of the plaintiffs, it ruled that British justice, following the precedent of the *Moçambique* decision, did not possess jurisdiction.[24]

Custom remains a means of creating international law, but varying practices of states make it an uncertain means. Justice Samuel Chase summarized the matter succinctly in 1796 when he wrote:

> The law of nations may be considered of three kinds, to wit, general, conventional, or customary. The first is universal or established by the general consent of mankind, and binds all nations. The second is founded on express consent, and is not universal, and only binds those nations that have assented to it. The third is founded on tacit consent; and is only obligatory on those nations, who have adopted it.[25]

The first of these categories is the third-ranked source identified in the Statute of the International Court of Justice. The acceptance of principles of law recognized as such by the international community presumes both that relevant legal norms exist and that they are binding on all governments. The concept derives from Vattel's notion of primary rules of law, to whose adherence all nations are obligated.

In a modern sense, general principles of law serve to lend support to the doctrine of human rights. In 1948, the General Assembly of the United Nations approved, by acclamation, the Universal Declaration of Human Rights, which is a statement of general principles. The concept of general principles may be either procedural or substantive. For instance, one may argue that due process and equal protection are principles derived from municipal codes and then applied in international jurisprudence.

Alternatively, the concept may refer to universal legal standards, such as good faith or restraint in the use of force.[26] International law recognizes the doctrine of *jus cogens*, defined as peremptory norms governing state behavior. The doctrine has its roots in Roman law and was used as a means of governing a far-flung empire. In sum, general principles of law are a means of bridging a presumed gap between customary and conventional law, but international tribunals prefer to rely upon state practice as codified in treaties.

Judicial decisions are the fourth category recognized as a source of international law. The International Military Tribunals convened first in Nuremberg and then Tokyo (1945–1948) articulated principles of international humanitarian law which apply to the War Crimes Tribunals established by the United Nations in 1992. The Permanent Court of International Justice of the League of Nations (1920–1940) and its successor, the International Court of Justice of the United Nations (1946–   ) have articulated doctrines of universal application. Finally bilateral arbitral tribunals convened to resolve a specific issue contribute precedents which clarify and advance the law. Examples include the *Alabama* claims (United States and Great Britain, 1871), the Alaska Boundary arbitration (United States and Great Britain, 1901), the Island of Palmas arbitration (United States and the Netherlands, 1928), and the English Channel economic zones (Great Britain and France, 1978).

---

[24]*Hesperides Hotels Ltd. v. Muftizade*, 2 All England Law Reports 1168, 1172–1174 (1978).
[25]*Ware (Jones) v. Hylton*, 3 U.S. (3 Dallas) 226 (1796).
[26]Peter Malanczuk, *Akehurst's Modern Introduction to International Law*, 7th ed. rev. (New York: Routledge, 1997), pp. 48–50.

In addition to the four sources identified in the Statute of the International Court of Justice, comity is sometimes cited as a source; yet comity should not be confused with customary international law, which is binding on governments. By comparison, comity is largely a matter of courtesy and protocol.[27] Since comity may evolve into customary law, the dividing line between the two may be indistinct. In 1993, the U.S. Supreme Court decided a case in which the litigants claimed that international comity barred it from considering claims against a London-based insurance firm.[28] Justice Antonin Scalia defined comity, in one sense, as ". . . substantive laws having extraterritorial reach." In doing so, he made a distinction between the "comity of the courts" and the "comity of nations" with the latter having the force of customary law. His opinion represented a dissent from the more traditional view held by the majority, which held that comity did not pose a legal obstacle to consider claims against overseas insurers.

THE WORLD SYSTEM

The question of whether the dominant theory of international law is monism or dualism should not obscure the necessity for rules and institutions capable of introducing a measure of order into world politics. The persistence of behavioral standards over time is a prerequisite for organized relations among governments. Even the balance of power—the essence of realpolitik—requires enforceable norms if the system is to succeed in limiting conflicts.[29] Writing in the heyday of the European balance of power, Georg Friedrich von Martens (1756–1821) observed:

> The greatest part of the states of Europe look, nowadays, upon this right of maintaining the balance of power, as a right that belongs to them.[30]

If we accept the thesis that the maintenance of the balance of power is not merely a tactic in diplomacy, but rather a legal right, then the relations of states take on the aura of an international legal regime. System and law have a symbiotic relationship, for the sum of diplomacy and law enables the balance of power to function. Despite their differing orientations, American and British courts have historically recognized the immanence of international law in the world system.

Topics for Discussion

1. Monism and dualism are the contending paradigms offering an explanation of the relationship of municipal to international law. How do these two frameworks of analysis differ? What assumptions set them apart? As the legal adviser to the government of a small state, which of the two approaches would you find more supportive of your diplomacy?
2. Anglo-American jurists share a common belief in the existence of international law, but they differ concerning its relation to municipal law. What is the principal

---

[27]Wesley L. Gould, *An Introduction to International Law* (New York: Harper & Bros., 1957), p. 137.
[28]*Hartford Fire Insurance Co. et al. v. California,* 509 U.S. 764, 817 (1993).
[29]Morton A. Kaplan and Nicholas de B. Katzenbach, *The Political Foundations of International Law* (New York: John Wiley, 1961), pp. 31–35.
[30]Georg Friedrich von Martens, *Summary of the Law of Nations,* trans. William Cobbett (Philadelphia: Thomas Bradford, 1795; reprint ed., Littleton, Co.: Fred B. Rothman, 1986), pp. 125–126.

difference in their respective legal philosophies? Is a convergence of these points of view possible?

3. What are the sources of public international law? As chief justice of the United States, John Marshall relied upon custom in the form of a common law of humankind. Since the formation of the United Nations, the emphasis has shifted to conventional law based on multilateral lawmaking treaties. Describe the elements of such treaties. How do they contribute to the universality of international law?

4. The Peace of Westphalia (1648) recognized the sovereignty of the territorial state and made it the basis of a balance-of-power system. How has the balance of power advanced the development of international law? Is the independence, sovereignty, and territorial integrity of individual states the foundation of modern international law?

CHAPTER 3

International Law within the State

In its opening decades the U.S. Supreme Court incorporated the law of nations into the municipal law of the republic. Principally through the writings of John Marshall and Joseph Story, the Court accomplished a twofold task. First it recognized the obligations of the new government to the international legal community; and second, its decisions made the law of nations a means of resolving disputes among the constituent states of the federation. In 1905, Chief Justice Melville Fuller applied a rule of customary international law to determine a maritime boundary between the states of Louisiana and Mississippi.[1] Fuller's reasoning was that the states were coordinate members of a federal union, and accordingly the rules of international law should govern the outcome of the case.[2]

FEDERALISM

The concept of a federal state lends itself to various interpretations. The emphasis in defining a federal relationship may either be on structure or process. The English historian Edward A. Freeman (1823–1892) identified two essential characteristics of a federation.[3] First each constituent member of the union must be independent of external authority in those matters reserved to it; and second, all members must be subject to the power of the commonwealth in those matters reserved to it. Questions of peace and war, diplomatic relations, and generally those issues within the realm of public international law are inherent in the sovereignty of the federal government, and the members of the federation must accede to the will of that sovereign. A century later, K. C. Wheare introduced the principle that the federal and regional governments are coordinate.[4] Each level of government would function within its own sphere of competence, and each would be independent of the other. The notion of an independent identity has subsequently lost support, for the prevailing belief is that the levels are mutually responsive in the performance of their respective tasks.

---

[1] *Louisiana v. Mississippi,* 202 U.S. 1, 49 (1905).
[2] Melville Fuller was an acknowledged specialist on boundary questions, and he served on the six-member tribunal assembled in 1899 to arbitrate a territorial dispute between Venezuela and British Guiana (today Guyana). See Willard Leroy King, *Melville Weston Fuller, Chief Justice of the United States, 1888–1910* (New York: Macmillan Co., 1950), chap. 19.
[3] Edward A. Freeman, *History of Federal Government from the Foundation of the Achaian League to the Disruption of the United States* (London: Macmillan Co., 1863), v.1:3.
[4] K. C. Wheare, *Federal Government,* 4th ed. (New York: Oxford University Press, 1964), p. 14.

Commenting in 1973 on the theories of federalism, M. J. C. Vile categorized a federal system as one possessing the qualities of both independence and interdependence.[5] Each level of government has its own identity, and no element is in every respect subordinate to the other. The relationship between the members of the federation and the unifying authority is a dynamic one and reflects their relative efficiency in the performance of functions. By comparison, Wheare's theory of the coordinate state appears rigid, but the structural approach is essential for an understanding of the position of federations under international law. Jerold Waltman offers a useful summary in his description of federalism as two levels of government, each with a source of authority beyond the reach of the other.[6] The conclusion is that both sources of authority possess a legal personality, but how does international law cope with this dualism? What level of authority represents the true legal personality of the state?

DUALISM AND INTERNATIONAL LAW IN THE UNITED STATES

Two incidents involving the receptivity of American society to immigrants highlight the American experience in reconciling the commitment to federalism with that to international law. Both cases focus on the issue of state responsibility, that is, the obligations incurred by a government upon acceptance of the status of a sovereign member of the international community. As noted in Chapter 2, Justice James Wilson in *Ware v. Hylton* (1796) argued that the United States was bound by the law of nations at the moment of its independence. Statehood and responsibility are inseparable. The Fourteenth Amendment (1868) guaranteeing equal protection and due process constitutes the necessary linkage between international and municipal law. On the basis of reciprocity, the rights of citizens are extended to aliens under the protection of the United States. The modality of securing such protection is a treaty of friendship, commerce, and navigation (FCN). One of the first acts of American diplomacy in the 1780s was to conclude a series of FCN treaties with European states, thereby safeguarding the rights of U.S. citizens abroad.[7]

On March 14, 1891, a mob broke into the sheriff's jail in New Orleans and lynched eleven inmates being held on a charge of homicide. Under the law of their homeland, the victims were subjects of the king of Italy, and the Italian consul lodged an immediate protest, which his embassy in Washington relayed to the Department of State.[8] An 1871 FCN treaty between the United States and Italy committed both states parties to the following:

> The citizens of each of the high contracting parties shall receive, in the States and Territories of the other, the most constant protection and security for their persons and property.[9]

---

[5]M. J. C. Vile, *Federalism in the United States, Canada and Australia,* Commission on the Constitution, research paper 2 (London: H.M. Stationery Office, 1973), pp. 2–4.

[6]Jerold L. Waltman, *American Government: Politics and Citizenship* (New York: West Publishing Co., 1993), p. 52.

[7]One of the first FCN treaties concluded was with the kingdom of Prussia. See United States—Prussia, Treaty of Amity and Commerce (September 10, 1785) in Malloy's *Treaties,* 2:1477.

[8]For a full account of this tragic episode, see 6 Moore 837-841.

[9]United States—Italy, Treaty of Commerce and Navigation (February 26, 1871) in Malloy's *Treaties,* 1:969.

After extended bilateral negotiations, during which Rome recalled its minister in Washington, the United States acknowledged that it had failed to meet its treaty obligation to defend the rights of the prisoners and agreed to pay an indemnity.

In his annual foreign affairs message dated December 9, 1891, President Benjamin Harrison declared:

> ... that the officers of the State charged with police and judicial powers in such cases must, in consideration of international questions growing out of such incidents, be regarded in such sense as Federal agents as to make this Government answerable for their acts in cases where it would be answerable if the United States had used its constitutional power to define and punish crimes against treaty rights.[10]

The dictum recognizes the centrality of international law as the basis for reciprocity, and the inability of the sheriff in Orleans Parish to safeguard his prisoners constituted a failure on the part of the United States to fulfill its duties under the FCN treaty with Italy. Payment of reparations was, therefore, obligatory.

The second incident involving federal responsibility for the actions of state and local government officials occurred in San Francisco, where the local school resolved in 1893 that children of Japanese immigrants must attend the city's Chinese elementary school.[11] The affair touched off a diplomatic controversy, whose outcome contributed to the conclusion of an FCN treaty between the United States and Japan. The Gresham-Kurino Treaty of Commerce and Navigation (November 22, 1894) opened with the following commitment:

> The citizens and subjects of the two High Contracting Parties shall have full liberty to enter, travel, or reside in any part of the territories of the other Contracting Party, and shall enjoy full and perfect protection for their persons and property.[12]

Despite this provision, the school board's discriminatory practice in assigning Japanese children to the Chinese school prevailed. An angry President Theodore Roosevelt condemned the policy as violative of international law and comity in a message to Congress in 1906.[13] Eventually the school board relented and retracted its policy.

The contretemps between public authority in California and the federal government was not yet at an end. The state of California enacted a statute that barred aliens from property ownership but allowed them to lease farmland for a period of three years. Meanwhile the United States and Japan had revised and expanded their FCN treaty to include a guarantee to each other's nationals the same rights and privileges held by native citizens.[14] Secretary of State William Jennings Bryan assured the Japanese ambassador that the United States would honor its treaty obligations even to the extent of compensating any Japanese subject whose property rights had been abridged

---

[10]Benjamin Harrison, Annual Message of the President, in F.R.U.S. 1891, vi.

[11]Roger Daniels, *Asian America: Chinese and Japanese in the United States since 1850* (Seattle: University of Washington Press, 1988), p. 111.

[12]United States—Japan, Treaty of Commerce and Navigation (November 22, 1894) in Malloy *Treaties,* 1:1028–1029.

[13]Theodore Roosevelt, Annual Message of the President, F.R.U.S. 1911, xlii.

[14]United States—Japan, Treaty of Commerce and Navigation (February 21, 1911), F.R.U.S. 1911, p. 315.

by California's restrictive laws.[15] Nevertheless the government in Tokyo remained concerned, and the foreign minister advised his ambassador in Washington that California's land law "...is not only in disregard of the letter and spirit of the existing treaty between Japan and the United States, but is essentially unfair and invidiously discriminatory against my countrymen."[16] As in New Orleans, the federal government could not claim immunity based on the doctrine of state's rights, and the United States accepted liability for violations of international law as embodied in treaty rights. Federalism does not limit a state's obligation to observe the reciprocity of treaties.

CONSULS AND STATE RESPONSIBILITY

The United Nations sponsored the Convention on Consular Relations (April 24, 1963), which is a multilateral treaty covering the rights and duties of consular officers charged with the duty, among others, of protecting their fellow citizens abroad. The convention stipulates that a consul has the duty of

> ...subject to the practices and procedures obtaining in the receiving State, representing or arranging appropriate representation for nationals of the sending State before the tribunals and other authorities of the receiving State, for the purpose of obtaining, in accordance with the laws and regulations of the receiving State, provisional measures for the preservation of the rights and interests of those nationals, where, because of the absence of any other reason, such nationals are unable at the proper time to assume the defense of their rights and interests.[17]

The foregoing provision established the obligation of the receiving or host government to notify the appropriate consulate in the event that an alien was detained and charged with a crime. A subsequent article recognized the right of the detainee to contact a consular officer. The fact that a person so detained might fail to request access to a consul was not a mitigating circumstance. The adherence of the United States to the convention meant that federal authority incurred the responsibility of implementing its provisions at all levels of government. As President Harrison observed, local and state officials were "Federal agents" when acting in fulfillment of treaty obligations.

In 1993, a criminal court of the Commonwealth of Virginia sentenced Angel Francisco Breard, a citizen of Paraguay, to death for the crime of murder.[18] Breard subsequently alleged and the prosecution conceded that the authorities of the Commonwealth had failed to notify the Paraguayan consulate in nearby Washington, D.C. As a consequence, the government of Paraguay sought relief in both the federal court system and in the International Court of Justice (ICJ) in The Hague. The U.S. Supreme Court ruled in 1998 that since the defendant had failed to raise the issue of notification during the trial, he had defaulted his claim that the proceedings against him

---

[15]Bryan to Viscount Chinda, (July 16, 1913), F.R.U.S. 1913, 644.
[16]Baron Kato to Viscount Chinda (June 9, 1914) as quoted by H. A. Millis, *The Japanese Problem in the United States* (New York: Macmillan Co., 1915), pp. 332–334.
[17]21 U.S.T. 77. The Convention entered into force for the United States on December 24, 1969.
[18]For a factual account of the *Breard* case, see Jonathan I. Charney and W. Michael Reisman, "*Breard:* The Facts," *American Journal of International Law* 92 (October 1998): 666–675.

violated international law.[19] The ICJ sought through provisional measures to delay the execution until it could review the merits of the case. Although Secretary of State Madeleine Albright also requested a delay in carrying out the sentence, the governor of Virginia declined to interfere with the sentence. During 1998 and 1999, similar cases arose in Arizona and Texas, in that the convicted murderers were foreign nationals who had not been represented by consular officers at their trials.[20]

The international legal issue in these cases was that of reciprocity. "Reciprocity is the permanent basis of the law of nations," wrote Chief Justice John Marshall in 1815.[21] Reciprocity consists of mutual and balanced obligations undertaken by both parties in fulfillment of an international agreement. The Convention on Consular Relations is such an agreement. The presumed inability of the federal government to act in *Breard* and parallel cases did not relieve the United States of its treaty commitment. The precedents set in New Orleans (1891) and in San Francisco (1906) are instructive on this point. As far as foreign governments are concerned, there exists only one legal personality for the United States, and it is articulated by federal authority. The issue of federal–state relations under the Constitution does not provide an escape clause from an FCN treaty or a multilateral convention.

THE SUPREMACY CLAUSE

Noting that the division of powers in a federation does not relieve the central government of its liability under the doctrine of state responsibility, the related question of legal personality deserves attention. International law recognizes both subject and object status. True subjects of international law possess legal personality, and with some exceptions these are sovereign states. The list of members of the United Nations provides an authoritative guide. The quality of sovereignty enables a government to assert the supremacy of its laws within its territory and of equal importance, to maintain a freedom of action in international affairs. Objects of public international law are usually natural or juridical persons, whose rights are protected by their governments. For example, in the *Breard* case, the government of Paraguay as a subject of international law could turn to the ICJ for relief. By comparison, Breard himself possessed object status and therefore did not have standing before the ICJ. In a federation, the locus of sovereignty may sometimes be unclear especially because of the practice of some constitutional theorists of referring to dual sovereignty, by which they mean a division of powers necessary for the internal governance of the state. In international law, the concept of dual sovereignty is a contradiction in terms.

James Madison put the matter succinctly during the debate at the Virginia convention on the ratification of the Constitution:

> Here the supremacy of a treaty is contrasted with the supremacy of the laws of states. It cannot be otherwise supreme. If it does not supersede their

---

[19]*Breard v. Greene, Warden* 523 U.S. 371, 378 (1998).
[20]The state of Arizona executed Karl and Walter LaGrand (Germany) and the state of Texas Joseph Faulder (Canada). In both instances the respective governments requested a stay of execution and the intercession of the Department of State.
[21]*The Nereide,* 13 U.S. (9 Cranch) 388, 400 (1815).

existing laws, as far as they contravene its operation, it cannot have any effect. To counteract it by the supremacy of state laws, would bring on the Union the just charge of national perfidy.[22]

The U.S. Supreme Court has ruled on constitutional challenges to the doctrine of the supremacy of treaties over state laws as embodied in the Constitution.[23] Justice Oliver Wendell Holmes wrote the definitive opinion on the supremacy doctrine in 1920. The United States and Great Britain had concluded a treaty designed to protect flocks of birds in their annual migration southward from Canada. Since the terms of the treaty were not automatically self-executing, Congress enacted the necessary implementing legislation.[24] When a federal game warden endeavored to enforce the law, the state of Missouri appealed to the U.S. Supreme Court with the argument that states have exclusive jurisdiction over game birds, and that the Constitution contains no grant of authority to Congress on this matter. In 1920, Holmes wrote the opinion for the Court and concluded that "... [t]he treaty in question does not contradict any prohibitory words to be found in the Constitution."[25] What is not prohibited is allowed.

The ability of state governments to nullify foreign policy decisions continued to be an issue. The normalization of relations between the United States and the Soviet Union in 1933 resulted from an executive agreement between President Franklin D. Roosevelt and Maxim Litvinoff, the Soviet foreign minister. The agreement included provisions for the settlement of claims advanced by U.S. citizens for the loss of property expropriated by the Soviet government. The arrangement appeared to override the banking law of the state of New York, and the U.S. Supreme Court again confronted the question of whether authority over foreign affairs is a concurrent power shared by the federal government and the states. Justice George Sutherland reasserted the supremacy clause when he wrote that "... the external powers of the United States are to be exercised without regard to state laws or policies."[26] In a parallel decision on an appeal by the insurance commissioner of the state of New York, Justice William O. Douglas wrote:

> No State can rewrite our foreign policy to conform to its own domestic policies. Power over external affairs is not shared with the States; it is vested in the national government exclusively.[27]

STATE-PROVINCE AGREEMENTS

Although the aforementioned decisions of the U.S. Supreme Court leave no real doubt as to the exclusive authority of the federal government over foreign policy, states continue to develop ties with foreign governments or their subnational authorities. In 1799,

---

[22]Jonathan Eliot (ed.), *The Debates in the Several State Conventions on the Adoption of the Federal Constitution,* 5 vols. (Philadelphia: J. B. Lippincott, 1836), 3:515.
[23]U.S. Constitution, art. 6, sec. 2.
[24]United States—Great Britain, Convention for the Protection of Migratory Birds Statutes at Large 39: 1702 (1916) and Migratory Bird Treaty Act, ibid. 40: 755 (1918).
[25]*Missouri v. Holland,* 252 U.S. 416, 433 (1920).
[26]*U.S. v. Belmont,* 301 U.S. 324, 331 (1937).
[27]*U.S. v. Pink,* 315 U.S. 203, 233 (1942).

Congress passed the Logan Act, which defined as a federal offense an unauthorized effort on the part of anyone to make representations to a foreign government for the purpose of influencing U.S. relations with that entity.[28] Nevertheless, since the 1930s, states and municipalities have concluded agreements with foreign authorities on administrative, cultural, and economic matters.[29] The states of California and New York took the lead, and other states were quick to follow. As of 1974, a survey commissioned by the U.S. Department of State showed that the state of Michigan had 108 agreements or arrangements with counterpart Canadian authorities, principally in the Province of Ontario.[30] The agreements cover such subjects as commerce, tourism, fisheries, and forestry. Of particular note is the cumulative impact of these arrangements, which in their totality contribute to an international legal regime for Lakes Michigan, Huron, and Superior. The outcome is the creation of a network of communications between governmental officials on both sides of the border. Federal authorities in Ottawa and Washington appear to be onlookers.

In the Southwest, local and state governments have followed the example set by their counterparts along the Canadian border and reached agreements with authorities of the Mexican states.[31] The states of Arizona and California have an arrangement to share the waters of the Colorado River with the authorities in Baja California. The formation of a regional organization encompassing Mexico and the states of the Gulf south offers the potential for regional economic development.[32] Such an arrangement would, however, run counter to the supremacy doctrine and the constitutional provision prohibiting agreements between states and foreign governments. In 1893, the U.S. Supreme Court addressed the issue, and Justice Stephen Field wrote that the "... prohibition is directed against the formation of any combination tending to the increase of political power in the States, which may encroach upon or interfere with the just supremacy of the United States."[33] The sentence is instructive because it leaves open the possibility of legitimating agreements that do not impinge upon the foreign-relations powers of the federal government. The constituent members of a federal system may indeed enter into international compacts, such as the cultural exchange between the state of Louisiana and the Province of Quebec (1967), without altering the legal personality of the federation or relieving it of its legal responsibility to the world community.

---

[28]Statutes at Large 1:613 (1799). The Logan Act was so named because Dr. George Logan, a Quaker, had undertaken a private peace mission to France, where he met with Prince Talleyrand, the foreign minister.
[29]Michael H. Shuman, "Dateline Main Street: Local Foreign Policies," *Foreign Policy* 65 (Winter 1986–1987): 154–156. Also see James Goldsborough, "California's Foreign Policy," *Foreign Affairs* 72 (Spring 1993): 88–96.
[30]Roger Frank Swanson, *State–Provincial Interaction: A Study of Relations between U.S. States and Canadian Provinces Prepared for the U.S. Department of State* (Washington, D.C.: The Canus Research Institute, 1974), pp. 153–167.
[31]The official name of Mexico is the United Mexican States, which reflects the federal nature of its constitution. Federalism facilitates agreements between the states of Mexico and the United States.
[32]In 1966, representatives of Mexico and six states of the Gulf south met in Biloxi, Mississippi, to prepare a draft agreement for a regional association in support of commerce and tourism. See Raymond Spencer Rodgers, "The Capacity of the States of the Union to Conclude International Agreements," *American Journal of International Law* 61 (October 1967): 1025–1027.
[33]*Virginia v. Tennessee,* 148 U.S. 503, 519 (1893). Also see American Law Institute, *Restatement of the Law: The Foreign Relations Law of the United States* (St. Paul, MN.: By the Institute, 1987), sec. 302 (d–f).

THE DOCTRINE OF PREEMPTION

Federalism achieves a balance between the local responsiveness of subnational governments and the efficiency of a national authority. The existence of two complementary, yet sometimes competing, levels of government can easily lead to a conflict of laws. Under U.S. practice, federal law supersedes state and local laws and through the preemption of state laws ensures a uniformity of legislation. State legislation is overridden whenever (a) the Constitution denies to states authority in a given field, or (b) Congress has already legislated on the matter.[34] In the performance of their functions, legislative and judicial organs of state government often render decisions that touch upon foreign relations. The question is one of the degree of overlap between federal and state authority rather than an absolute separation of the two.

In 1967, the U.S. Supreme Court addressed the issue of the role of states in the formulation of foreign policy.[35] The state of Oregon had invoked the concept of reciprocity in a 1951 law that barred foreign nationals from inheriting property if their governments would, as a matter of policy, confiscate the inheritance. The law was aimed at those governments of Eastern Europe whose legal code called for the nationalization of properties held abroad. Justice William O. Douglas wrote the opinion for the Court and concluded:

> State courts, of course, must frequently read, construe, and apply laws of
> foreign nations. It has never been suggested seriously that state courts are
> precluded from performing that function, albeit there is a remote possibility
> that any holding may disturb a foreign nation.[36]

The opinion acknowledged that public authority at all levels of government must address questions of international law despite James Madison's argument that in foreign relations there is only one government competent to speak for the United States.[37]

Zschernig did not, however, solve the problem. During the war in Vietnam the legislature of the Commonwealth of Massachusetts passed a resolution challenging the constitutionality of the commitment of U.S. forces in a foreign conflict without a declaration of war by Congress. Justice Douglas attempted unsuccessfully to persuade the Court to hear the case, but a majority of the justices assumed that the conflict was a question best reserved to the political branches.[38] Similarly, the Massachusetts legislature enacted a statute in 1996 to ban state-funded contracts with companies doing business in Myanmar (formerly Burma). The legislation was in response to confirmed reports of human rights violations by the military regime in Rangoon. A federal district court struck down the statute in 1998 because it violated the constitutional doctrine that foreign policy is the exclusive responsibility of Congress and the president.

---

[34]Harold G. Maier, "Preemption of State Law: A Recommended Analysis," *American Journal of International Law* 83 (October 1989):833.

[35]Peter J. Spiro, "Taking Foreign Policy Away from the Feds," *Washington Quarterly* 1 (Winter 1988): 200. For a commentary on Spiro, see Richard B. Bilder, "Role of States and Cities in Foreign Relations," *American Journal of International Law* 83 (October 1989): 821.

[36]*Zschernig v. Miller,* 389 U.S. 429, 433. For a precedential decision, see *Asakura v. Seattle,* 265 U.S. 332, 344 (1924).

[37]James Madison, "No. 42," in *The Federalist* (1788).

[38]*Massachusetts v. Laird,* 400 U.S. 886 (1970).

Defenders of the Massachusetts law argued that the Commonwealth has the authority to decide with whom it will do business, and that the Constitution does not circumscribe this right.[39]

The issue is one of creating a dynamic equilibrium between the rights of the states and the responsibility of the federal government to fulfill its obligations as a unified international legal personality. The accession of the United States to multilateral agreements designed to achieve the liberalization of international commerce has revived interest in the right of federal authority to preempt state laws and local ordinances. In the instance of the putative sanctions imposed by Massachusetts on corporations, both the government of Japan and the Commission of the European Union filed briefs with the court, alleging that the state law was violative of the principle of free trade and therefore of the charter of the World Trade Organization (in effect on January 1, 1995). Actions by state and local governments, contrived to use trade as a means of influencing the domestic policies of foreign governments, do not go unnoticed by the international community. As approved by Congress in the form of a 1993 "fast-track" resolution, the North American Free Trade Agreement (NAFTA) offers a workable formula for maintaining the balance in federal–state relations. The agreement states in Article 1206:

> Each Party may set out ... within two years of the date of entry into force of this Agreement, any existing non-conforming measure maintained by a state or province, not including local government.[40]

The clause acknowledges the political reality that federalism requires a mutual and balanced adjustment between the central government and subnational authorities. Although the Constitution stipulates the supremacy of federal law and treaties, the political reality of cooperative federalism is more complex. The interests of constituent states must be taken into account, and these often result in concessions to state laws in the form of reservations to international agreements. Accordingly, the negotiations leading to the conclusion of NAFTA result in a web of compromise, which is the essence of federalism.

The role of federations under international law lends itself to two interpretations. The first reflects a formalistic approach whereby state governments may not enter the realm of foreign affairs. The decision in *Zschernig v. Miller* reflects that approach as does the judicial negation of state resolutions expressing disapproval of overseas military intervention or trade with authoritarian regimes. The globalization of political life presages an intensification of the problem. The end of the Cold War did not remove the occasion for states to assume activist roles in the field of foreign policy. Conversely, federalism denies to the central authority the argument that national security may curtail the constitutional rights of states. Under the guise of an international emergency, the federal government could not, for example, alter the constitutional guarantee of a republican form of government to the states.[41] Nevertheless, the doctrine of powers reserved to the

---

[39]Fred Bayles, "Burma law in Mass. ruled unconstitutional," *USA Today,* 6 November 1988, sec. A, p. 3; and Carey Goldberg, "Limiting a State's Sphere of Influence," *New York Times,* 15 November 1998, sec. I, p. 22

[40]Office of the President, Executive Document, *North American Free Trade Agreement* (Washington, D.C.: Government Printing Office, 1992), Article 1206(2), 1:12–13. See William J. Clinton, "Proclamation 6641— To Implement the North American Free Trade Agreement (December 15, 1993)," *Weekly Compilation of Presidential Documents* (December 20, 1993) 29: 2596–2599. Hereafter *Presidential Documents.*

[41]U.S. Constitution, art. 4, par. 4.

states expressed in the Tenth Amendment does not compromise federal supremacy in the conduct of foreign relations.[42]

The first interpretation focuses on formal legal doctrine and presumes that international law consists of a set of neutral rules applicable to all relevant situations. The second interpretation focuses on the role of international law as a means of making policy choices. Accordingly, the law is flexible and can be adapted to a variety of political conditions. The genius of federalism is that it allows for such adaptation. Myres S. McDougal has addressed the question of policy formulation within a federal system and concluded that federalism is a ". . . fuzzy hierarchy of responsibility." What legal formalists view as a disadvantage, McDougal and others of the policy school regard as an asset enabling a political system to respond to challenges at various levels of authority.[43] For example, in July 1999, the state of California empowered state courts to hear cases arising from slave labor during World War II.[44] Unless federal law preempts that of California, courts in that state will rule on allegations of war crimes committed abroad, thus propelling the judiciary of the state into an international legal controversy. According to the Statute of the International Court of Justice, judicial decisions are a source of international law. In this instance state courts will render decisions contributing to the development of the humanitarian law of war.

THE RESOLUTION OF DISPUTES BETWEEN MEMBERS OF A FEDERATION

As one body of law informs another, so international law provides a framework for the resolution of disputes over title to territory within a federation.[45] Three cases, two American and the other Canadian, stand out as examples of how decisions of courts on matters internal to a federation contribute to the growth of world law. The first was *Louisiana v. Mississippi* (1905) in which Chief Justice Fuller drew upon the work of publicists as well as custom to delimit the maritime boundary between the two Gulf coast states. In competition over the valuable resource of oyster beds, Louisiana and Mississippi disputed the control of the adjacent waters lying between them. The case was an early initiative in environmental law, in that Louisiana forbade the use of a dredge to harvest oysters on the thesis that this technique destroyed the oyster beds. Conversely, Mississippi permitted dredging. The environmental issue hinged upon the delimitation of the maritime boundary between the two adjacent states. Mississippi proposed that the boundary should follow the mid-channel—a thesis originally advanced by Hugo Grotius. Louisiana rejected the Grotian rule and argued instead for the principle of the *thalweg;* that is, the most navigable channel should determine the

---

[42]Ibid., Tenth Amendment (1791). See Louis Henkin, *Foreign Affairs and the United States Constitution,* 2nd ed. (New York: Oxford University Press, 1996), 165–167.

[43]Myres S. McDougal, "The Comparative Study of Law for Policy Purposes: Value Clarification as an Instrument of Democratic World Order," in *Studies in World Public Order,* ed. Myres S. McDougal et al. (New Haven, CT: New Haven Press, 1987), 970–972.

[44]Paul Abrahams, "Tokyo grapples with lawsuits for war conduct," *Financial Times,* 9 December 1999, sec. I, 6.

[45]A pathbreaking study of the contribution of federal courts to the development of international law on such questions as the economic use of rivers and the rights of downstream riparians is Ivan Bernier, *International Legal Aspects of Federalism* (Hamden, CT: Archon Books by the Shoe String Press, 1973), chap. 6.

boundary. Begun by the French navy in the early 1700s and continued by the U.S. Coast Survey (1846–1854), hydrographic charts of the coast accurately located the *thalweg*. Based on this data, the chief justice accepted Louisiana's interpretation and chose the *thalweg* rather than the mid-channel, thus establishing a precedent for other governments.[46] In 1986, the Soviet Union and China resolved a long-standing boundary dispute along the Ussuri River, and they relied upon the *thalweg*.

The second case also concerns the ownership of water. Like the preceding case, this one also came under the original jurisdiction of the U.S. Supreme Court. In 1916, Wyoming initiated a suit to secure a share of the waters of the Laramie River, which rises in Colorado. At issue was the question of whether the rights of riparian users in the two states were protected by customary international law. Counsel for Colorado advanced the following argument:

> Each State depends for its existence primarily upon its natural resources, of which water in the arid regions is frequently the most valuable. Self-defense compels the State to withhold its resources for the benefit of future as well as present generations and for the welfare and perpetuity of the State. With independent Nations, these natural resources, if need require, must be defended by the sword. But with States of the Union this court must decide the controversy.[47]

Principles of international law govern the outcome of a dispute over sovereignty and the distribution of waters. Within a federation a constitutional court is empowered to provide an answer, but the international system may allow only for self-help in the threat of or use of force. The principles in both instances are the same, yet the structure within which they are applied is different.

Justice Willis Van Debater wrote a precedential opinion for the Court. He overruled the argument that each state exercises unrestricted sovereign authority over the waters within its borders and decreed that, as a matter of equity, Colorado must continue to share the water of the Laramie River with farmers and ranchers in Wyoming.[48] The international community recognized this precedent in the Lake Lanoux arbitration of 1957. Lake Lanoux is located in France near the Spanish border. As was the case with Colorado and the Laramie River, French authorities asserted exclusive jurisdiction over the lake and its tributaries although one of them flowed into Spain and provided Spanish agriculture with a needed resource. As part of a hydroelectric project, a French power company planned to build a dam at the lake and thereby reduce the outflow of water, to the ultimate disadvantage of Spanish farmers. The Spanish government protested and insisted upon retention of a share of the lake's runoff. Stalled diplomatic efforts led both governments to turn to arbitration to resolve the dispute. A five-member arbitral tribunal ruled that the waters of Lake Lanoux must be shared with Spain.[49] The tribunal applied the customary rule requiring the equitable apportionment of waters used by two adjacent states and cited the decision in *Wyoming v.*

---

[46] *Louisiana v. Mississippi*, 202 U.S. 1, 49 (1905).

[47] *Wyoming v. Colorado*, 259 U.S. 419, 435 (1922).

[48] Ibid., pp. 496–497. Also see William L. Griffin, "The Use of Waters of International Drainage Basins under Customary International Law," *American Journal of International Law* 53 (January 1959): 50, 67–68.

[49] Also see United Nations, "Affaire du Lac Lanoux," in *U.N.R.I.A.A.* 12:281–282.

Colorado as a precedent.[50] The relationship between international and municipal law is that of a seamless web, and judicial decisions within federations provide useful precedents for international tribunals. As for the issue of international watercourses, it remains open as indicated by the construction in Turkey of a dam which will lower the level of the Euphrates River as it flows through Syria and Iraq.

The third exemplary case derives from the constitutional history of Canada. In 1927, when Canada was a self-governing but not yet sovereign polity, the Privy Council of Great Britain served as the highest court of appeal for constitutional cases arising from the dominions—constituent members of the then–British Commonwealth of Nations. The issue in question was a territorial dispute between Labrador, a province of Canada, and Newfoundland, a member of the Commonwealth with dominion status.[51] Evidence presented by the contending parties consisted largely of historic maps presented in support of one or another claim. Cartographic evidence is subject to challenge, and the Privy Council in its ruling on admissibility stated:

> [T]he fact that throughout a long series of years, and until the present dispute arose, all maps issued in Canada either supported or were consistent with the claim put forward by Newfoundland, is of some value as showing the construction put upon Orders in Council and statutes by persons in authority and by the general public in the Dominion.[52]

The dictum that "all maps issued in Canada" reveal an official and public perception supporting the claim of Newfoundland confirms the importance of cartography as evidence in territorial disputes. There must, however, be an obvious and continuing acceptance by mapmakers, both public and private, of the perception that the disputed territory belongs to a given polity. As stipulated by the Privy Council, a single map is not conclusive. The dictum that cartographic evidence must reveal a clear-cut trend was applied by the ICJ in 1953 in a dispute between France and Great Britain over two groups of islets in the English Channel. The ICJ examined the maps offered by both governments and observed the absence of a uniform interpretation over time.[53] In this instance, the ICJ applied the *Labrador* standard in the obverse by pointing out the lack of agreement among cartographers.

The foregoing three cases illustrate the contribution made by judicial decisions in federations to the development of customary international law. The assumption that international law is something apart from municipal law is misleading, and to this extent the monist view of the universality of the legal system receives support. A 1951 case decided by the ICJ is illustrative.[54] The kingdom of Norway had by royal decree enclosed a broad belt of adjacent waters for purposes of protecting its fishing industry.[55] The British government protested the enclosure and argued that fishing on what it regarded as the high seas should be open to all. After a trial lasting almost two years, the ICJ ruled in favor of Norway and set a precedent to the effect that in defense of its economic in-

---

[50]Brunson MacChesney (ed.), "Judicial Decisions: Lake Lanoux Case (France–Spain)," *American Journal of International Law* 53 (January 1959): 156, 162.

[51]In 1949, Newfoundland became a province of Canada.

[52]*Re Labrador Boundary,* 2 *Dominion Law Reports* 427 (1927).

[53]*The Minquiers and Ecrehos case* (*United Kingdom v. France*), Judgment of November 17, 1953: *ICJ Reports,* 47, 62.

[54]*Fisheries Case* (*United Kingdom v. Norway*), Judgment of December 18, 1951, *ICJ Reports 1951,* 116.

[55]As discussed above, the case of *Mortensen v. Peters* focused on the same issue.

terests a state could designate exclusive or restricted fishing zones.[56] The British member of the ICJ, Lord McNair, wrote in favor of restricting the authority of a state to enclose, for economic reasons, coastal waters and insisted instead that the seas constitute *res communis*—the common property of nations. To support his argument McNair cited two decisions by the U.S. Supreme Court, which restricted efforts by California and Texas, respectively, to extend their seaward jurisdiction. His attention was drawn to the statement in the latter case to the effect that

> [W]hatever any nation does in the open sea, which detracts from its common usefulness to nations, or which another nation may charge detracts from it, is a question for consideration among nations as such, and not their separate governmental units.[57]

As noted in the preceding chapter, the International Court of Justice recognizes general principles of law as one of the sources of public international law. In the *Anglo-Norwegian Fisheries* case the ICJ turned to decisions in the municipal law of a federation in an effort to define the relevant general principles of law. The debate over the extent of a coastal state's jurisdiction over adjacent waters continues, but the principle that the oceans represent the historic commons of the international community is well established through the interrelationship of municipal and international law. C. Wilfred Jenks, a noted British barrister, correctly assessed the importance of the case that the ICJ established principles which could then be applied in other areas of the world. The decision moved international law away from what Jenks terms "formless and debatable custom" to the establishment of judicial precedent.[58] The outcome is a process of codification of historical custom and the formation of a universal code of law capable of linking legal systems worldwide. The universality of international law runs counter to the balance-of-power thesis granting governments immunity to those principles of law that they did not accept. The corollary of Jenks's interpretation is a model of world order.

Topics for Discussion

1. In terms of the organization of territorial space, what features distinguish a federation from a unitary state? What role do principles of international law play in resolving disputes between constituent members of a federation?
2. Federal legislation by treaty is an established practice under the U.S. Constitution. Discuss an example of such legislation and describe how it may alter the division of powers between federal and state authorities.
3. With reference to the doctrine of state responsibility, can the U.S. government absolve itself of blame for the transgressions against international law committed by state authorities? What was President Benjamin Harrison's dictum on this issue?
4. How do decisions of constitutional courts in a federation influence the development of international law? Is there a meaningful dividing line between municipal and international law, or does one body of law inform another?

---

[56]Gerald Fitzmaurice, "The Law and Procedure of the International Court of Justice, 1951–1954" (The Anglo-Norwegian Fisheries Case), *British Year Book of International Law, 1954* 31 (New York: Oxford University Press, 1956), 371–374.

[57]*U.S. v. Texas,* 339 U.S. 707, 718 (1950). See also *U.S. v. California,* 332 U.S. 19, 35 (1946).

[58]C. Wilfred Jenks, *The Common Law of Mankind* (London: Stevens & Sons, 1958), pp. 102, 180.

CHAPTER 4

Subjects of International Law

Traditional works on international law treated subject status in a straightforward manner by identifying the true subject as a sovereign state. Now the definition of a subject of international law has become complex. Indeed some argue that the criteria for subject status are so broad that the question of who qualifies has lost much of its meaning. The classical distinction was that of subject and object status.[1] The former characterized a sovereign entity with an acknowledged international legal personality. The latter referred to individuals, either natural or corporate persons, who lacked the attributes of statehood and were therefore not entitled to the rights associated with subject status. For example, the Statute of the International Court of Justice stipulates: Only states may be parties in cases before the Court.[2] Individuals, associations, corporations, charities, foundations need not apply. The modern trend is, however, one of eroding the distinction between subjects and objects, if not universally, at least within the framework of regional international law.

STATEHOOD

The Charter of the United Nations identifies states as eligible members and in doing so adheres to the historical notion that only sovereign entities possess true subject status under international law.[3] Indeed classical writers viewed international law as the link between the state and diplomacy, and they regarded the balance of power as an expression of positive law.[4] Customary international law recognizes four indispensable characteristics of statehood: (a) an indigenous population, (b) a defined territory, (c) an autonomous government, and (d) a capacity to establish relations with other states.[5] The first two criteria are objective and are relatively easy to establish, but the subjective nature of the third and fourth criteria makes it a political issue. Acceptance of a new state as a member of the United Nations reflects a political judgment rather than a legal determination. The entry of the West African republic of Guinea-Bissau offers a case in point. Originally a colony of Portugal, Guinea-Bissau gained its independence in 1974 after a prolonged guerrilla war. Even prior to the withdrawal of Portuguese authority, an estimated eighty governments had granted recognition to the new republic.

---

[1]Paul Sieghart, *The International Law of Human Rights* (New York: Oxford University Press, 1983), p. 20.
[2]United Nations, Statute of the International Court of Justice (New York: Office of Public Information, 1945), Art. 34.
[3]*Charter of the United Nations* (New York: Office of Public Information, 1945 et seq.), Art. 4(1).
[4]Travers Twiss, *The Law of Nations*, 2nd ed. (1884; reprint Littleton, CO.: Fred B. Rothman, 1985), pp. 187–188.
[5]Inter-American Convention on the Rights and Duties of States (Montevideo, December 26, 1933), in 3 Bevans' *Multilateral Treaties*, 145–149.

Did the liberation movement meet the standard of an autonomous government in control of its territory? The answer is doubtful, but political considerations override legal tests in the matter of establishing whether an entity qualifies for statehood.

Breakaway or secessionist regimes always present a special problem, and the legal history of the American Civil War (1861–1865) illustrates the complexity of the issue. In 1869, Chief Justice Salmon P. Chase grappled with the question of whether the governments of the several Confederate states possessed a legal personality. He concluded that the bonds between the state of Texas and the Union were indissoluble, but of greater long-term significance was the dictum that the public acts of the government of Texas were lawful insofar as they were not overtly hostile to the United States. Chase argued that every society required a government competent to carry out its duties. Specifically, he offered the following rather broad definition of statehood:

> A state, in the ordinary sense of the Constitution, is a political community of free citizens, occupying a territory of defined boundaries, and organized under a government sanctioned and limited by a written constitution, and established by the consent of the governed.[6]

Therefore, the nonbelligerent laws and administrative acts of the government of Texas merited judicial recognition in the courts of the United States. Separatist communities of today may well draw upon this statement as a basis for their claim of legitimacy. Notably, the U.S. Supreme Court affirmed this position in two decisions reached after Chase's demise in 1873.[7]

The precedent set by the U.S. Supreme Court in the post–Civil War cases has experienced a revival in the modern period. In 1924, the Court of Appeals of the State of New York faced the question of whether acts of the government of the Russian Socialist Federated Soviet Republic, then unrecognized by the United States, were lawful and deserving of judicial recognition. The Court decided in the affirmative. In presenting the opinion of the Court, Justice Benjamin Cardozo observed:

> Juridically, a government that is unrecognized may be viewed as no government at all, if the power withholding recognition chooses thus to view it. In practice, however, since juridical conceptions are seldom, if ever, carried to the limit of their logic, the equivalence is not absolute, but is subject to self-imposed limitations of common sense and fairness, as we learned in the litigations following our Civil War. In those litigations acts or decrees of the rebellious governments, which, of course, had not been recognized as governments de facto, were held to be nullities when they worked injustice to citizens of the Union, or were in conflict with its public policy. . . . On the other hand, acts and decrees that were just in operation and consistent with public policy were sustained not infrequently to the same extent as if the governments were lawful.[8]

---

[6] *Texas v. White,* 74 U.S. (7 Wallace) 700, 721.

[7] *Horn v. Lockhart,* 84 U.S. (17 Wallace) 570, 580 (1873) and *Williams v. Bruffy,* 96 U.S. (6 Otto) 176, 192 (1877). For a commentary see Edwin D. Dickinson, "Unrecognized Government or State in English and American Law," *Michigan Law Review* 22 (November 1923): 1–42.

[8] *Sokoloff v. National City Bank,* 145 Northeastern Reporter 917–918 (1924).

Following Cardozo, courts may grant judicial recognition to the acts of unrecognized governments as a matter of "common sense and fairness." The decision serves to protect the human rights of persons in territories under the sway of revolutionary authorities, and it established an often-cited precedent. In 1965, the House of Lords invoked *Sokoloff* and reached a conclusion that in the interest of justice and the practical need to administer policy, courts may indeed accord judicial standing to the acts of an unrecognized government.[9]

The foregoing should not be interpreted to mean that all acts of an unrecognized breakaway government are lawful. Violations, for example, of basic human rights (i.e., general principles of law in the sense of the Statute of the International Court of Justice) do not fall under the expedient doctrine articulated by Chief Justice Chase in *Texas*. In 1965, authorities in the Crown colony of Rhodesia (now Zimbabwe) declared themselves independent and established an autonomous regime, which had effective control of the country. The secessionist government instituted the practice, not unknown in European law, of preventive detention, whereby an individual is held without a formal charge being preferred. In times of political unrest a government may seek to neutralize opposition groups by detaining their leaders. Such an act is a denial of the right of habeas corpus, which requires that charges be brought against an individual before he or she can be held in prison.[10]

The Rhodesian government applied the tactic of preventive detention to those opposed to its secessionist policy. One of the detainees was Daniel Madzimbamuto, whose wife succeeded in instituting an appeal to secure her husband's release. In London, the Privy Council heard the case and rendered a decision that denied judicial recognition to the Rhodesian regulations on preventive detention.[11] In its 1968 decision the justices of the Privy Council reviewed extensively the doctrine of the U.S. Supreme Court developed after the Civil War and reached two conclusions. First, the American decisions were reached after the end of the war and the dissolution of the Confederacy, whereas the separatist government in Rhodesia was still in power. Second, the right of habeas corpus is so fundamental that its suspension cannot be compared with the civil suits, that is, issuance of municipal bonds, on which the U.S. Supreme Court had ruled. True, the Privy Council recognized the doctrine of the implied mandate, which may extend validity to the acts of a usurper to maintain order in society, but such a mandate, while it may apply to wills and conveyances, does not endow legitimacy to the suspension of a basic constitutional guarantee. The *Madzimbamuto* case set a limit to the extent to which an unrecognized government could claim the validity of its acts. Where the limit is and how it should be applied remain difficult questions. Yet despite the abstract nature of the question, contemporary legal doctrine makes clear that the subject status linked to statehood carries an obligation to uphold basic rights.

---

[9]*Carl-Zeiss Stiftung v. Rayner and Keeler Ltd.*, 2 All England Law Reports 536, 581–582 (1966). The court of appeal (Lord Denning) affirmed the doctrine of judicial recognition of the acts of an unrecognized government in *Hesperides Hotels Ltd. v. Aegean Turkish Holidays Ltd.*, 1 All England Law Reports 277, 282–283 (1978).

[10]At the outbreak of the Civil War, President Abraham Lincoln suspended the right of habeas corpus in the border states. He took this action based on the constitutional authority granted the commander in chief.

[11]*Madzimbamuto v. Lardner-Burke*, 3 All England Law Reports 561, 578 (1968).

THE DOCTRINE OF NECESSITY

In a dissenting opinion on *Madzimbamuto,* Lord Pearce made reference to the principle of necessity, under which a revolutionary government may, in the interest of public order, suspend guarantees of constitutional rights.[12] The first case resulted from a military takeover in Pakistan in 1958. General Ayub Khan, the new head of government, proclaimed martial law and annulled the constitution. The Supreme Court of Pakistan received appeals regarding the suspension of constitutionally protected rights. Chief Justice Muhammad Munir responded by articulating the doctrine of necessity, which stipulates:

> A revolution is generally associated with public tumult, mutiny, violence and bloodshed but from a juristic point of view the method by which and the persons by whom a revolution is brought about is wholly immaterial. The change may be attended by violence or it may be perfectly peaceful. It may take the form of a *coup d'état* by a political adventurer or it may be effected by persons already in public positions. Equally irrelevant in law is the motive for a revolution, inasmuch as a destruction of the constitutional structure may be prompted by a highly patriotic impulse or by the most sordid of ends. For the purposes of the doctrine here explained a change is, in law, a revolution if it annuls the Constitution and the annulment is effective. If the attempt to break the Constitution fails those who sponsor or organize it are judged by the existing Constitution as guilty of the crime of treason. But if the revolution is victorious in the sense that the persons assuming power under the change can successfully require the inhabitants of the country to conform to the new regime, then the revolution itself becomes a law-creating fact because thereafter its own legality is judged not by reference to the annulled Constitution but by reference to its own success.[13]

The opinion seems to suggest that might does indeed make right. A seizure of political power through violence and intrigue appears to create an accomplished fact meriting judicial recognition. The argument for such a point of view hinges on the requirement for a legal order, no matter how frayed, as a prerequisite for the maintenance of society. The second decision affirming the doctrine of necessity arose from internal strife in the Republic of Cyprus (1963–1964). A former British Crown colony, Cyprus became an independent republic in 1960. As a precondition of independence, the government of the new state accepted a bicommunal constitution designed to provide for political participation by both the Greek majority and the Turkish minority on the island. Precipitated by acts of a Greek Cypriot militia, intercommunal violence broke out at Christmastime 1963, and in the ensuing breakdown of public order the Greek Cypriot government adopted emergency measures, among which was the creation of an extraconstitutional body with broad powers—the Supreme Council of the Judiciary. This act led to a constitutional challenge, which was overruled by the Supreme

---

[12]Ibid., p. 581.
[13]*The State v. Dosso,* 2 Pakistan Supreme Court Reports 180, 184–185 (1958).

Court of Cyprus.[14] Pointing out that the duty of the government is to ensure order, the court cited the doctrine of necessity as an inherent constitutional power. The dissident view is that the fundamentals of the constitution ought to be preserved, and that the doctrine of necessity merely served to camouflage a *coup d'état.*

SOVEREIGNTY

The authority of a government to suspend constitutional guarantees and rule by decree derives from the classical definition of *sovereignty.* At the onset of the modern period, the French political philosopher Jean Bodin (1530–1596) defined sovereignty as " ... absolute and perpetual power vested in a commonwealth which in Latin is termed *majestas.*"[15] The definition contains the core concept of the modern state, which acknowledges no authority other than itself, either internally or externally. For Bodin sovereignty was associated with the person of the monarch, a supreme lawgiver, but one bound by the law of nature. Sovereignty was not the arbitrary and capricious use of power.[16] In the eighteenth century, the age of revolution ushered in constitutions which assigned sovereignty to the people—however that term might be defined. The difficulty with the interpretation of sovereignty as power is that international law becomes merely a cluster of conveniences useful for the administration of foreign policy and ceases to be a code governing the behavior of states. International law may regulate relations among states, but it does not rise above them. In its historic sense sovereignty is a juridical notion at variance with the belief in an international community based on law—a belief articulated by James Madison and John Marshall.

Finding a way in which to reconcile sovereignty with the obligation to abide by the law of nations as expressed in the U.S. Constitution may pose a dilemma, but an influential British legal theorist has offered a useful solution. J. L. Brierly has reviewed the development of the doctrine and concluded that in its present-day form sovereignty is "...merely a term which designates an aggregate of particular and very extensive claims that states habitually make for themselves in their relations with other states."[17] The flexibility of Brierly's definition reflects the realities of the modern international system and relieves us of the burden of a doctrinaire point of view. If Brierly is correct, however, the claims of courts first in Pakistan and then in Cyprus to hand down rulings based on necessity lose much of their luster, for necessity endows the state as a juridical person with absolute power. The reasoning is circular: The state is sovereign, and sovereignty is absolute. The reality of world politics places the state in a complex web of relationships far removed from Bodin's belief in *majestas.* Today the state has rivals, for it is no longer the exclusive claimant to legal personality under international law. Other international entities have developed an authentic subject status, causing a revision of the historic concept of sovereignty.

---

[14]*Attorney General of the Republic v. Mustafa Ibrahim,* 3 Cyprus Law Reports (Triantafyllides, J.) 1, 227 (1964). See also Criton G. Tornaritis, *Cyprus and Its Constitutional and Other Legal Problems,* 2nd ed. (Nicosia: Office of the Attorney-General, 1980), pp. 74–76.

[15]Jean Bodin, *Six Books of the Republic* (1576) quoted in *The Great Political Theories,* ed. Michael Curtis (New York: Avon Books, 1961) 1:272.

[16]Charles Howard McIlwain, *The Growth of Political Thought in the West, from the Greeks to the End of the Middle Ages* (New York: Macmillan, 1932), pp. 286–287.

[17]J. L. Brierly, *The Law of Nations: An Introduction to the International Law of Peace,* 6th ed. (New York: Oxford University Press, 1963), p. 47.

INTERNATIONAL ORGANIZATIONS

While international history encompasses examples of non-state actors, the growth of their influence is a contemporary development.[18] For example, the number of intergovernmental organizations (IGOs) increased from about thirty in 1910 to over a thousand at the end of the century, and the number continues to grow. Added to this figure are increasingly important nongovernmental organizations (NGOs), including such human rights organizations as Amnesty International. International organizations, both public and private, have assumed a critical role in world politics. They contribute to the development of international law by pressing the cause of codification through the formulation of multilateral lawmaking conventions, as exemplified by the United Nations Convention on the Law of the Sea (1982).

The concept of *complex interdependence* links international law with international organization. Interdependence alone is a broad term indicating a reciprocal relationship between two states. In the field of arms control, the United States and the Soviet Union were interdependent during the 1980s. Complex interdependence describes a web of relations among a given set of states. Although the costs and benefits will be shared unequally by the states in this relationship, all participants will show some positive results.[19] Characteristically, complex interdependence takes the form of a proliferation of linkages among the various components of the involved governments.[20] A transnational conference of legislators and a binational commission to administer a frontier zone serve as examples of the multitiered series of cross-boundary ties representative of complex interdependence. The outcome of this relationship is the growth of IGOs capable of formulating and implementing those rules of state behavior which contribute to the development of international law.

International organizations may be either universal[21] or regional. The United Nations system, including its subsidiary organizations, provides an institutional forum within which customary law can evolve into multilateral conventions. As noted earlier, among the organs of the United Nations the International Court of Justice possesses the authority to resolve questions of law and to interpret treaties. Decisions of the Court, such as the one in the *Anglo-Norwegian Fisheries* (1951) case, contribute to the evolution of international law. Similarly, policies implemented by the International Bank for Reconstruction and Development (World Bank) require clearance by the bank's legal staff, whose work serves to clarify, for example, the rights of downstream riparians whenever a hydroelectric project is constructed. A loan from the World Bank must comport with international legal standards as defined by the institution. Even if the bank does not provide full funding, its start-up capital is enough to provide the necessary influence to assure compliance with internationally acceptable environmental

---

[18]Robert O. Keohane, "International Institutions: Can Interdependence Work?" *Foreign Policy* 110 (Spring 1998): 82–84.

[19]Robert O. Keohane and Joseph S. Nye, Jr., "*Power and Interdependence* revisited," *International Organization* 41 (Autumn 1987): 731. See also by the same authors, *Power and Interdependence,* 2nd ed. (Reading, MA.: Addison-Wesley Educational Publishers, 1989).

[20]Robert O. Keohane and Joseph S. Nye, Jr., "Transgovernmental Relations and International Organizations," *World Politics* 27 (October 1974): 43.

[21]The concept of *universal* should not be confused with *global.* The former refers to an organization open to all states, e.g., the United Nations, and the latter to a worldwide grouping of those states sharing a given political culture, e.g., the Commonwealth of Nations.

requirements.[22] In sum, the United Nations system has become a source of international law binding on member states. In a parallel development, regional international organizations have established lawmaking institutions. Established in 1949, the forty members of the Council of Europe created the European Court of Human Rights, whose decisions are in many, but not all instances binding on the states party to the European Convention on Human Rights (1950).

The classical theory of realpolitik recognized only the sovereign state as the source of international law, which in turn originated from the state practice of the leading members of the international community. Complex interdependence and its concomitant growth of international organizations stressed the formation of conventional law, the acceptance of which became a precondition for entry into the international community. International organizations originated in the 1800s as a means to satisfying such functional requirements as the delivery of the mail (e.g., the Universal Postal Union, 1874), and a century later they had evolved into institutions essential for economic development and the maintenance of world order. The status of a true subject of international law is no longer limited to statehood, but includes the IGOs that governments have created as a multilateral response to universal or regional challenges. Necessity has replaced the balance-of-power model with complex interdependence and in doing so has developed a new pattern of international legal relations.

BREAKAWAY STATES

When the San Francisco Conference opened on April 25, 1945, fifty governments joined in the effort to formulate the Charter of the United Nations. By the end of the century, the world organization had 185 members and was still growing. The proliferation of states has led to a series of complications in international law and diplomacy.[23] One problem is the indefinite status of secessionist regimes. Under the banner of national self-determination, peoples formerly under colonial rule have achieved independence, and the dissolution of existing states, notably the Soviet Union in 1991, has added even more members to the international community. Many of the new entities have a doubtful subject status because the major powers deny them recognition of their statehood and bar their entry into international organizations. Are unrecognized and breakaway states subjects or objects of international law? The question lends itself to an answer based on historical precedent.

The Republic of Texas provides a useful analogue of a newly independent, yet unrecognized polity. Through military action the people of Texas severed their ties with Mexico and established an autonomous republic in 1836. Although diplomatic recognition of statehood was not forthcoming from the powers, the governments of Great Britain and the United States did enter into international agreements with the fledgling republic. The British government agreed to serve as a mediator between Mexico and Texas in an effort to facilitate the conclusion of a peace settlement between the

---

[22]Argentina and Paraguay jointly sponsor a hydroelectric project (Yacyreta) on the Paraná River. Construction began in 1983 with capital from the World Bank, and the loan agreement specified adherence to international environmental law. See John Barham, "Argentina and Paraguay in Dam Project," *Financial Times,* 28 October 1993, sec. 1, p. 5.

[23]Elmer Plischke, *Microstates in World Affairs: Policy Problems and Options* (Washington, D.C.: American Enterprise Institute, 1977).

two contending parties, and in a second treaty Texas agreed to join Great Britain in a collaborative effort to suppress the slave trade.[24] Nevertheless, British diplomacy withheld formal diplomatic recognition of the independence of Texas from Mexico and sought to play a mediatory role between the two contending parties. Recognition of statehood for Texas would have cost Great Britain its credibility as a mediator. In both legal and diplomatic terms, the expedient solution was one of treating the Republic of Texas as if it were a sovereign state, but stopping short of making a declaration to that effect.

Initially, the United States pursued a similar policy. In a message sent to Congress before it adjourned in 1836, President Andrew Jackson expressed sympathy for Texas but he withheld recognition. The message concluded:

> Prudence, therefore, seems to dictate that we should stand aloof, and maintain our present attitude, if not until Mexico itself, or one of the great foreign powers, shall recognize the independence of the new Government, at least until the lapse of time or the course of events shall have proved beyond cavil or dispute the ability of the people of that country to maintain their separate sovereignty and to uphold the Government constituted by them.[25]

Three months later Congress dispensed with the policy of prudence and enacted an appropriations measure covering the cost of sending a confirmed diplomatic representative to present his credentials to the president of the Republic of Texas and to commence a dialogue on claims advanced by U.S. citizens against the Republic.[26] On March 7, 1837, the United States recognized the independence of Texas and a year later concluded two treaties with the Republic.[27] Popular sentiment overrode the cautious policy of the president and forced recognition at an early date. From an international legal perspective, however, Jackson could have dealt with the government of Texas on the same indeterminate basis as the British, thereby avoiding exacerbating relations with Mexico. Statehood in the final analysis is largely what diplomats choose to make of it.

The question of whether a breakaway state is a true subject of international law remains largely one of perspective. The experience of the Republic of Texas sets a precedent for Kosovo. With a population of two million, a majority of whom are ethnic Albanians, the province of Kosovo sought to follow the path of autonomous political development only to face a policy of repression by the government of Serbia. In the spring of 1999, the combined forces of the North Atlantic Treaty Organization (NATO) led by the United States and Great Britain carried out a campaign of sustained air bombardment to force a withdrawal of Serbian military and police units from Kosovo. After Serbian forces disengaged in May, NATO deployed a peacekeeping force (KFOR) in Kosovo and reestablished a civilian administration predominantly under the control

---

[24]Great Britain–Texas, Convention relative to the Public Debt of Mexico (November 14, 1840), in 29 B.F.S.P., pp. 84–85 (1840–1841), and Treaty for the Suppression of the African Slave Trade (November 16, 1840), in ibid., pp. 85–86.

[25]Texas message, December 21, 1836, reprinted in 1 Moore's *Digest* 101.

[26]An act making appropriations for the civil and diplomatic expenses of Government, Statutes at Large 5:170 (1837). The measure was unique, in that Congress took the lead in calling for the recognition of a foreign government. Normally, the president initiates the process.

[27]United States–Texas, Claims Convention (April 11, 1838) in 2 Malloy's *Treaties* 1778–1779, and Boundary Convention (April 25, 1838) in ibid., 1779–1780.

of Kosovar Albanians. Kosovo was a secessionist province, but was Kosovo deserving of statehood?

The solution developed by Lord Palmerston, the British foreign secretary, for the Republic of Texas applies to Kosovo. The province is not a state and remains, therefore, a part of Serbia, yet political control is a function of an international force and local authorities. The Serbian government's writ no longer runs in Kosovo. As a matter of necessity, the international community must deal with the provincial government, regardless if it is recognized as sovereign. Legal formalism notwithstanding, Kosovo has acquired the practical equivalent of subject status. Again, the reality of diplomacy requires a departure from the traditional definition of statehood and the acceptance of the notion that legal personality may attach to entities lacking sovereignty in a formal sense.

SUCCESSOR STATES

One of the most intricate of international legal issues to arise in the post–Cold War period is the question of successor states. On Christmas Day, 1991, Mikhail Gorbachev announced his resignation as president of the Union of Soviet Socialist Republics, and President George Bush quickly moved to grant recognition to each of the fifteen successor republics of the former Soviet Union.[28] Although expected, the announcement that over seventy years of Communist Party rule had ended was a shock. Suddenly instead of one state, there were fifteen. A few of the resultant legal problems included arms control agreements, debts, boundary delimitation, membership in international organizations, and representation abroad. Would international agreements entered into by the now-extinct Soviet Union be honored? If so, by whom? Who would control nuclear weapons? Who would be responsible for debts?

The list of questions is almost unending, and an historical case study provides a guide to coping with this problem. In 1783, the Anglo-American Treaty of Peace ended the War of Independence and resulted in the recognition of the United States as a successor state of thirteen British colonies.[29] Obligations, notably the reciprocal responsibility for debts, accompanied the peace agreement. Independence meant that the United States was free to act within the limits of the law of nations. A subsequent treaty normalizing relations between the two countries emphasized that the United States must pay the debts of its citizens whenever these could not otherwise be collected.[30] The experience of the United States set the precedent that a new state is admitted to the world community on the basis of a commitment to adhere to the rules of international law. A successor state inherits treaty obligations that make possible its role as an actor in international affairs.

MAYBE YES, MAYBE NO?

In the discussion of subject status the quality of sovereignty associated with statehood initially emerged as the decisive criterion. Then other entities, such as international organizations or breakaway states, are also true subjects of international law. An addi-

---

[28]"Gorbachev, last Soviet Leader, resigns; U.S. recognizes Republics' Independence," *New York Times,* 26 December 1991, p. A1.

[29]Definitive Treaty of Peace (September 3, 1783), 1 Malloy's *Treaties,* pp. 586, 588.

[30]Treaty of Amity, Commerce and Navigation (November 19, 1794), ibid., pp. 590, 594.

tional category of subjects includes organizations, some of whose functions give them the necessary standing. A premier example is the International Committee of the Red Cross organized in 1863 to provide humanitarian relief for the victims of war. Later the Red Cross joined with the Red Crescent Society to form an international federation with a universal mission. The Red Cross and Red Crescent movement has sponsored multilateral treaties designed to spare civilians and prisoners in time of war, and through these conventions the organizations have achieved the status of recognized subjects. The Order of St. John (Knights of Malta), originally a medieval religious order and secularized in 1879 for the purpose of humanitarian work, provides a further example of functional recognition of subject status. The order maintains diplomatic relations with nineteen governments and enters into international agreements with the same. Modern international law recognizes a type of subject status that transcends both the criteria or territoriality and nationality.[31] The traditional notion linked to a sovereign and territorial state is giving way to new definitions of international legal personality.

These organizations demonstrate the futility of establishing hard and fast categories for subject status. As international society evolves, previous doctrines identifying only territorial states as subjects give way to new interpretations, which endow a nongovernmental international organization (NGO) with subject status in the performance of specified functions. The functional dimension of international legal personality is still developing against a background of globalism, and international law must adapt to new circumstances. The law of nations of the Constitution is now giving way to an authentic transnational law encompassing entities of many different kinds.

OBJECT STATUS

Standard international law treatises of the interwar period emphasized a categorical distinction between subject and object status. One authoritative text asserted that states alone possess a corporate character, and that international law is binding on the state and not on the individual officers of a government.[32] In the aftermath of World War II the barrier between subject and object status began to erode. A revision of L. Oppenheim's standard work repeats the accepted formulation identifying only states as subjects but adds that states may endow individuals with rights and thereby accord them subject status.[33] Kurt von Schuschnigg, a former chancellor of Austria, carried the process a step further by advancing the argument that the need to prevent war and to uphold human rights implies a rebirth of the doctrine of natural law, that is, the existence of a law of nations by which all governments are bound. The logic of positivist theory must require statehood as a precondition for subject status, but natural law redirects our attention to the individual.[34] Does the individual have a capacity to act on the basis of international law? Scholarly opinion remains divided. Even as increased attention is given to the rights and obligations of the individual, a leading text asserts the

---

[31]Arthur C. Breycha-Vauthier and Michael Potulicki, "The Order of St. John in International Law: A Forerunner of the Red Cross," *A.J.I.L.* 48 (October 1954): 554–556.
[32]Charles G. Fenwick, *International Law,* 2nd ed. (New York: D. Appleton-Century Co., 1934), p. 86.
[33]Lauterpacht's *Oppenheim* 1: 21, 579.
[34]Kurt von Schuschnigg, *International Law: An Introduction to the Law of Peace* (Milwaukee: Bruce Publishing Co., 1959), pp. 69–72.

traditional positivist doctrine confining legal personality and therefore true subject status to sovereign states.[35] The debate between the naturalists and the positivists is by no means resolved.

Case law may provide an answer, especially with respect to those charged with the commission of war crimes. In Nuremberg, Germany, the International Military Tribunal (IMT) convened on November 14, 1945, to commence a lengthy trial of twenty-two defendants charged with crimes against peace, humanity, and the law of war. Robert Jackson, a sitting justice of the U.S. Supreme Court, served as one of the prosecutors. In his opening statement, Justice Jackson addressed the issue of state as opposed to individual responsibility under international law. He acknowledged that prior to World War I the responsibility for violations of the law of war attached to states, for they alone possessed subject status, but he continued that only those sanctions which reach individuals have meaning. Consequently, the concept of responsibility must be expanded, and in his opening remarks he asserted:

> Of course, the idea that a state, any more than a corporation, commits a crime is a fiction. Crimes are always committed only by persons. While it is quite proper to employ the fiction of responsibility of a state or a corporation for the purpose of imposing a collective liability, it is quite intolerable to let such legalism become the basis for immunity.[36]

The Nuremberg doctrine led to a recognition of the rights and duties of individuals under international law. In 1993, the United Nations Security Council revived this doctrine and established an international tribunal to prosecute persons charged with the commission of war crimes in the territory of the former Yugoslavia.[37] Contemporary humanitarian law places individuals as well as states within the purview of international law.

Topics for Discussion

1. Describe the traditional criteria of statehood. Apart from territorial states, what other international actors have subject status under international law?
2. What is the doctrine of necessity? As defined in the *Dosso* case (1958), does this doctrine enable a government to evade its duties under international law, especially with regard to human rights?
3. How has the concept of sovereignty evolved from Bodin (1576) to Brierly (1963)? Does the change in definition reflect a transformation of the world system?
4. Can an individual claim immunity from international law by asserting that he or she was acting on behalf of a sovereign state? Or has the purview of modern international law expanded to encompass individuals and other non-state actors?

---

[35]Von Glahn, p. 52.
[36]International Military Tribunal, *Trial of the Major War Criminals: 14 November 1945–1 October 1946* (Nuremberg: By the Tribunal, 1947), 2:150.
[37]U.N., Security Council, Resolution 827, 25 May 1993, Official Records, S/RES/827 (1993).

CHAPTER 5

Recognition of States and Governments

In the study of international law, no question had led to greater misunderstanding than that of the meaning of *diplomatic* recognition. Official opinion as to why or why not a government is unable to recognize a new state or a revolutionary regime is an old one that invariably relies on legal arguments, which presumably tie the hands of policy-makers. The truth lies elsewhere. The recognition of a new state or government is a political act with legal consequences, and political expediency governs the decision to grant recognition. Anglo-American diplomacy and the Republic of Texas is instructive on this point. Great Britain withheld recognition, and the United States granted it. The legal fact of a secessionist state was the same in both instances. The difference lies in the differing policy objectives of the two powers.

LATIN AMERICAN DOCTRINES

Latin American diplomacy has always emphasized international law and organization.[1] The governments of South America and the Caribbean couch their foreign policy in the rhetoric of international law, and this practice invariably leads to the related questions of statehood and recognition of governments. The wars of independence leading to the formation of Latin American republics (1810–1825) established new states based on the doctrine of *uti possidetis* (as you possess it). Boundaries reflected the course of military campaigns and established the geopolitical basis for the modern republics of Central and South America. Secretary of State John Quincy Adams moved quickly to grant recognition to the newly independent states, and the keystone of his foreign policy— the Monroe Doctrine (1823)—guaranteed their sovereignty against European intervention. In this political context recognition came to mean both the acknowledgment of statehood and the acceptance of a new government.[2]

The recurrent question in Latin American diplomacy was whether the seizure of power by a military clique merited recognition as a lawful government. The Ecuadoran jurist and diplomat Carlos Tobar y Borgoño (1884–1923) argued the thesis that international recognition of a dictatorial regime established by armed force encouraged

---

[1]See especially H. B. Jacobini, *A Study of the Philosophy of International Law as seen in the Works of Latin American Writers* (The Hague: Martinus Nijhoff, 1954).

[2]For a discussion of President Monroe's policy recognizing the new states of Latin America, see Julius Goebel, *The Recognition Policy of the United States* (New York: Columbia University Faculty of Arts and Sciences, 1915), pp. 135–140.

political adventurers to try and overthrow constitutional governments.[3] In 1907, the Tobar doctrine, as it came to be known, was incorporated into a multilateral treaty committing the five governments of Central America to a peaceful resolution of disputes. Article 1 of the treaty stipulated:

> The Governments of the High Contracting Parties shall not recognize any other Government which may come into power in any of the five Republics as a consequence of a *coup d'etat,* or of a revolution against the recognized Government, so long as the freely elected representatives of the people thereof have not constitutionally reorganized the country.[4]

The test of recognition under the Tobar doctrine is subjective. Who are the representatives of the people? What are the criteria for a *free* election? At first blush, the answers to these questions may appear self-evident, but the application of these standards to political change in a specific state will quickly reveal their complexity.

Seventeen years later the five Central American republics concluded a revised version of their treaty of amity, but they retained the original language barring recognition of any group that seized power by violent and illegal means.[5] The second treaty was signed in Washington with the U.S. secretary of state in attendance, signifying the endorsement of the Tobar doctrine by his government. By this time, state practice had incorporated the Tobar doctrine into the customary international law of the Americas. As early as 1913, President Woodrow Wilson had invoked the principle of nonrecognition of an authoritarian regime when he withheld recognition from the Mexican dictator, General Victoriano Huerta. At the end of his first year in office Wilson bluntly informed the Congress:

> We are the friends of constitutional government in America; we are more than its friends, we are its champions; because in no other way can our neighbors, to whom we would wish in every way to make proof of our friendship, work out their own development in peace and liberty. Mexico has no Government. The attempt to maintain one at the City of Mexico has broken down, and a mere military despotism has been set up which has hardly more than the semblance of national authority.[6]

A year later, General Huerta went into exile.

Nevertheless, as a result of growing European and North American influence, governments of Latin America gradually began to withdraw their support from the Tobar doctrine. They criticized the Wilsonian approach as one of unwarranted interference

---

[3]Marjorie M. Whiteman, 2 *Digest of International Law,* U.S. Department of State Pubn. 7553 (Washington, D.C.: Government Printing Office, 1963), pp. 84–87. Hereafter cited as Whiteman.
[4]Additional Convention to the General Treaty between the Governments of Costa Rica, Guatemala, Honduras, Nicaragua, and Salvador respecting Recognition of Governments, Intervention and Re-election of Presidents (December 20, 1907) in 100 *B.F.S.P.* 840–841 (1906–1907).
[5]General Treaty of Peace and Amity between the Central American States (February 7, 1923) in *American Journal of International Law: Official Documents* 17 (April 1923): 118.
[6]Woodrow Wilson, Annual Message of the President, *F.R.U.S. 1920,* p. x. Notably Wilson applied the precondition of constitutional and representative government only to the Americas. See Green Haywood Hackworth, *Digest of International Law,* U.S. Department of State (Washington, D.C.: U.S. Government Printing Office, 1940) 1:185. Hereafter cited as Hackworth.

and insisted that recognition of new governments was an obligation. The Mexican foreign minister, Genaro Estrada, published a press release in 1930 in which he stated:

> After a careful study of the subject, the Government of Mexico has transmitted instructions to its Ministers or Charges d'Affaires in the countries affected by the recent political crises, informing them that the Mexican Government is issuing no declarations in the sense of grants of recognition, since that nation considers that such a course is an insulting practice and one which, in addition to the fact that it offends the sovereignty of other nations, implies that judgment of some sort may be passed upon the internal affairs of those nations by other governments, inasmuch as the latter assume, in effect, an attitude of criticism, when they decide favorably or unfavorably, as to the legal qualifications of foreign regimes.[7]

The thrust of the Estrada doctrine achieved the status of regional international law in the Montevideo Convention of 1933. Article 3 stated:

> The political existence of a state is independent of recognition by other states. Even before recognition the state has the right to defend its integrity and independence, to provide for its conservation and prosperity, and consequently to organize itself as it sees fit, to legislate upon its interests, administer its services, and to define the jurisdiction and competence of its courts.
>
> The exercise of these rights has no other limitation than the exercise of the rights of other states according to international law.[8]

The constitutive act of the Organization of American States (1948) opened with a declaration of principles, among which were:

a. International law is the standard of conduct of States in their reciprocal relations;

b. International order consists essentially of respect for the personality, sovereignty and independence of States, and the faithful fulfillment of obligations derived from treaties and other sources of international law.[9]

The charter then incorporated the Montevideo convention's article of recognition as stated.

The Good Neighbor Policy as proposed by President Herbert Hoover and carried out by President Franklin D. Roosevelt was an implicit rejection of the Wilsonian view that recognition of a government bestowed legitimacy upon it. Noninterference by the United States in the affairs of a Latin American republic entails acceptance of the Estrada doctrine. In the 1990s, however, the countervailing Tobar doctrine experienced a revival. In 1991, the popularly elected president of Haiti, Jean-Bertrand Aristide, was overthrown by a military cabal, whose leader, General Raoul Cédras, organized a government. First the

---

[7]Estrada Doctrine of Recognition (September 27, 1930) as reprinted in Whiteman 2:85. Also see Richard N. Swift, *International Law: Current and Classic* (New York: John Wiley & Sons, 1969), p. 60.
[8]Inter-American Convention on the Rights and Duties of States (December 26, 1933) in 3 Bevans *Multilateral Treaties,* p. 147.
[9]Charter of the Organization of American States (Bogotá, April 30, 1948) in 2 *United States Treaties 1951* (Washington, D.C.: Government Printing Office, 1952), pp. 2394, 2418.

Bush and then the Clinton administration declined to recognize the legitimacy of the new regime on the grounds that it violated the constitution and therefore lacked legitimacy.[10] After futile attempts to negotiate a restoration of constitutional government and pursuant to an enabling resolution of the U.N. Security Council, President Clinton resorted to armed intervention and justified the action by stating in a televised address:

> There's no question that the Haitian people want to embrace democracy; we know it because they went to the ballot box and told the world. History has taught us that preserving democracy in our own hemisphere strengthens America's security and prosperity. Democracies are more likely to keep the peace and to stabilize our region.[11]

General Cédras went into exile, and President Aristide was restored to office. Wilsonianism may well have had the final word.

TWO THEORIES OF RECOGNITION

Closely related to the contrapuntal doctrines of Tobar and Estrada are the theories of *declaratory* and *constitutive* recognition, which may be applied to governments as well as states. The declaratory theory is a statement of political fact acknowledging that a state or government exists and therefore merits recognition. The constitutive theory asserts that the act of recognition itself constitutes a new state or government.[12] Although governments are not always consistent in adhering to one theory or another, in general Great Britain favors the declaratory approach while the United States adheres to the constitutive practice.

Advocates of realpolitik will find support in the declaratory theory, which stresses the acceptance of a political fact irrespective of the legitimacy bestowed by a democratic and constitutional form of government.[13] The interest of a state requires diplomatic relations with all other members of the international community, and accordingly recognition is extended without implying approval or disapproval. If international law is to regulate the relations of states, then it must be universal. To withhold recognition from a state is to deny its right to exist. From this perspective recognition becomes a necessary act, even a duty.[14] The state exists and its sovereignty and independence are not subject to external approval. In the tradition of realist diplomacy the legal fact of statehood is above question. For another state to question the legitimacy of a new state runs counter to the doctrine of territorial supremacy.[15] The assumption that the international system is a loose anarchy of sovereign entities leads to the conclusion that the declaratory principle is the correct one.

---

[10]Sean D. Murphy, "Democratic Legitimacy and Recognition of States and Governments," *International and Comparative Law Quarterly* 48 (July 1999): 545–548.

[11]William J. Clinton, Address to the Nation on Haiti (September 15, 1994) in *Presidential Documents* (September 1994–January 1995) 30:1781.

[12]Brierly, pp. 138–140. Also see James Crawford, *The Creation of New States in International Law* (New York: Oxford University Press, 1979), pp. 15–19.

[13]For a discussion of democratic entitlement and the rights of statehood, see Thomas M. Franck, "The Emerging Right to Democratic Government," *American Journal of International Law* 86 (January 1992): 46, 90.

[14]Ti-chiang Chen, *The International Law of Recognition* (New York: Frederick A. Praeger, 1951), pp. 3–6.

[15]Malcolm N. Shaw, *International Law,* 4th ed. (New York: Cambridge University Press, 1997), pp. 296–303.

Constitutive theorists argue that recognition not only bestows rights, but stresses the obligation of the newly formed state to fulfill its duties as a member of international society. The government of a new state must affirm a readiness to enter into constructive relations with other states on the basis of international law. As noted earlier, by incorporating an international law clause into its 1787 Constitution, the government of the United States accepted an obligation to uphold the principles of international law. The constitutive theory applies the same standard. The political fact of existence is not enough. Accordingly, no state is obligated to recognize a new state or government.[16] Again, the argument is that the international system lacks a superior authority to set and enforce the standards of recognition, and consequently the decision must depend upon the convenience of each government. If recognition is primarily an expedient political act with legal consequences, the notion of linking it to specific governmental forms and policies is reasonable.

STATES AND GOVERNMENTS

The combined forces of decolonization and the fragmentation of multinational states have increased the number of states from the forty-nine that participated in the founding conference of the United Nations[17] to the world organization's 185 members in 1999. The proliferation of states has altered the international system and contributed to the complexity of the question of recognition. Among the issues in law and diplomacy is the distinction made between extending recognition to a state as opposed to its government and thereby implying that the government is illegal and consequently devoid of legal rights.

Classical diplomacy did not make a distinction between states and their governments. The recognition of one was tantamount to the recognition of the other. The Tobar doctrine represented a departure from the traditional approach and meant that a state could be recognized as an independent legal personality, but its government could not express the rights or fulfill the duties of that personality. U.S. policy has often drawn a line between states and governments with the result that Washington has recognized the existence of a state but not its government. President Wilson made this point with reference to the Huerta regime. Later he refused to recognize the Soviet government established in Russia after the revolution of November 7, 1917. Instead the United States continued to regard the representative of the ousted government of Alexander Kerensky as the authentic voice of the Russian state, and this awkward state of affairs continued until 1933, when the administration of President Franklin D. Roosevelt recognized the Soviet regime. The difficulty in recognizing a state but not its actual government is self-evident. Nonrecognition of a government means that U.S. citizens traveling in the country in question do not have the protection of an embassy, which may be interpreted as a denial of a constitutional right.[18]

---

[16]N. A. Maryan Green, *International Law,* 3rd ed. (London: Pitman Publishing, 1987), pp. 33–36.
[17]The Ukraine and White Russia also had delegations at the San Francisco Conference (1945), but these republics did not become sovereign states until 1991.
[18]Edwin D. Dickinson, "Unrecognized Government or State in English or American Law," *Michigan Law Review* 22 (December 1923): 132–134. Also see Donald G. Bishop, *The Roosevelt-Litvinov Agreements: The American View* (Syracuse, N.Y.: Syracuse University Press, 1965).

EVOLUTION OF U.S. POLICY

In the world of diplomacy "creative ambiguity" may sometimes offer a temporary advantage, but over the long run consistency in the application of standards of international law and policy endows a government's foreign policy with credibility. Clarity and continuity in applying a policy of recognition of states and governments is illustrative of the point. Long associated with the constitutive orientation, presidential decisions have not always hewed this line.[19] Secretary of State Henry L. Stimson (1929–1933 term) articulated the doctrine that the United States would not recognize as lawful the acquisition of territory by conquest. The Stimson doctrine, as it came to be known, derived its legitimacy from the Pact of Paris (1928), which outlawed war as an instrument of policy.[20] When Japan took control of Korea in the aftermath of the Russo-Japanese War (1904–1905), the United States recognized Japanese suzerainty and converted its diplomatic mission in Seoul into a consulate general subordinate to the American embassy in Tokyo.[21] The somewhat bureaucratic acceptance of the extinction of a sovereign state through conquest was not to be repeated in the case of China. Starting in September 1931, the Japanese army occupied the northeastern Chinese province of Manchuria and announced the formation of the puppet state of "Manchuko." The League of Nations condemned the move as an act of aggression. Although not a member of the League, the United States supported the world organization, and Secretary Stimson informed the American ambassador in Tokyo that the United States would not recognize any situation or agreement brought about by the unprovoked use of armed force.[22] The following month, Stimson assured a senior member of the Senate Committee on Foreign Relations that the United States favors ". . . a system of orderly development by the law of nations including the settlement of all controversies by methods of justice and peace instead of by arbitrary force."[23]

Similarly, the Stimson doctrine applied to the incorporation of the Baltic republics. In 1978, President Jimmy Carter issued a directive blocking the assets of Latvia, Lithuania, and Estonia in accordance with a policy of nonrecognition of the forcible incorporation of these countries into the Soviet Union.[24] The partitioning of Eastern Europe in the Hitler–Stalin pact of 1939 led to the Soviet occupation of the republics, and they did not regain their independence until the dissolution of the Soviet Union in 1991. During this period, the United States continued to recognize the legal personalities of the three states, albeit with the understanding that de facto governance was in the hands

---

[19]Thomas Galloway, *Recognizing Foreign Governments: The Practice of the United States* (Washington, D.C.: The American Enterprise Institute, 1978), pp. 145–147. For an editorial view of a failure to abide by principle, in this instance the recognition of the Cambodian dictator Pol Pot, see "Hold-Your-Nose Diplomacy," *Washington Post,* 17 September 1980, A18.

[20]Pact of Paris (August 27, 1928), 2 Bevans 732.

[21]1 Hackworth 84. A memorandum agreed to by William Howard Taft, then the secretary of war, and Count Taro Katsura, on November 23, 1905, recognized the dominant position of the Japanese resident general in Korea. The following day the U.S. minister in Seoul received instructions to depart.

[22]Secretary of state to the ambassador in Japan (January 7, 1932) in *F.R.U.S., Japan, 1931–1941,* 1:76.

[23]Letter to Senator William E. Borah (February 23, 1932) reprinted in ibid., 1:83–87.

[24]Marian Lloyd Nash, *Digest of United States Practice in International Law, 1978,* Department of State (Washington, D.C.: Government Printing Office, 1980), 1359.

of Soviet authorities. Specifically, the American consulate in Leningrad (today St. Petersburg) included the three republics in its administrative district, which reflected a tacit acceptance of Soviet control.

By comparison, U.S. policy toward the Himalayan mountain state of Tibet lacked the consistency shown the Baltic republics. In 1951, the army of the People's Republic of China occupied Tibet, and its leadership, notably the Dalai Lama, sought refuge in India. The requirements of the Stimson doctrine applied: An act of aggression does not merit recognition. The end of the Cold War and the development of Sino-American commercial and cultural ties suggested the expediency of resolving the Tibetan question. Principle gave way to the necessity of realpolitik. Following a state visit to China in 1998, President Clinton summarized his government's policy as follows:

> We have not advocated independence for Tibet, separation, civil war,
> anything disruptive. We have advocated, if you will, autonomy with integrity.
> It's supposed to be an autonomous region anyway.[25]

The issue of Taiwan (formerly Formosa) is equally complex. In 1949, the Chinese Communist Party consolidated its control in the aftermath of a prolonged armed struggle, and the vanquished elite of the Nationalist Party withdrew to Taiwan, where it established an autonomous government. President Harry S. Truman responded to the regime change in China by asserting the traditional policy of nonrecognition:

> We shall refuse to recognize any government imposed upon a nation by the
> force of any foreign power. In some cases it may be impossible to prevent
> forceful imposition of such a government. But the United States will not
> recognize any such government.[26]

The president argued that the government of Taiwan was the legitimate representative of the Chinese people and therefore deserved the support of the United States.[27] Following the war in Korea (1950–1953), relations between Washington and Beijing were in a condition of diplomatic permafrost. The thaw came in 1972, when President Nixon visited China and issued a joint statement as a first step toward the normalization of relations. The document asserted that "...Taiwan is a part of China."[28] In 1979, Congress passed the Taiwan Relations Act, which ended formal diplomatic representation to the government of Taiwan and foresaw the peaceful unification of the island with the mainland.[29] The Shanghai communique and the subsequent legislation are efforts to achieve a compromise solution: The territorial integrity of the Chinese state is to be restored, but not through the use of armed force. The means of unification are to be democratic and peaceful, but an agreed formula for the realization of this goal remains elusive.

---

[25]Interview with Radio Free Asia (June 24, 1998), in *Presidential Documents* (June 29, 1998) 34: 1210.
[26]Quoted in Warren Christopher, "Normalization of Diplomatic Relations," Bureau of Public Affairs, Department of State (June 11, 1977), p. 2.
[27]Chinese government on Formosa (June 27, 1950) in *Public Papers of the Presidents: Harry S. Truman, 1950* (Washington, D.C.: Government Printing Office, 1965), p 172.
[28]Shanghai communique (February 27, 1972) in *Public Papers of the Presidents: Richard Nixon, 1972* (Washington, D.C.: Government Printing Office, 1974), p. 378.
[29]Taiwan Relations Act (April 10, 1979) in *Statutes at Large* 93: 14.

THE BRITISH APPROACH

While constitutive theory dominates American thinking, British diplomacy adheres to the declaratory principle. The Wilsonian doctrine requiring a distinction between the recognition of a state and of its government is incompatible with the British test of whether a government is in effective control. If that test is passed, the government merits recognition, which is a political act and does not connote approval or disapproval. Reaction to the seizure of power by the Chinese Communist Party in 1949 is illustrative. The United States refused to recognize the new government in Beijing until the passage of the Taiwan Relations Act. Great Britain moved quickly and extended recognition in 1949, shortly after the takeover. Essentially, British diplomacy reflects the Estrada doctrine to the effect that to withhold recognition of a new government is an affront to its sovereignty.

The Tinoco affair is illustrative of the problem resultant from nonrecognition. In January 1917, Federico Tinoco, the minister of war of Costa Rica, seized power and ruled for some thirty-one months after which he went into exile. Tinoco's government was unconstitutional, but it did exercise effective control of the republic. It was therefore a government de facto. Nevertheless, Great Britain and the United States suspended relations with the insurgents and denied them diplomatic recognition. In 1919, the restoration of a government committed to constitutionalism did not resolve the issue of whether acts of state under Tinoco were legally binding. In particular, British entrepreneurs complained to their government that the contracts protecting their investments were being invalidated. The American consul in San José summarized the issue as follows:

> Lack of recognition of this Government by our Government is placing it in jeopardy and threatens its very existence. This British question is one of many which it cannot handle properly without recognition by the United States, and American interests in general are affected injuriously as a result.[30]

Despite this plea, the United States and Costa Rica did not restore relations until 1922.

The plight of British investors, whose guarantees had been washed away by a torrent of political changes, led London to consider economic countermeasures. Eventually, strained relations gave way to a bilateral agreement committing Great Britain and Costa Rica to arbitration, that is, recourse to an arbitral tribunal for the resolution of their dispute over the validity of contracts concluded under the Tinoco regime. In 1923, the two governments signed the arbitral agreement, and William H. Taft (the serving chief justice of the United States and president from 1909 to 1913) was designated the sole arbitrator.[31] The Costa Rican case rested on the argument that the British government had not recognized Tinoco's government on the grounds that its seizure of power was unconstitutional. How could a contract with an extralegal government be regarded as binding? The British conceded that recognition had been withheld but insisted that the Tinoco regime was a de facto government exercising control over the republic. Such a government could create rights for British citizens, and these rights deserve the pro-

---

[30]The consul at San José to the secretary of state (July 16, 1920), *F.R.U.S.* 1920, 1:836–837.
[31]Arbitration Agreement between Great Britain and Costa Rica (Washington: October 18, 1923), *American Journal of International Law* 18 (January 1924): 147.

tection of international law. The Costa Rican rebuttal stressed that nonrecognition brought into play the doctrine of estoppel, whereby a government which refuses to assert its rights loses them. In his concluding statement Taft acknowledged the contradiction inherent in the British position, and noted that recognition would have enhanced the British claim. In the end, both governments accepted a settlement based on a compromise. The Tinoco arbitration illustrates the negative legal consequences of nonrecognition based on the application of constitutive principles and undoubtedly contributed to the British acceptance of a declaratory theory.

The declaratory theory presumes that an executive decision preempts a judicial determination. Two cases serve to illustrate the relationship between law and foreign policy. The first was *Luther v. Sagor* (1921), which focused on the legality of the acts of an unrecognized government.[32] The plaintiff manufactured timber for a British company situated in Russia. Following the revolution of 1917, the Bolshevik government nationalized the company and expropriated its assets. The trade representative of the new Russian government then attempted to sell the timber in Great Britain. The purpose of the suit was to block the sale on the grounds that the British government had not recognized the Bolshevik authorities and therefore the act of expropriation had no standing under British law. The timber should, therefore, revert to its original owner, the A. M. Luther Company. Two judgments followed. In the initial one, the court ruled for the plaintiff despite evidence that the new regime in Moscow was in effective control. The position taken by the court was that it must defer to guidance from the Foreign Office, and that meant nonrecognition. When the Foreign Office eventually did grant recognition to the de facto government, the decision was reversed in favor of the defendant.

The second case involved an interned German national, one Kuechenmeister, who at the end of the Second World War sued for a writ of habeas corpus (i.e., a court order requiring his release from detention).[33] Through his counsel, Kuechenmeister argued that the military collapse of Germany and the unconditional surrender of its armed forces ended the state of war, which justified his detention. The Court of Appeal took judicial note of a certificate from the Foreign Office to the effect that a state of war continued to exist between Great Britain and Germany despite the cessation of hostilities. Consequently habeas corpus was denied, and the plaintiff continued to be detained as an enemy alien. A reference to the opinion of Justice Cardozo in the *Sokoloff* case[34] reveals a critical distinction between American and British courts in the adjudication of cases on recognition and international legal personality. Cardozo was under no obligation to accept as binding a certificate from the U.S. Department of State regarding the legal status of the Soviet Russian government, even if one had been offered. In the cases of *Luther* and *Kuechenmeister,* judicial authorities sought and received guidance from the Foreign Office, which they were obligated to follow. As applied in Great Britain, the doctrine of judicial self-limitation[35] ensures a unity of policy between the executive and the judiciary. By comparison, federal and state courts in the United States are not obligated to follow the lead of the executive branch.

---

[32] *A. M. Luther v. James Sagor,* 90 All England Law Reports 1202 (1921).
[33] R. v. Bottrill: Ex parte Kuechenmeister, 2 All England Law Reports 434 (1946).
[34] See Chapter 4 (note 7) for the background of the *Sokoloff* case as decided by the Court of Appeals of the State of New York.
[35] Chen, p. 7.

In sum, the declaratory interpretation of British policy presumes that recognition of a state is tantamount to recognition of its government. Indeed the act of withholding recognition of a government constitutes a violation of international law because that government cannot exercise its rights under international law.[36] Recognition of a new government, even one whose constitutional legitimacy is in question, is a duty. The Estrada doctrine appears in most cases to have gained acceptance, yet the question of what to do about a government practicing genocide (e.g., the "killing fields" of the Pol Pot regime in Cambodia, 1975–1979) remains. A proposed solution involves introducing a third or intermediate category of recognition. Such a category would provide for the extension of recognition on a limited basis permitting routine contacts, but full recognition would not be forthcoming.[37] In February 2000, a new Austrian government based on a coalition of a centrist party with a populist movement of the right took office. The European Union responded to this development by downgrading its relations with Vienna, and the United States summoned its ambassador home for consultation.[38] Recognition, however, was never an issue, yet the diplomatic response to the new government did impair its ability to achieve foreign policy goals. Considerations of policy continue to outweigh legal theory on the issue of recognition.

BELLIGERENCY AND INSURGENCY

In an era when states implode under the impact of divisive internal forces, the question of the standing of insurgent forces under international law becomes critical. Angola, the Congo, and the Sudan offer tragic examples. Within the framework of customary international law, Justice Joseph Story formulated the basic policy on the recognition of belligerency in 1818. Santo Domingo (now Haiti and the Dominican Republic) experienced a revolution with the result that rival insurgent movements controlled the island. In 1794, Congress had enacted a neutrality law requiring the forfeiture of any vessel employed in the service of a foreign state, and a ship carrying munitions to one of the warring parties on Santo Domingo was indeed seized. The question arose as to whether an unrecognized revolutionary movement with local authority qualified as a foreign *state*. If not, the federal statute could scarcely be said to apply to the vessel. Justice Story responded:

> No doctrine is better established, than that it belongs exclusively to governments to recognize new states in the revolutions which may occur in the world; and until such recognition, either by our own government, or the government to which the new state belonged, courts of justice are bound to consider the ancient state of things as remaining unaltered.[39]

Although the legal personality of a state experiencing internal war remains in tact, international law does not relegate secessionist forces to the level of bandits. Instead

---

[36]Hersh Lauterpacht, *Recognition in International Law* (New York: Cambridge University Press, 1947; reprint, New York: AMS Press, 1978), pp. 4–5.

[37]Colin Warbrick, "The New British Policy on the Recognition of Governments," *I.C.L.Q.* 30 (July 1981): 591.

[38]Robert H. Reid, "Dangerous' regime to be sworn in," *USA Today,* 4 February 2000, p. 8A.

[39]*Gelston v. Hoyt,* 16 U.S. (3 Wheaton) 246, 324 (1818).

law and diplomacy recognize two special categories: belligerency and insurgency. To qualify for the status of belligerency, three criteria must be met: rebellion must be organized around a government, the revolt must extend a local uprising, and a substantial area must be under the de facto control of antigovernment forces.[40] The American Civil War provided a setting for a test of these standards.

In April 1861, President Lincoln declared a blockade first of the Gulf Coast ports of the Confederacy and shortly afterwards of those on the East Coast. The following month the British government issued a proclamation acknowledging the Confederacy as a belligerent community subject to the rules of the law of war and entitled to the protection thereof.[41] France and Spain adopted the same policy.

Shortly thereafter, the U.S. Supreme Court confronted the issue in the *Prize Cases,* which involved four neutral vessels seized as they attempted to run the blockade. A hostile blockade is an act of war and creates a state of belligerency. The Court had to decide first if the president had acted within the limits of his constitutional authority and second if the declaration of a blockade conferred the character of belligerents on Confederate forces. In its response to the first question, the Court was divided; but it supported the proposition that the blockade implied a status of belligerency.[42] The precedent set in the *Prize Cases* became an issue during the war in Vietnam, when the war powers of the president were again debated. The administration of President Lyndon Johnson (1963–1969) referred to this decision in support of the argument that a presidential proclamation had created a legal condition of belligerency, which meant, among other issues, that the Vietcong guerrillas in South Vietnam were members of a belligerent community.[43] Judicial decisions often serve to clarify customary international law.

Insurgency precedes belligerency. Insurgents are not yet in control of an identifiable territory, and they are not successful enough to form a government. Accordingly, their rights are more limited. The distinction between belligerency and insurgency was the essential issue in a case involving American filibustering during the Cuban uprising against Spanish rule in 1896. *The Three Friends,* a privately owned American-flag vessel, had been fitted out with arms and munitions for the purpose of supporting the insurrectionists. U.S. authorities libeled the ship (i.e., they instituted legal proceedings against it) on the grounds that its sailing would violate a presidential proclamation of neutrality, which barred rendering assistance to a foreign power in time of war. The U.S. Supreme Court ultimately dismissed the libel on the grounds that the relevant law covered either a war between states or a civil war, but not a revolt that had not yet gained control over substantial territory and thereby won the status of a belligerency.

Writing for the Court, Chief Justice Melville Fuller commented:

> The distinction between recognition of belligerency and recognition of a condition of political revolt, between recognition of the existence of war in a material sense and of war in a legal sense, is sharply illustrated in the case

---

[40]Von Glahn, pp. 72–73.
[41]Moore, 1:184–193. Also see Adams to Seward (June 14, 1861) in *Diplomatic Correspondence, 1861* (Washington, D.C.: Government Printing Office, 18): 103–105.
[42]*The Prize Cases,* 67 U.S. (2 Black) 635, 669 (1861).
[43]John Norton Moore, *Law and the Indo-China War* (Princeton, NJ: Princeton University Press, 1972), pp. 198–200.

before us. For here the political department has not recognized the existence of a *de facto* belligerent power engaged in hostility with Spain, but has recognized the existence of insurrectionary warfare prevailing before, at the time and since this forfeiture is alleged to have occurred.[44]

Nevertheless, the line between belligerency and insurgency remains unclear, for considerations of policy guide a government's decision to extend recognition to a de facto regime representing a revolutionary movement. Fuller's decision to redirect the issue to the executive branch was prudent.

Closely related to the complexity of distinguishing between belligerency and insurgency is the problem of *premature* recognition. Ideological commitment to a revolutionary cause may move a government to grant recognition to an insurrectionary movement first as a belligerent community and then as a de facto government. Guinea-Bissau, until 1974 a Portuguese colony on the west coast of Africa, offers a case in point. A national liberation movement waged an eleven-year struggle for statehood, during which some eighty governments, principally in the global south, recognized the independence of the new state prior to the withdrawal of the Portuguese colonial administration. Yugoslavia provides a second example. Starting with unilateral declarations of independence by Slovenia and Croatia in 1991, the Federal Republic began to dissolve, and open warfare soon erupted. Influenced by ties of religion and history, Germany and Austria moved quickly to recognize the sovereignty of Slovenia and Croatia. Some observers insist that a delayed act of recognition might have given diplomacy time to work out a more peaceful separation of the two new republics. History permits only one interpretation, and the rest remains speculative. Premature recognition of a state or a government may be politically attractive, but the long-term effect is violative of international law. Adherence to the declaratory standards of effective control of territory and the absence of a credible challenger requires recognition under the terms of the Montevideo Convention (1933). The constitutive approach links legitimacy to political democracy, but as noted, the advocates of this doctrine have historically been prepared to make exceptions in the name of expediency. From the standpoint of the role of international law in the administration of foreign policy, adherence to the historic standard of realpolitik is usually the best course of action.

DIVIDED POLITIES

The bipolarity of the Cold War led to the formation of blocs of states integrated under the regional leadership of the two superpowers. Strategic designs and economic interests spawned by the confrontation of the rival alliances led to the dismemberment of historic states. Austria was reunified in 1955, and the destruction of the Berlin Wall in 1989 removed the final barrier to German unification. Despite the growing multipolarity of the international system, two states—Cyprus and Korea—remain tragically divided. Both were sovereign and independent states in the modern period, and their division is part of the tragic legacy of the Cold War. In each instance, dialogues are now in progress to reduce the barriers that divide these states in the hope that a political solution will

---

[44]*Three Friends,* 166 U.S. 1, 64 (1897).

evolve. The international community, particularly the United Nations, is capable of providing the incentives necessary to overcome the demilitarized zones of the past.

The international law of recognition may serve a purpose by providing a framework for a settlement. Both Cyprus and Korea suffer from a de facto partition between north and south. Overcoming the partition will require a comprehensive formula crafted to meet the unique conditions of the state in question. Nevertheless, a single precondition must be met in both instances: Each party to the dialogue must recognize the legitimacy of the other. Without such reciprocity, productive negotiations will not take place. At this point, the declaratory theory of recognition makes its contribution. Immediately prior to unification each government and/or authority extends recognition to its negotiating partner. Two flags are hoisted for a prescribed period, possibly twenty-four hours, and then lowered to be replaced by a single banner representing the unified state. The advantage of reciprocal recognition followed by unification is that of resolving the myriad of legal problems which would arise if the lawfulness of the statutes or treaties of one of the governments was subsequently called into question. Of course, retroactive recognition is possible, as the U.S. Supreme Court demonstrated in its post–Civil War decisions regarding the Confederacy, but uncertainty encumbers such a process. Prior recognition as a precondition to union resolves the issue and enhances the chances of success of the new government. Used in this sense, the doctrine of recognition becomes a means for restoring the unity of a divided polity.

Topics for Discussion

1. Is the withholding of recognition from a revolutionary government a violation of its rights under international law? Under what circumstances may a new government be denied recognition? If recognition is subsequently granted, is the legal effect retroactive?
2. Does international law provide for a meaningful distinction between the recognition of a state and/or a government? How do the policies of Great Britain and the United States differ on this question?
3. Under what circumstances may courts extend judicial recognition to the acts of an unrecognized regime even though it has not been granted de facto recognition? Does discretionary authority on the part of an independent judiciary serve the cause of human rights, or does it weaken the foreign policy of the government in question?
4. How does international law distinguish between belligerency and insurgency? Could insurgents be tried as pirates or terrorists? Is a transnational revolutionary movement protected by international law?

CHAPTER 6

State Responsibility

In the first instance recognition is usually de facto, in that it acknowledges a political fact, namely the formation of a new state or the triumph of a new government over its adversary in a civil war. The establishment of normal diplomatic relations, often in the form of a friendship, commerce, and navigation (FCN) treaty, leads to *de jure* recognition, which confirms the willingness of the new government to fulfill its legal obligations and abide by international law. Entry into the United Nations or regional organizations invariably signifies *de jure* recognition. Recognition in law as well as in fact carries with it the obligation of state responsibility. The expression historically had a meaning limited to the international liability of government officials for their acts. In 1980, the International Law Commission (ILC), a committee of experts appointed by the General Assembly of the United Nations, addressed the problem of international responsibility and concluded:

> There is an internationally wrongful act of a State when:
> **a.** conduct consisting of an action or omission is attributable to the State under international law; and
> **b.** that conduct constitutes a breach of an international obligation of the State.[1]

Although the ILC is not a political body, its membership of thirty-four reflects the diversity of legal cultures encompassed by the United Nations, and its annual reports to the General Assembly merit consideration. The notion of state responsibility is inherent in international law. Vattel observed that statehood carried with it obligations to the international community, and Madison incorporated the notion into the international law clause of the Constitution. Two world wars threatened the disappearance of this concept as one government after another flouted basic legal norms. The ILC revived interest in state responsibility, and in doing so the commission's work stimulated an important development in international law.

RIGHTS OF STATES

Through the achievement of statehood, a political community acquires the rights of a subject under international law. Following the Charter of the United Nations, these rights include sovereignty, territorial integrity, independence, and the right of existence, that is, individual or collective self-defense. As noted in Chapter 4, the classical doctrine

---

[1]International Law Commission, 37th session (1985), *Yearbook of the International Law Commission, 1980* (30th session) 2 (Pt. 2):30, reprinted in Marina Spinedi and Bruno Simma (eds.), *United Nations Codification of State Responsibility* (New York: Oceana Publications, 1987), Appendix 1:325.

of sovereignty stressed the absolute authority of the state over its territory and subjects (not always citizens), and the modern view interprets the concept as an aggregation of rights claimed by a state. Regional integration in the interest of economic development and military security is bringing states together and creating a new notion of sovereignty.[2] The once definitive outlines of the idea have become blurred.

The Charter of the United Nations retains in its second article a commitment to the sovereign equality of the member states. Skeptics of international law rarely fail to point out the difficulty of applying this phrase to the real world of politics.[3] The phrase does not, however, mean an equality of power and influence among states. Even the charter recognizes the special position of the five permanent members of the Security Council.[4] Juridical equality rarely matches equality in fact. The disparity of power among states is too great, and no controlling authority exists to check the ambitions of the strong against the weak.[5] In 1970, the General Assembly adopted a resolution defining equality as a legal concept, which focused on sovereignty and independence.[6] Four years later the General Assembly enhanced the meaning of equality by linking it to the concept of distributive justice and calling for a sharing of resources with the developing countries of the Global South.[7] Although resolutions of the General Assembly have a declaratory as opposed to a mandatory character, their adoption represents a general acceptance of principles, which may then be said to constitute shared political and legal goals.

Territorial integrity is a sensitive issue for many states, whose frontiers are subject to constant violations. The traditional view of the problem was one of ravages by armed bands, which would then flee to the sanctuary offered by an international border. While depredations of this kind still occur, modern technology has increased the vulnerability of the state as a territorial unit. In an unseen fashion, political and economic penetration can erode the territorial supremacy of a government and leave the symbol of the state untouched. For many governments, territorial integrity is a juridical notion rather than a political reality.[8]

Independence represents the freedom of action which a government is presumed to enjoy in making foreign policy decisions. New states, however, often come into existence with restrictions placed on their role in world affairs. Treaties of guarantee limit a government in the defense of its interest. Such a treaty usually involves a concession,

---

[2]Stanley Hoffmann has defined sovereignty as a "divisible nexus of powers" in "International Systems and International Law," *World Politics* 14 (October 1961):235.

[3]Robert H. Bork, "The Limits of 'International Law,'" *The National Interest* 18 (Winter 1989):4–5.

[4]Article 23 assigns permanent seats and special voting rights to China, France, Russia, the United Kingdom, and the United States.

[5]Werner Levi, *Law and Politics in International Society,* Sage Library of Social Research (Beverly Hills, CA: Sage Publications, 1976), pp. 121–125.

[6]Resolution 2625, Declaration on Principles of International Law concerning Friendly Relations and Cooperation among States in accordance with the Charter of the United Nations in United Nations, General Assembly, 25th session, 1883rd plenary meeting, 24 October 1970, *Official Records* (A/8082), pp. 121–124.

[7]Resolution 3201, Declaration on the Establishment of a New International Economic Order, in United Nations, General Assembly, Sixth Special Session, 2229th plenary meeting, 1 May 1974, ibid. (S-VI), pp. 3–5.

[8]For an overview of "transsovereign problems," see Maryann K. Cusimano (ed.), *Beyond Sovereignty: Issues for a Global Agenda* (Boston: Bedford/St. Martin's, 2000), especially Chap. 1.

which may be political, economic, or military. For example, a new government may commit itself to a policy of nonalignment and a concomitant rejection of alliances, or it may guarantee itself to a continuation of a special commercial or banking arrangement, such as the use of the former colonial power's currency. Military guarantees abound and usually take the form of granting privileges for bases and logistical facilities. Independence under these circumstances remains an abstract notion.

From the perspective of the theory of international relations, the right to preserve the state through a resort to self-defense is the most problematic. The modern international system is based on the Peace of Westphalia (1648), which gave rise to a balance of power among sovereign and independent polities. The rules of the system required the preservation of, minimally, five major actors, among whom a fluidity of movement would maintain an equilibrium flexible enough to deter aggression. Diplomacy was the first means of coping with a crisis, and the use of force was the ultimate argument. The preservation of the state became a moral duty.[9] Article 51 of the Charter of the United Nations guarantees the right of self-defense and affirms that the use of force is compatible with international law. The question of whether a multistate balance of power is truly indicative of present-day world politics is debatable, yet international law assumes a priori the persistence of the Westphalian system.

ACT OF STATE DOCTRINE

What immunity should a government possess in the exercise of its sovereign authority? Diplomats and jurists find answering this question difficult. Customary international law extended immunity to a sovereign entity on the assumption that it is supreme within its own territory. Melville Fuller, the chief justice of the United States, articulated this standard in the *Underhill* case when he wrote that the courts of one country should not sit in judgment on the acts of public officials in their own territory.[10] The doctrine of immunity was subsequently expanded to encompass revolutionary regimes. In 1914, civil war raged in Mexico, and the forces of guerrilla leader Francisco Villa imposed military levies on the civilian population. Among the goods requisitioned was a supply of leather owned by an American company. The guerrillas operated under the nominal authority of President Venustiano Carranza, and the U.S. Supreme Court ruled that the requisition was a lawful act of state, which could not be challenged in foreign courts.[11]

The foregoing interpretation of an act of state was sufficiently broad to ensure immunity to any sovereign authority, even a partisan band, for actions taken in its own territory. The rise of totalitarian regimes in the twentieth century called such blanket immunity into question. The act of state doctrine was never intended to provide a legal screen for state-sponsored campaigns of terror. A reappraisal was in order, and the result was the Bernstein "exception." The plaintiff was a German citizen against whom specious charges of violating foreign currency laws had been brought under the National

---

[9]Hans J. Morgenthau, "The Mainsprings of American Foreign Policy: The National Interest vs. Moral Aspiration," *American Political Science Review* 44 (December 1950): 854.
[10]*Underhill v. Hernandez,* 168 U.S. 250 (1897).
[11]*Oetjen v. Central Leather Co.,* 246 U.S. 297 (1918).

Socialist dictatorship. The secret state police (the Gestapo) imprisoned him and seized his property, in this instance merchant ships. During the Second World War a Belgian firm acquired the ships, and after the cessation of hostilities the plaintiff, now resident in the United States, sued the company in federal court to recover his assets. Judge Learned Hand wrote the opinion and concluded that the political branch should deal with the claims.[12] Hand did not, however, rule out the legitimacy of the claim and in doing so gave credence to the principle that the actions of a government within its own territory could still be subject to review by external authorities. Nevertheless, an executive act was essential before a court could suspend the act of state doctrine.[13] The wall of exclusive sovereign authority had been weakened but not breached.

The true judicial challenge to the act of state doctrine came in 1964, when the U.S. Supreme Court decided a case dealing with the expropriation of property by a foreign government. Beginning in 1959, the government of President Fidel Castro consolidated its control over Cuba, and a year later it enacted Law 851, which stated in part:

> *Whereas,* it is the duty of the peoples of Latin America to strive for the recovery of their native wealth by wresting it from the hands of foreign monopolies and interests which prevent their development, promote political interference, and impair the sovereignty of the underdeveloped countries of America.
> *Whereas,* the Cuban Revolution will not stop until it shall have totally and definitely liberated its fatherland.
> *Whereas,* Cuba must be a luminous and stimulating example for the sister nations of America and all the underdeveloped countries of the world to follow to free themselves from the brutal claws of Imperialism.[14]

The implementation of Law 851 led to the nationalization of foreign property in Cuba, and the Sabbatino case was an effort to challenge the expropriation without compensation before the U.S. Supreme Court. In his opinion, Justice John M. Harlan argued that customary international law is unclear. It may, in fact, not prescribe unqualified adherence to the rule that the courts of this country must recognize the sovereign acts of foreign authorities. Despite this ambiguity the argument concluded that:

> [t]he act of state doctrine does, however, have "constitutional" underpinnings. It arises out of the basic relationships between branches of government in a system of separation of powers. It concerns the competency of dissimilar institutions to make and implement particular kinds of decisions in the area of international relations. The doctrine as formulated in past decisions expresses the strong sense of the Judicial Branch that its engagement in the task of passing on the validity of foreign acts of state may hinder rather than further this country's pursuit of goals both for itself and for the community of nations as a whole in the international sphere.[15]

---

[12]*Bernstein v. van Heyghen Freres Société Anonyme,* 163 F. 2d 246 (1947).
[13]Richard Falk, "Sequel to Sabbatino," *American Journal of International Law* 59 (April 1965): 937.
[14]Reprinted in *Banco Nacional de Cuba v. Sabbatino,* 376 U.S. 398, 404n. (1964).
[15]Ibid., p, 423.

The *Underhill* case issue was one of coercion by public authority, and in *Sabbatino* it was the confiscation of property. Without directly challenging the act of state doctrine, Congress moved to create an opening whereby courts could review economic reprisals taken by foreign governments against aliens. In the so-called Hickenlooper amendment (1964) to an authorization bill on foreign aid, Congress stipulated:

> Notwithstanding any other provision of law, no court *in the United States* [italics added] shall decline on the ground of the federal act of state doctrine to make a determination on the merits giving effect to the principles of international law in a case in which a claim of title or other right is asserted by any party including a foreign state (or a party claiming through such state) based upon (or traced through) a confiscation or other taking after January 1, 1959, by an act of state in violation of the principles of international law.[16]

Notably, the act stipulated courts *in* the United States rather than courts *of* the United States.[17] The distinction being that Congress intended the rule to apply to state as well as federal courts, there being a possibility that a state court would apply an un-restricted interpretation of the act of state doctrine as opposed to the more restrictive view of the federal judiciary. The law also applied specifically to *a violation of the principles of international law,* which raised the question of whether a government's seizure of property is indeed an offense under public international law. The customary rule is that the expropriation must be carried out by a public authority, be nondiscriminatory, and be accompanied by a good faith effort at compensation. Satisfying these require-ments entitles a government to exercise its sovereign prerogatives within its territory without interference from foreign powers. The Hickenlooper amendment presumed that the government of Cuba had failed to adhere to the customary standards, and therefore citizens of the United States should have access to the judicial process. The amendment will, however, probably prove to be the exception rather than the rule as far as the act of state doctrine is concerned.

In 1996, Congress took a further step toward modifying the act of state doctrine as applied to Cuba by passing the Helms-Burton Act, which imposed negative sanctions on foreign commercial interests alleged to be using property expropriated from Amer-ican owners in 1959.[18] The law represents a legislative enactment designed to deny Cuban authorities of the protection afforded by the act of state doctrine. Moreover, the proposed punitive action against overseas commercial interests (i.e., Canadian and Eu-ropean firms) doing business in Cuba raised the issue of the rights of third parties.[19] Legislation enacted to interpret and thereby modify an accepted principle of custom-ary international law is fraught with problems, and for that reason the retaliatory pro-visions of the law remain unfulfilled.

---

[16]Foreign Assistance Act of 1964, sec. 301 (2), *Statutes at Large* 78: 1009, 1013 (1964).

[17]Donald T. Kramer, "Modern Status of the Act of State Doctrine," *American Law Reports* (federal) 12: 707, 728; and Howard S. Levie, "Sequel to Sabbatino," *American Journal of International Law* 59 (April 1965): 366, 368.

[18]Cuban Liberty and Democratic Solidarity (Libertad) Act of 1996, *Statutes at Large* 110 (1996): 785.

[19]John H. Jackson and Andreas F. Lowenfeld, "Helms-Burton, the U.S. and the W(orld) T(rade) O(rganiza-tion)," *American Society of International Law: Flash Insight* (March 1997): 2; and Guy de Jonquières, "Keeping the Lid on Helms-Burton," *Financial Times,* 31 July 1997, p. A4.

SOVEREIGN IMMUNITY

Closely related to the act of state doctrine is the premise of sovereign immunity. Traditional international law guards the person of the sovereign and bars civil or criminal action against a chief of state in the performance of his or her duties.[20] The charges of waging a war of aggression and of crimes against humanity in the trials of major war criminals following the Second World War created a basis for holding a head of government accountable. Nevertheless the notion of sovereign immunity persists. In a contemporary sense, the case of General Augusto Pinochet may have the effect of redefining state practice regarding sovereign immunity. Chapter 2 addressed the issue of the jurisdiction of national courts over internationally recognized offenses against human rights, in this case homicide and torture. The discussion must now focus on the historic view of immunity as a derivative of state sovereignty.

Chief Justice John Marshall summarized the historic doctrine in 1812, when he wrote that the practice of states granted an ". . . exemption of the person of the sovereign from arrest or detention within a foreign territory."[21] Adding that the rule is ". . . universally understood to apply," Marshall concluded that immunity applies to the sovereign, to diplomatic agents, and to those foreign armies to whom permission had been granted to cross the territory of the home country. The doctrine evolved from a pattern of international relations in which the activities of a sovereign were exclusively political, and the concept of immunity was held to be absolute.

An exception to the foregoing concerns the position of a sovereign who sues in a foreign court. Following the Civil War, the United States instituted three suits in equity in British courts, the purpose of which was to recover the assets of the Confederacy in Great Britain. Once attorneys for the United States filed their motion, the United States became subject to a countersuit for purposes of discovery, a process allowing the defendants to secure information essential to their case. The counterclaim named the "United States and Andrew Johnson" as the defendants. Arguing on behalf of the defendants, the attorney general pointed out that ministers of the Crown could not be summoned, adding:

> So again in the case of a suit by a foreign sovereign state, every member of the government might, upon the theory advanced on the other side, be made a party and compelled to reveal important state secrets as the price of the right to bring the original suit to a hearing. Any such rule would be opposed to the plainest principles of international comity, would occasion monstrous inconvenience, and would result in a practical denial of justice. At all events the President has been improperly made a Defendant, and in order to obtain the required discovery some officer of state should have been selected who is under the control of the sovereign state, and whose oath could bind it.[22]

Sovereign immunity applies even in the case of a counterclaim. For reasons of law and policy, the court determined that the president could not be named as a defendant although an officer of his government might be.

---

[20]Lauterpacht's Oppenheim, pp. 239–240.
[21]*Schooner Exchange v. McFaddon,* 11 U.S. (7 Cranch) 116, 137 (1812).
[22]*Prioleau v. United States and Andrew Johnson,* Court of Chancery, Law Reports: Equity Cases, ed. G.W. Hemming 2:659, 662–663 (1866).

Contemporary developments in international law suggest, however, a restrictive interpretation of the concept. Governments may own and operate commercial enterprises, such as airlines, which are not immune from suit. In 1952, the U.S. Department of State released the Tate letter and in doing so drew a line between the public acts of a sovereign and private acts, usually of a commercial nature. This policy established an avowedly restrictive theory of sovereign immunity and made foreign governments liable to suits for damages.[23] The letter offered, however, little guidance for distinguishing between public and private acts, but it did enunciate the principle. Sovereign immunity was no longer absolute.[24] In 1976, Congress acted to lessen the ambiguity by passing the Foreign Sovereign Immunities Act (FSIA), which restated the classic doctrine and then added three principal exceptions. The first involved a waiver of immunity by a foreign government, the second dealt with a commercial activity or the use of property for that purpose, and the third focused on the rights of property owners whose assets had been seized in violation of international law.[25] The third exception points directly to Cuba. Finally the FSIA exempted the military activities of a foreign sovereign as the basis of a suit. In deference to the language of both law and diplomacy, a suit under the FSIA is technically *in rem* (i.e., for the recovery of property) rather than *in personam* (i.e., against the person of the sovereign).[26]

The first test of the FSIA came in 1976, when Orlando Letelier, an exiled Chilean diplomat, and Ronni Moffitt, an American citizen, fell victim to a car bomb detonated in Washington, D.C. Subsequent investigation revealed the complicity of the Chilean intelligence service, the DINA, which had suborned the plot. U.S. authorities conducted an investigation, and a civil tort action resulted. Ultimately, the culpability of Chilean authorities under the FSIA was established to the satisfaction of a federal jury, and damages were awarded.[27] In this connection a comparison with the *Filartiga* case (1980), as discussed in Chapter 2, is useful. *Filartiga* was a suit for damages resulting in death by torture at the hands of a Paraguayan official in Paraguay. The Alien Tort Act (1948) placed the matter under the jurisdiction of a federal district court, which found for the plaintiff. In theory the case could also have been tried under the FSIA because the use of torture is a violation of international law, and an appeal to sovereign immunity does not protect the torturer.[28]

The FSIA was enacted in 1976, yet its application is retroactive as demonstrated in a suit arising from the armed intervention of Turkey in the Republic of Cyprus during the summer of 1974. Acting under the terms of a treaty of guarantee, the Turkish army landed in Cyprus and occupied the northern third of the island. Real property belonging to Greek Cypriots and others of Greek heritage was expropriated without compensation. In 1996, three U.S. citizens of Greek descent brought suit against Turkey

---

[23]Jack B. Tate, acting Legal Adviser, "Changed Policy Concerning the Granting of Sovereign Immunity to Foreign Governments," *Department of State Bulletin* 26 (June 23, 1952): 984–985.
[24]Whiteman 6:657.
[25]Foreign Sovereign Immunities Act, *Statutes at Large* 90: 2891, 2893 (1976).
[26]James Crawford, "Execution of Judgments and Foreign Sovereign Immunity," *American Journal of International Law* 75 (October 1981): 820, 847.
[27]*De Letelier v. Chile,* U.S. District Court, District of Columbia, 488 F. Supp. 665 (1980) and 502 F. Supp. 259 (1980). The decision was appealed, and the U.S. Supreme Court denied certiorari in 471 U.S. 1125 (1985).
[28]The FSIA makes a distinction between *jure imperii* (actions of a sovereign nature) and *jure gestionis* (actions of a private or commercial nature), the latter being subject to civil suit for compensatory and punitive damages. See *De Letelier v. Republic of Chile,* Second Circuit Court of Appeals, 748 F. 2nd 790 (1984).

under the provisions of the FSIA covering unlawful expropriation. They argued that the seizure of their property was discriminatory, that the action was taken without the knowledge or consent of the recognized government of Cyprus, and that they were denied access to the appellate process established by local authorities in northern Cyprus. A federal district court dismissed the suit on the grounds that it exceeded the statute of limitations for such an action. The plaintiffs appealed, and the Court of Appeals for the District of Columbia, interpreted the FSIA as follows:

> Although the term "foreign state" in the context of FSIA's sovereign immunity exceptions encompasses an agency or instrumentality of a state, the converse is not true; that is, the term "agency or instrumentality" does not include the foreign state itself.[29]

The court ruled that the exceptions to sovereign immunity would not apply to the operations of the Turkish army and concluded that no basis exists to exercise jurisdiction over the merits of the dispute. Sovereign immunity regarding the actions of an army in the field remained uncontested.

The *Crist* case offers an insightful contrast to the decision in *Letelier.* In the latter the Chilean clandestine service was held to be an "agency or instrumentality" of the state, which meant that the exceptions to immunity stipulated in the FSIA applied. The Republic of Chile was accountable for the actions of its secret agents. Federal authorities could take action, and the plaintiff could initiate a suit for damages. By contrast, in the former case whatever damages resulted from the war on Cyprus in 1974 might well be attributed to the Turkish army but not to the Turkish state as a legal personality. The apparent discrepancy remains to be clarified. In sum, the exceptions to the traditional doctrine of sovereign immunity have scarcely taken root in case law.

International terrorism may, however, lead to a breakthrough on the subject of sovereign immunity. The *Letelier* case occasioned a review of existing legislation, and in 1996 Congress passed an antiterrorism act. The law authorized the executive to brand those governments named as sponsors of terrorism, and several states were shortly thereafter so identified. A state on this list could not claim the full protection of sovereign immunity in a federal court. Funding, training, and equipping a terrorist organization could no longer be regarded as acts of state. Whatever doubts may have existed on this point were removed by the bombing on Pan Am Flight 103 over Lockerbie, Scotland, in 1988. Sovereign immunity no longer provided a shield for state terrorism.[30]

BRITISH LAW

A comparative approach serves to clarify the meaning of concepts in international law, and British jurisprudence makes a significant contribution to this process. Legal theory in Great Britain and on the continent takes an absolutist approach to the act of state doctrine. A government exercises its sovereign power in the interest of the state, *raison d'état,* and is not subject to challenge by courts at home or abroad. By extension, British

---

[29]*Crist v. Republic of Turkey and the Army of the Republic of Turkey,* U.S. Court of Appeals, District of Columbia Circuit, 103 F. 3rd 922 (1997).
[30]Anti-Terrorism and Effective Death Penalty Act of 1996: Subtitle B—Jurisdiction for Lawsuits Against Terrorist States, *Statutes at Large* 110: 1214, 1241 (1996).

courts do not possess the authority to compel the Crown to fulfill obligations contracted through an act of state. By virtue of an international agreement, the Crown may receive an indemnity for injuries done to its subjects, but a court may not compel the government to make payment to the subjects in question, nor can a court require the government to implement all the terms of an international treaty.

Central to an understanding of the sovereign prerogatives of the Crown is the concept of acts of state.[31] Examples include decisions on a state of war, on the recognition of a state or its government, or on the territorial extent of the jurisdiction of the Crown. Such matters are not subject to review by the courts, which must adhere to guidance from the government department concerned. As discussed in Chapter 4, the decision of the Court of Appeals of New York in *Sokoloff* (1924) demonstrated that a state court could extend judicial recognition to the acts of a then unrecognized government without deferring to the policy of the Department of State. Under the acts-of-state doctrine, British courts would not have the same latitude. In 1921, British courts addressed the problem of whether the revolutionary regime in Russia could be said to have carried out an act of state when it expropriated a store of timber owned by a British company. The commercial agent of the Russian government, not yet recognized by Great Britain, attempted to sell the timber on the British market, and the original owners sought an injunction arguing that the sale was illegal because no lawful authority had carried out the expropriation. The agent insisted that the Russian government existed de facto, and that its internal acts were those of a state. His legal representative pointed to post–Civil War decisions of the U.S. Supreme Court that accepted as valid routine acts of civil administration of Confederate authorities. In an initial decision, a presiding judge ruled that the actions of an unrecognized government lacked validity, and that the timber did indeed belong to its British owners. The Court of Appeals, however, reversed this decision on the grounds that in the interim the Foreign Office had recognized the Russian government and instructed the judiciary accordingly.[32] Unlike *Sokoloff,* there was no question of departing from the political guidance of the executive.

LETTERS ROGATORY

In ancient Rome the consuls sought to ascertain popular opinion on proposed laws through a process known as rogation. The concept evolved into a procedural device whereby the courts of one jurisdiction request the assistance of another judicial system in the acquisition of evidence. In the decades following the founding of the United States, courts of one state would turn to those of another state for relevant judicial records. The practice of issuing *letters rogatory* as a formal statement eventually assumed an international dimension. The act of state doctrine guarantees the independence of judicial systems, but does not preclude their collaboration. In this regard international law recognizes the comity of courts.

Conventional international law now sets the procedural standards for letters rogatory. In 1975, the Organization of American States sponsored a multilateral treaty au-

---

[31]*Halsbury's Laws of England* (London: Butterworths, 1977) 18: 724–728.
[32]*Luther v. Sagor,* All England Law Reports 90: 1202, 1215 (1921).

thorizing the use of letters rogatory in civil and commercial (not criminal) cases for the purpose of:

a. The performance of procedural acts of a merely formal nature, such as service of process, summonses or subpoenas abroad;

b. The taking of evidence and the obtaining of information abroad, unless a reservation is made in this respect.[33]

The Hague Convention on Evidence facilitates the exchange of information among courts, but the treaty's application is far from universal.[34] Nevertheless the concept of state responsibility has evolved to the stage at which courts of different national systems are obligated to assist each other in civil cases.

INTERNATIONAL ORGANIZATIONS

The related issues of responsibility and immunity take on a special meaning when applied to public international organizations. Intergovernmental organizations (IGOs), whether universal or regional, contribute to the stabilization of the international system. They possess a legal personality, and their officials enjoy the immunity associated with a territorial state. In 1945, pursuant to the drafting of the Charter of the United Nations, Congress enacted legislation recognizing the legal status of international organizations by guaranteeing that:

> [r]epresentatives of foreign governments in or to international organizations and officers and employees shall be immune from suit and legal process relating to acts performed by them in their official capacity.[35]

The foregoing incorporates conventional international law into the municipal law of the United States. Two multilateral treaties are of particular note. The first is the Vienna Convention on Diplomatic Relations (1961), which extends to diplomats the rights associated with sovereign immunity.[36] A diplomatic agent represents not the self, but the legal personality of the sending state. The receiving state is, therefore, obligated to treat foreign diplomats as an extension of the sovereignty of their respective governments. The rule of reciprocity requires all governments to observe the principle of mutual obligation in facilitating the work of each other's diplomatic representatives. The Convention on Privileges and Immunities of the United Nations (1946) applied the customary rule regarding diplomats to the country delegations and officials of the world organization. Having entered into force in the United States only in 1970, the convention recognizes the juridical personality of the United Nations and derives from this recognition the immunity of its officials and staff.[37]

---

[33]Inter-American Convention on Letters Rogatory (January 30, 1975), reprinted in I.L.M. (March 1975) 14: 339. See also Additional Protocol to the Inter-American Convention on Letters Rogatory (May 8, 1979), reprinted in I.L.M. (September 1979) 18: 1238.

[34]Convention on the Taking of Evidence Abroad in Civil and Commercial Matters (March 18, 1970), U.S.T. 23:2555.

[35]International Organizations and Immunities Act (December 29, 1945), *Statutes at Large* 59: 669, 572.

[36]Vienna Convention on Diplomatic Relations (April 18, 1961), U.S.T. 23: 3227, 3245.

[37]Convention on Privileges and Immunities of the United Nations (February 13, 1946), U.S.T. 21: 1418. On April 29, 1970, the convention was proclaimed in force in the United States.

Regional and functional organizations, too, enjoy privileges and immunities. As of 1997, the United States recognized seventy-five IGOs as having a special status under federal law. The list included IGOs devoted to such purposes as the lessening of trade barriers, law enforcement, arms control, public health, intellectual property rights, and investment and developmental banking.[38] Remarkably, the fifteen-member European Union (EU) was not on the list until recently, which implies problems in both law and protocol. The application of the concept of legal personality to regional or specialized IGOs is indicative of the changing nature of international politics, for in many instances the decisive actors are no longer territorial states but rather their collaborative arrangements, which have now become a force in their own right.

PROSPECTS

The discussion opened with a description of the work of the ILC and its report on state responsibility. Draft articles are, of course, a long way from becoming conventional international law, but they do represent an incipient international consensus, which might evolve into a multilateral treaty. The implications for the international system are far-reaching, for state responsibility alters the theory of the classical balance of power. Realpolitik presumes an ongoing competition among states for power, and in this setting international law served to protect the rights of states in peace and war. Yet state responsibility imposes duties upon states and emphasizes their commitment to the international community. Rules serve to restrict the play of power politics. Sovereignty is no longer the absolute and perpetual quality conceived by Bodin. States are accountable for their actions and may be held to have committed a wrongful act for which they cannot evade responsibility. Indeed the fact that such an act is not illegal under the municipal code of the state involved does not mitigate the international responsibility of its government. How far this doctrine will progress remains an open question.

Topics for Discussion

1. Describe the traditional theory of sovereign immunity. How has the U.S. Supreme Court historically interpreted it?
2. Congress has endeavored to restrict sovereign immunity. How successful has this effort been, especially with regard to U.S. relations with Cuba?
3. Is the notion of state responsibility dependent upon reciprocity between governments or does the concept derive its importance from a sense of customary obligations to the international community?
4. State responsibility applies primarily to commercial and civil torts. Should the doctrine now be expanded to cover political offenses?

---

[38]Privileges and Immunities of International Organizations, *United States Code* (1994): Supplement III (1997), Title 22, Sec. 288.

CHAPTER 7

Human Rights

The primacy of the state as the true subject of international law overshadows the rights of the individual, yet multilateral lawmaking conventions have over the past fifty years focused on the duty of government to protect human rights. The defense of social, economic, and cultural rights is becoming an obligation *erga omnes,* that is, a commitment to the international community. While the concept of international human rights law is modern, the legal premises reflect the teachings of classical philosophy. The Roman jurist Cicero (106 to 43 B.C.) argued that law is not merely a product of human reason, but that it is rooted in nature. *Jus naturale*—the law of nature—joins together humankind.[1] In the tradition of the Greek Stoics, law represents the highest form of reason, and justice is the means through which philosophers may discover the true nature of things. Although the positivist theory of scientific jurisprudence edged naturalist thought into relative obscurity, the concept of universal human rights has revived interest in the classic doctrine of *jus naturale.*

The Peace of Westphalia ending the Thirty Years' War in 1648 established a benchmark in the development of human rights law. The Treaty of Münster, one of the two principal agreements constituting the peace settlement, guaranteed religious rights in Bohemia, now the core province of the Czech Republic, as well as the principle of liberty in the "exercise of religion."[2] For the first time in modern legal history a multilateral treaty, adhered to by powers great and small, embodied a commitment to religious liberty and thereby imposed a limit on the exercise of sovereign authority by the states party to it.[3] Similarly, the final act of the Congress of Paris ending the Crimean War (1854–1856) encompassed a guarantee of freedom of worship in the Balkan provinces of Wallachia and Moldavia, then a part of the Ottoman Empire.[4] These concessions may well have been small, but the principle they embodied was to have far-reaching ramifications.

---

[1]Cicero's major works are *The Laws* and *On the Commonwealth,* extensive excerpts of which appear in William Ebenstein, *Great Political Thinkers* (New York: Rinehart and Co., 1951), Chap. 4; and Curtis, *The Great Political Theories,* 1: Chap. 3. For the background of Ciceronian theory, see Paul E. Sigmund, *Natural Law in Political Thought* (Cambridge, MA: Winthrop Publishers, 1971), Chap. 2.

[2]See Articles 46 and 49 of the Treaty of Peace, Münster, October 24, 1648, reprinted in Clive Parry (ed.), *The Consolidated Treaty Series* (Dobbs Ferry, NY: Oceana Publications, 1969) 1:332. Hereafter cited as Parry.

[3]Bilateral treaties also served to guarantee the religious liberty of minorities, an important example being the commitment of the Treaty of Kutschuk-Kaïnardji (Russia and the Ottoman Empire on July 10, 1794) to protect the Christian subjects of the Sublime Porte. See 2 Parry 913, 917.

[4]Treaty of Paris (March 30, 1856) reprinted in Michael Hurst (ed.), *Key Treaties for the Great Powers, 1814–1914* (New York: St. Martin's Press, 1972), 1: 317, 324. Hereafter cited as Hurst.

SLAVERY

As an offense against the law of nations, slavery is defined as the treatment of an individual as a chattel (property), and in doing so denying that person all rights and freedom. The struggle to establish the criminality of chattel slavery under international law was long and arduous. The historical record of this ongoing effort illustrates the difficulty in bringing about the transition from customary to conventional international law. The campaign against slavery reflects the incremental nature of international law and beyond that the loose anarchy of the international system, as the following detailed account reveals.

At the Congress of Vienna (1814–1815), the representatives of the major powers assembled to construct a Concert of Europe after the defeat of Napoleon at Waterloo. A series of treaties encouraging the growth of international law resulted from the Congress, and among these was a declaration of the powers that they would collaborate to eradicate the slave trade.[5] Further international action came in the form of a commitment to suppress the slave trade in the Congo.[6] The focus on the Congo led to a second multilateral agreement in 1890. This time the terms specified slave trading as a criminal act, the punishment of which was a duty incurred by the states parties.[7] Situated on Zanzibar, an international bureau served to implement the terms of the treaty.[8] Criminalizing the offense and creating an institution for enforcement of the rule represented the first steps toward putting in place an international regime capable of coping with the problem. Declaratory statements by themselves do not suffice and must, therefore, be translated into policy administered by a formal institution. The development of the international law regarding slavery provides a case study of this process.

The formation of universal international organizations strengthened the antislavery regime. In one of its early acts, the League of Nations moved in 1926 to sponsor a convention to suppress both the slave trade and slavery itself.[9] The convention broadened the definition of slavery to include compulsory and forced labor. States parties committed themselves to enact the necessary laws and to assist each in the enforcement of these statutes. In the event of an interstate dispute, the signatory governments accepted an obligation to resolve it either through adjudication before the League's Permanent Court of International Justice or through arbitration. The United Nations assumed the responsibility for the administration of the League's convention.[10] In 1956, the United Nations sponsored a revised multilateral convention with the avowed purpose of abolishing slavery and related practices.[11] For example, the updated convention

---

[5]Declaration relative to the Universal Abolition of the Slave Trade (February 8, 1815), 63 Parry 473.
[6]General Act of Berlin (February 26, 1885), Parry 165: 485, 493. The United States signed but did not ratify the agreement. See 2 Hackworth 667.
[7]General Act of Brussels for the Repression of the African Slave Trade (July 2, 1890), 2 Malloy 1964.
[8]In 1922, Belgium accepted the mission of coordinating the international effort against the slave trade. See 2 Hackworth 668.
[9]Although the United States was not a member of the League of Nations, it did sign and ratify the treaty. See International Convention to Suppress the Slave Trade and Slavery (September 25, 1926), 46 Stat. 2183.
[10]Protocol amending the Slavery Convention (December 7, 1953), U.S.T. 7:479. The United Nations Convention on the Law of the Sea (December 10, 1982) also imposed a duty on signatory governments to suppress the slave trade and to provide refuge for fleeing slaves. See 21 I.L.M. 1261 (1982).
[11]Supplementary Convention on the Abolition of Slavery, the Slave Trade, and Institutions and Practices similar to Slavery (September 7, 1956), 18 U.S.T. 3201.

condemned debt bondage (i.e., peonage), serfdom, and involuntary child labor. A commitment was made to the rights of women in marriage. The slave trade, slavery, and such associated offenses as the mutilation and marking of an individual to show servile status were declared criminal acts. Finally the signatory governments accepted a duty to provide asylum for those fleeing slavery.

The 1956 United Nations Convention would appear to have resolved an age-old problem through the creation of an international legal regime, but the success of the effort should not lead to a false sense of optimism. Christian Solidarity International (CSI), a human rights group based in Zurich, Switzerland, campaigns against the continued practice of slavery in some less-developed countries. The CSI's activism so irritated a group of countries that their representatives at the United Nations stripped the organization of its standing as an accredited adviser to the world organization on human rights problems.[12] Sadly, slavery persists in different parts of the world, despite international efforts to the contrary. Reports abound from the Ivory Coast and from the Sudan.[13] Skeptics will insist that the imperfect effort to eliminate slavery exposes the inefficacy of international legal responses to violations of human rights. Nongovernmental international organizations, like CSI, committed to the defense of human rights assert that the overall record is positive. Progress is being made, but a concerted effort is required to finish the task.

THE RIGHTS OF WOMEN

Perhaps the severest test of a human rights regime is the international protection of the rights of women. Although lawmaking treaties and observer groups exist in the field of women's rights, progress toward realizing the goal of these efforts is slow. In this regard, one is reminded of the Austinian view that law must be based on a command, which is enforceable by a sovereign. International law is therefore little more than an appeal to ethical precepts. Nevertheless, a concern with its prestige will lead a government to seek the legitimacy associated with adherence to declarations of compliance with human rights standards, and therein lies the hope for an international law of the rights of women.

Contrary to popular opinion, the concept of women's rights has deep historical roots as typified by Christine de Pizan (1364–1431), a political theorist, who stressed the essential equality of men and women—a doctrine which undergirds modern human rights conventions.[14] With the founding of the United Nations, the opportunity arose to develop the conventional international law needed to realize the goal of equality. In 1953, the United Nations sponsored a multilateral treaty guaranteeing the political

---

[12]A.M. Rosenthal, "On My Mind: The World of Slavery," *New York Times*, 3 September 1999, A19; and "Write versus Wrong," *The New Republic* (November 22, 1999): 10.

[13]Howard W. French, "Age-old Curse of Slavery Alive in the Ivory Coast," *New York Times*, 23 June 1998, p. A4; and "Slave Redemption: Sudan," *Christianity Today* 43 (August 9, 1999): 29–33. See also the testimony of Kevin Bales, University of Surrey, before the Senate Foreign Relations Committee, which held hearings on "Slavery Throughout the World" on September 28, 2000 (unpublished manuscript).

[14]Edward M. Wheat, " 'Now a New Kingdom of Femininity Is Begun . . .': The Political Theory of Christine de Pizan's *The Book of the City of Ladies*," *Women & Politics* 20 (1999): 23, 36. Also see Arvonne S. Fraser, "Becoming Human: The Origins and Development of Women's Rights," *Human Rights Quarterly* 21 (November 1999): 853, 905.

rights of women. Significantly the treaty addressed the need to protect both active and passive rights. Women possessed the entitlement to run for public office as well as the franchise. "One man, one vote" now became "one citizen, one vote," and votes were of equal value.[15]

The major contemporary breakthrough occurred in 1979, when the United Nations opened for signature the Convention on the Elimination of All Forms of Discrimination Against Women (CEDAW). By March 2000, 165 governments had ratified the convention, all but twenty-two members of the United Nations.[16] CEDAW serves two purposes: It defines the concept of discrimination against women and proceeds to set up an agenda for action under municipal codes of law. Article 1 of the convention defines discrimination as:

> . . . any distinction, exclusion or restriction made upon the basis of sex which has the effect or purpose of impairing or nullifying the recognition, enjoyment or exercise by women, irrespective of their marital status, on the basis of equality of men and women, of human rights and fundamental freedoms in the political, economic, social, cultural, civil or any other field.

States parties to CEDAW undertake a commitment to promulgate legislation premised on the principle of equality of men and women to include the abolition of discriminatory laws and administrative practices. To achieve these goals, the states parties obligate themselves to the following: (a) the incorporation of the principle of equality into their municipal codes, (b) the formation of judicial and administrative bodies capable of implementing the principle by working to eliminate discrimination against women in the public and private sectors, and (c) the protection of women against the social forms of unequal treatment that is characteristic of some traditional societies. Of note is the freedom of a woman to choose her own nationality rather than, as was previously the case, being bound to the nationality of her spouse. Under the auspices of the United Nations, the Commission on the Status of Women (CSW) reports to the General Assembly and monitors the implementation of the convention. Through periodic conferences attended by representatives of governments and human rights organizations, the CSW turns a spotlight on violators of CEDAW. In 1995, the first of such universal conferences convened in Beijing, and five years later the delegates reconvened in New York, where the division between the progressives and the gradualists became apparent.[17]

Parallel to developments within the United Nations, regional organizations have also recognized the international legal rights of women. One of the first efforts in this direction was undertaken by the Organization of American States (OAS) in 1948. At a meeting in Bogotá, Columbia, delegates of the OAS agreed to adhere to a multilateral treaty guaranteeing the political rights of women, in particular the right to vote.[18] The

---

[15]Convention on the Political Rights of Women (March 31, 1953), 27 U.S.T. 1911. The United States ratified the convention on April 8, 1976.

[16]Convention on the Elimination of All Forms of Discrimination Against Women (December 18, 1979), 19 I.L.M. 33. CEDAW incorporated a 1957 Convention on the Nationality of Women and the 1962 Convention on Consent to Marriage, Minimum Age for Marriage and Registration of Marriages. It thereby served to codify customary and conventional law regarding the rights of women. The United States signed the CEDAW on July 17, 1980 but never deposited the instrument of ratification.

[17]Barbara Crossette, "Egyptian at Center on Rights of Women," *New York Times,* 8 June 2000, A7.

[18]Inter-American Convention on the Granting of Political Rights to Women (May 2, 1948), 27 U.S.T. 3301.

initiative undertaken by member governments of the inter-American system illustrates the significance of regional international law. A regional organization is often capable of providing the impetus needed to compel a universal body to act. The topic of the rights of women is a case in point.

UNRESOLVED ISSUES

CEDAW and related advances have provided the question of the rights of women with a salience that it never previously possessed. Yet two important and related issues remain to be addressed. The first is spousal abuse and the second is genital mutilation. Is domestic violence an acceptable ground for granting asylum? U.S. law and practice are vague on this question.[19] Similarly, the practice of infibulation or female mutilation is prevalent in certain regions of the world.[20] CEDAW may well be the most promising international legal response, because the convention obligates governments adhering to it to modify those social policies which reinforce a pattern of discrimination against women. Mutilation is certainly one of these.

Although both customary and conventional international law condemn torture and discrimination, legal remedies are often unavailable. For example, U.S. law on the granting of asylum stipulates that the attorney general cannot act without proof of a "well-founded fear of persecution" based on such factors as race, religion, or political opinion.[21] But gender is not one of the reasons cited. By extrapolation we may infer that brutality against women does constitute a basis for asylum, and the argument receives support from the classical doctrine of natural law. Nevertheless, the positivist reply is that unless a government gives its explicit consent, normally in the form of a treaty ratification, it is not bound to take action against those practices violative of CEDAW's commitment to equality.

THE RIGHTS OF THE CHILD

The case of Elián González, a six-year-old Cuban boy rescued at sea by fishermen and brought to the United States in 1999, has served to illustrate the special needs of children under international law. Slavery, brokered marriages of minors, and other offenses against children have until recently failed to attract the attention of the international legal community. In 1980, an international convention was designed to cope with the manifold problems accompanying the wrongful removal of a child from one state to another. The *wrongful removal* of a child under the age of sixteen years from one state to another occurs whenever there is a breach of either custody or access rights of one or both parents. For example, a judicial settlement in a divorce case invariably assigns custody of children to one parent and guarantees the other a right

---

[19]Anna Shelton, "Battered Women: A New Asylum Case," *The Progressive* 63 (November 1999): 25–27.
[20]Jaimee K. Wellerstein, "In the Name of Tradition: Eradicating the Harmful Practice of Female Genital Mutilation," *Loyola of Los Angeles International and Comparative Law Review* 22 (October 1999): 99, 117. Also see Barbara Crossette, "Mother Cites New U.S. Law on Torture to Fight Return to Nigeria," *New York Times,* 3 December 1998, A10.
[21]Refugee Act of 1980 (March 17, 1980), 94 Stat. 106. Also see Migration and Refugee Assistance Act (June 28, 1962), ibid. 76:121.

of access. If the custodial parent then leaves the country of residence, the access rights of the other parent have been breached. Each contracting state agrees to establish a central authority whose purpose is the administration of the convention.[22]

As is the case in most lawmaking conventions defining the duties of governments, the Convention on Child Abduction allows for exceptions. Essentially, these are as follows:

a. A year has elapsed from the date of the abduction, and the child has settled into a new and secure environment,

b. The parent claiming custodial or access rights was not actually exercising them, or

c. Evidence indicates that the repatriation of the child would expose him or her to "physical or psychological harm."

Considerations of humanity serve to mitigate the legal doctrine that the rights of the parent in the state of habitual residence take precedence. The question of determining the best interests of the child is within the purview of judicial authorities of the state receiving the request for repatriation. The discussion in the previous section about the unresolved problems confronting women of all ages is relevant here.

The United States has ratified the convention, but Cuba has not. Article 35 of the treaty is specific:

This Convention shall apply as between Contracting States only to wrongful removals or retentions occurring after its entry into force in those States.

In the matter of Elián González, the government of Cuba has demanded the protection afforded by the convention but has refused to make a reciprocal commitment vis-à-vis other governments. Reciprocity is a basic principle of international law without which the community of states cannot exist. Chief Justice John Marshall pointed out in his opinion on *The Nereide,* as discussed in Chapter 1, that the U.S. Supreme Court is bound by the law of nations, which depends for its existence on a reciprocal acknowledgment of obligations by all governments. Rights are always the companion of duties.

The issue of abducted children is one of general concern because of the hundreds of cases which have developed in the past decade. Human rights activists have sponsored the opening in Washington, D.C., of the Center for Missing and Exploited Children—a nongovernmental organization (NGO) seeking to mobilize support for the 1980 convention. On the official level, President Jacques Chirac of France has twice raised with Chancellor Gerhard Schröder of Germany the abortive appeal of French mothers whose children have been taken by German spouses. In this regard, President Chirac has reportedly spoken of the "law of the jungle." The convention requires states parties to process applications for the return of abducted children to their lawful parent or guardian within six weeks. British courts have established a record of meeting the deadline.[23] But German courts often extend the process to a year, enabling the parent who

---

[22]Convention on the Civil Aspects of International Child Abduction (October 25, 1980) 19 I.L.M. 1501.

[23]In England and Wales the government has chosen to vest jurisdiction over child abduction cases involving two states in a single high-level authority, thereby assuring a uniformity of decision making. By comparison, the administration of the convention in Germany and the United States is decentralized giving multiple state courts jurisdiction, a circumstance which engenders delay and inconsistency in rulings. Does decentralization comport with the treaty requirement for a *central authority*? See Nigel Lowe and Alison Perry, "International Child Abduction—The English Experience," *International and Comparative Law Quarterly* 48 (January 1999): 127.

has taken the children to claim an exception as just described. Perhaps the best commentary was provided by Joschka Fischer, the foreign minister of Germany and a leader of the ecological party, the Greens. With regard to protests from American mothers over German court decisions concerning their children taken to Germany, Fischer observed:

> I do not accept the interpretation of all those affected. But we now have a political problem, which during the Cold War would essentially have been a human problem.[24]

The United Nations has enhanced the protection afforded by international law to children in 1989, when the General Assembly approved a comprehensive treaty on the rights of the child. The revised and expanded convention explicitly extended to children the care and assistance guaranteed under the General Assembly's Universal Declaration of Human Rights (1948). The multilateral commitment is one of enabling a child, defined as anyone under the age of eighteen, to develop in a positive environment—one free of discrimination based on gender, nationality, religion, or political orientation. The dominant principle appears in article 3 of the 1989 convention:

> In all actions concerning children, whether undertaken by public or private social welfare organizations, courts of law, administrative authorities or legislative bodies, the best interests of the child shall be a primary consideration.[25]

It is notable that the language identifies the best interests of the child as "a" and not "the" primary consideration.

Regional international law again plays a critical role. In 1996, the Council of Europe, an association of some forty European states committed to the federalist ideal, sponsored its own convention designed to uphold the rights of children. Chapter 4 focused on a discussion of the true subjects of international law, that is, sovereign states. Contemporary human rights law, especially as it relates to children, raises the question of whether the individual may claim subject status. The European experience suggests that the person can, and the convention on the rights of children is instructive on this point.

The European convention contains a pathbreaking provision recognizing the procedural rights of the child. Article 3 states:

> A child considered by internal law as having sufficient understanding, in the case of proceedings before a judicial authority affecting him or her, shall be granted, and shall be entitled to request the following rights:
> **a.** to receive all relevant information;
> **b.** to be consulted and express his or her own views;
> **c.** to be informed of possible consequences of compliance with these views and possible consequences of any decision.[26]

Those exercising parental responsibilities may not represent the child if there is a conflict of interest. The cumulative result of these provisions is the recognition of individual rights, in this case of a child, under international law. The progressive development

---

[24]"Interview with Joschka Fischer," *Der Spiegel* 20 (May 15, 2000): 39, 42.
[25]Convention on the Rights of the Child (November 20, 1989), 28 I.L.M. 1456.
[26]European Convention on the Exercise of Children's Rights (January 25, 1996), 35 I.L.M. 653.

of human rights law as it relates to children signifies the gradual erosion of the distinction between subject and object status, for in the field of human rights the individual is now becoming a recognized subject with authentic standing rather than an object on whom the law may act.

ETHNIC GROUP RIGHTS

Public and private endeavors in the field of human rights center on the individual rather than a collectivity, but there exists a parallel tradition whereby the protection of the individual is conceived of as a function of the integrity of the group, defined in ethnic or religious terms. The governance of the Ottoman Empire (ca. 1300–1919) provides an example of a polity organized on the basis of group rights. The *millet* or religious communities of the Empire, which stretched from the Danube River to the Arabian Peninsula, possessed constitutional standing and were the social units that made possible the administration of government. The *rum-millet* or Greek Orthodox community functioned under the Patriarch of Constantinople (modern Istanbul); the government appointed an *ephor* to supervise the Jewish community; and the Armenian community had a patriarch of its own.[27] The historian Arnold Toynbee in commenting on the *millet* system pointed out that at the very time Moslems were being expelled or massacred in European countries the Ottoman Turks organized their state to protect ethnic and religious minorities.[28] The concept of international group rights has an Eastern rather than a Western origin.

The rights of minorities became a European issue starting with the Greek war of independence (1821–1832), which sparked the progressive breakup of the Ottoman Empire. In 1876, Turkish irregulars carried out massacres in Bulgarian villages, and William Gladstone, leader of the Liberal Party in the House of Commons, published a pamphlet in which he denounced these atrocities as violative of international law and morality. Gladstone's argument rested on the assumption that every government was accountable for misdeeds committed against its subjects—the fundamental thesis of human rights law. Prime Minister Benjamin Disraeli, leader of the Conservative Party, argued that British strategic interests necessitated good relations with the Ottoman Empire, and these precluded interference in its internal affairs.[29] The debate between Gladstone and Disraeli was one of principle versus expediency. Efforts to uphold the norms of international law may indeed founder on the barrier of the interest of the state.

The Paris Peace Conference opened in 1919 for the purpose of drafting the treaties of peace ending the First World War. The Allied and Associated Powers (the United States was one of the latter) crafted agreements designed to create a system of mutual security in Europe, and guarantees of minority rights, especially in newly created states, were an integral part of the system. Nine treaties of guarantee of minority rights were

---

[27]Geoffrey Lewis, *Modern Turkey* (New York: Praeger, 1974), pp. 33–35.
[28]Arnold J. Toynbee, *The Western Question in Greece and Turkey: A Study in the Contact of Civilizations* (London: Constable and Co., 1922), p. 267.
[29]Marvin Swartz, *The Politics of British Foreign Policy in the Era of Disraeli and Gladstone* (New York: St. Martin's Press, 1985), pp. 37–44.

incorporated into the peace settlement.[30] All of the treaties incorporated essentially the same principles, and the treaty with Czecho-Slovakia, known as the Convention of Brünn with regard to citizenship and the protection of minorities, served as a prototype. The treaty recognized the multiethnic character of the Czecho-Slovak Republic, one of the successor states of the Austro-Hungarian Empire, and guaranteed cultural and political rights to the German, Hungarian, Polish, and Ruthenian peoples within its borders. Each national group could use its own language in commerce and government, operate its own schools, and participate in the political process. Citizenship was not linked to ethnicity, assuring equal protection in the administration of government. The League of Nations was to monitor the implementation of the treaty, and an aggrieved minority could appeal to it for assistance. At the Paris Peace Conference some governments complained that the minority treaties compromised their sovereignty, to which President Woodrow Wilson replied that the Powers had the right to censure the new states they had, by and large, created.[31]

During the interwar period, revisionist governments cynically exploited the plight of minorities to redraw the borders of Eastern Europe. As a consequence the peacemakers endeavoring to restore order after the Second World War tended to view with skepticism the minority treaties of the 1920s and to favor a general commitment to individual human rights. The Universal Declaration of Human Rights approved by the General Assembly of the United Nations in 1948 was but a case in point. Nevertheless, Europe did provide two successful examples of a revival of minority treaties, the first based on territorial autonomy and the latter on individual autonomy. Failed attempts in the Mediterranean world, notably Cyprus and Lebanon, offset the continental European record. The cases about to be considered should not be taken as precedents for other parts of the world.

The first example is that of Italy's German minority. The peace arranged at Paris in 1919 created the Republic of Austria and defined its borders in such a way that the kingdom of Italy acquired a German-speaking population of about 200,000 in the province of South Tyrol. The transfer of territory resulted from secret negotiations, which precluded a democratic solution in the form of a referendum. The Fascist government of Benito Mussolini imposed a harsh regime on the South Tyroleans and ultimately planned to expel them in an effort which later was to be known as ethnic cleansing.[32] The defeat of fascism in 1945 created an opportunity for the governments of Austria and Italy to renegotiate the status of the South Tyrol, and the result was the Gruber-de Gasperi agreement of 1946.[33] The agreement guaranteed the German population equality of linguistic rights, provided for autonomous legislative and executive authorities in

---

[30] Austria (September 10, 1919), 3 Israel 1535, 1560; Bulgaria (November 27, 1919), 3 Israel 1727, 1743; Czecho-Slovakia (June 7, 1920), 3 L.N.T.S. 189, 225; Greece (August 10, 1920), 28 L.N.T.S. 244; Hungary (June 4, 1920), 3 Israel 1863, 1885; Poland (June 28, 1919), L.N.T.S.: not reproduced; Roumania (December 9, 1919), 5 L.N.T.S.:336, 343; Turkey (July 24, 1923), 28 L.N.T.S. 12; and Yugoslavia (October 21, 1920), L.N.T.S.: not reproduced.

[31] F. P. Walters, *A History of the League of Nations* (New York: Oxford University Press, 1969), pp. 91–92.

[32] For a detailed account of these developments, see Anthony Alcock, *The History of the South Tyrolean Question* (London: Joseph Publ., 1970).

[33] Paris Agreement on the South Tyrol (September 5, 1946) in Treaty of Peace with Italy (February 10, 1947), 61 Stat. 1369, 1427–1428. Karl Gruber, Chancellor of Austria, and Alcide de Gasperi, Prime Minister of Italy, signed for their respective governments.

the province of Bozen/Bolzano, recognized the need for bilingual education, and abrogated the Fascist decrees calculated to alter the demographic character of the region. As promising as was this undertaking, ethnic tension remained at a high level until the governments of Austria and Italy agreed on the "package" of 1969.[34] The omnibus agreement contained fifteen discrete provisions designed to realize the goal of territorial autonomy and to guarantee equality of opportunity for all citizens of the Republic of Italy. Parliamentary statutes and executive decrees provided for the implementation of the separate provisions.

The Italian approach to minority rights is territorial. The ethnic German community would have an autonomous province and the institutions essential for the maintenance of its identity. Austria as the former sovereign functions as a guarantor of the arrangement. The military significance of the South Tyrol has long since disappeared, for both Austria and Italy are members of the European Union, whose integrative processes have removed any possibility of armed conflict between the two former enemies. We may speak of a gradual washing out of frontiers brought about by the rise of regional organizations, and this process rather than formal treaties is the ultimate guarantor of minority rights.

Regional autonomy is, however, not always a feasible approach to protecting minorities, whose dispersion within a larger population may make the formation of an ethnically homogeneous province a practical impossibility. The alternative form of autonomy is personal, whereby the individual possesses enumerated rights irrespective of his or her place of residence. In 1955, the four powers occupying Austria (France, Great Britain, the Soviet Union, and the United States) agreed to restore the sovereignty and independence of the republic and accordingly signed the Austrian State Treaty. Article 7 stipulated:

> Austrian nationals of the Slovene and Croat minorities in Carinthia,
> Burgenland and Styria shall enjoy the same rights on equal terms as all other
> Austrian nationals, including the right to their own organizations, meetings
> and press in their own language.[35]

Personal autonomy avoids the pitfall of having to draw territorial boundaries around language islands in order to create self-governing areas. The Austrian solution, rather than the Italian, is to be recommended.

UNIVERSALISM AND HUMAN RIGHTS

Regional perspectives serve as building blocks for a universal system of human rights. The Charter of the United Nations (1945) commits the world organization in article 55 to promote:

> ... universal respect for, and observance of, human rights and fundamental
> freedoms for all without distinction as to race, sex, language, or religion.[36]

---

[34]For the text of the Austro–Italian agreement, see "South Tirol Dispute," *Keesing's Contemporary Archives* 17 (1969–1970): 23846 and "South Tirol," ibid. 18 (1971–1972): 24747.
[35]Austrian State Treaty (May 15, 1955), 6 U.S.T. 2369, 2411.
[36]Charter of the United Nations, Article 55(c).

The principle was elaborated and adopted three years later in the Universal Declaration of Human Rights. As a resolution of the General Assembly one may well argue that the declaration constituted a statement of intent setting goals for governments to attain as opposed to an obligation in the form of the black letter law of a convention.[37] The countervailing view is that the declaration represents *jus cogens,* that is, peremptory norms of international law, governing state behavior. While no authoritative list of what constitutes a violation of *jus cogens* exists, the complicity of a government in acts involving aggressive war, crimes against humanity, slavery, or piracy would be a breach of international law.[38] In this respect the Hispanic tradition in the study of international law proves helpful, for it acknowledges the linkage between natural law (*jus naturale*) and human rights, a relationship which positivists deny.[39] The rationale of human rights law is a difficult problem for positivists and suggests the potential of a revival of naturalist theory.

The first major lawmaking treaty formulated under the charter was the Genocide Convention (1948). The twentieth century witnessed crimes against humanity on an unparalleled scale, and the United Nations moved at its initial session to brand any effort to destroy or forcibly deport an ethnic or religious minority as an offense against the law of nations.[40] President Truman signed for the United States, but the Senate declined to give its approval in part because of concern over states' rights. In 1988, President Reagan successfully pressed the Senate for its concurrence, and the following year he ratified the convention. By joint resolution Congress enacted the Genocide Convention Implementation Act of 1988, which both recognized genocide as an offense under international law and a federal crime under the municipal law of the United States.[41] Congress included in its definition of the offense not only conspiracy to commit genocide, but also complicity in the commission of the crime. Notably genocide is an extraditable criminal act. The legislative history of the Genocide Convention illustrates the process whereby international law is incorporated into the municipal law of the United States.

In keeping with its obligation under the charter, the United Nations has addressed a wide range of social and economic issues and in doing so has broadened the concept of human rights to include positive duties on the part of governments. In 1966, the United Nations opened for signature two separate but mutually supporting conventions. The first was the Covenant on Economic, Social and Cultural Rights, which promised self-determination for all peoples, elevated the principle of collective bargaining to a right under international law, promised an adequate standard of living to everyone, protected the family, and outlawed gender bias.[42] The United States did not adhere to this treaty, but President George Bush did ratify the second in 1992—the International

---

[37]Ian Brownlie, *Principles of Public International Law,* 5th ed. (Oxford and New York: Oxford University Press, 1998), pp. 574–576.

[38]Oscar Schachter, *International Law in Theory and Practice* (Boston: Martinus Nijhoff, 1997), pp. 342–344.

[39]José-Luis Cascajo Castro et al., *Los derechos humanos* (Human rights) (Seville: University of Seville, 1979), p. 23.

[40]Convention on the Prevention and Punishment of Genocide (December 9, 1948), reproduced in Dusan J. Djonovich (ed.), *United Nations Resolutions: Resolutions of the General Assembly* (Dobbs Ferry, N.Y.: Oceana Publications, 1973), II: 238–241.

[41]Genocide Convention Implementation Act (November 4, 1988), 102 Stat. 3045. For congressional documentation with an introductory analysis by Christopher C. Joyner, see 28 I.L.M. 754 (1989).

[42]International Covenant on Economic, Social and Cultural Rights (December 19, 1966), 6 I.L.M. 360 (1967).

Covenant on Civil and Political Rights. The rights covered included participation in the political process, freedom of movement and expression, equality of marriage partners, judicial due process, and the defense of minority rights. These commitments were, however, subject to the requirement of maintaining national security and public order (*ordre public*) and accordingly could be circumscribed in the interests of the state.[43]

Reaction to the two covenants is mixed. On the positive side, they represent a moral consensus of humankind, for they are indeed a codification of general principles of law regarding the rights of the individual and of groups. Critics are quick to point out that there is no means of enforcement apart from the courts of the country in question. To be sure, an appeal to the United Nations Commission on Human Rights and the high commissioner for human rights (as of 1999, Mary Robinson of Ireland) is evident, but the reality is that the commission's competence is limited to investigating complaints and reporting to the General Assembly, where political roadblocks can be raised by governments determined to avoid embarrassing disclosures on such matters as slavery.

Secretary General Kofi Annan has called for reforms designed to support the commission, but the response has not been encouraging.[44] Taking the broader view, progress toward the codification of human rights law over the past fifty years is remarkable. Conventions guaranteeing the rights of women, protecting children, criminalizing ethnic cleansing, and recognizing the economic, social, and political rights of the individual as a part of the law of nations have had an effect. The struggle against the slave trade required two centuries, and it is not yet over. By comparison, the achievements under the aegis of the United Nations are impressive. The law is in place, and the immediate challenge is one of securing compliance.

Topics for Discussion

1. Human rights law involves two concepts: (a) obligations *erga omnes,* and (b) *jus cogens* or peremptory norms. What is the relationship between the two? Acting together, how do they provide a basis for an international commitment to human rights?

2. How has the definition of human rights expanded since the founding of the United Nations? The original notion of "offenses against the law of nations" required governments to suppress international criminality, such as piracy. What duties do governments now have under modern human rights law?

3. Historically, only the sovereign and territorial state could claim the status of being a true subject of international law. Individuals and ethnic groups were limited to object status. Has the growth of human rights law endowed persons and groups with subject status independent of the civil liberties guaranteed by municipal law?

4. As one body of law informs another, so the international norms of human rights are incorporated into codes of municipal law. Give examples of how the process of incorporation functions.

---

[43]International Covenant on Civil and Political Rights (December 19, 1966), ibid., 368.
[44]John Tessitore and Susan Woolfson, *A Global Agenda: Issues Before the 54th General Assembly of the United Nations,* United Nations Association of the United States of America (Lanham, MD.: Rowman & Littlefield Publishers, 1999), pp. 154–160.

CHAPTER 8

Citizenship

Political obligation is the bond that links the individual to the state. The political theory of ancient Greece bound the individual to the polis (city-state) and postulated that only through the acceptance of the rights and duties of citizenship could one become a member of the community. Citizenship was essentially a question of identity, which was manifested in a legal relationship. This relationship resulted in the theory of natural rights possessed by all who had accepted the duties of citizenship. Modern international law views citizenship largely as a function of jurisdiction. Whether a given government has the responsibility for an individual depends upon his or her passport, which may change during a lifetime. Citizens of the member states of the European Union (EU) have passports bearing the inscription "European Community," suggesting two levels of citizenship—one European and the other national. The evolution of the concept of citizenship based on the exclusive prerogatives of the sovereign to commitment to political values, including human rights, reflects the changing nature of international law.

ACQUISITION OF CITIZENSHIP

Historically citizenship derives its meaning from membership by birth in a basic social unit, such as the clan. Kinship distinguished the citizen from outsiders, whose acceptance may be cordial but always tentative. The development of the modern territorial state shifted the emphasis from family ties to loyalty to the sovereign. The citizen became one who accepted the supremacy of the state and owed a permanent allegiance to it. From this transition evolved the two predominant modes of acquiring citizenship at birth: *jus sanguinis* (law of the blood) and *jus soli* (law of the soil). While the former is generally recognized, many governments will not accept *jus soli*.

Jus sanguinis may appear to be straightforward, but the application of this doctrine may involve complications. For example, is a child born out of wedlock entitled to claim the citizenship of his or her parents? If the parents are of different nationalities, whose blood line is determinative? Is the guiding principle one of matriarchy or patriarchy? These and other questions make the application of *jus sanguinis* far from simple. Persons born abroad of American parents are entitled to claim U.S. citizenship, but only if they reside in the United States for five consecutive years before attaining the age of twenty-three. In practice, however, returning from abroad to attend college will, in large measure, meet the residence requirement. In such an instance, an administrative or judicial decision is required to confirm that the individual has indeed complied with the law. The statute then provides guidelines, which must then be interpreted.

By comparison, *jus soli* is less judgmental because the place of birth is usually recorded by a public authority. Most governments are, however, reluctant to accept the standard of place of birth in view of the mass movement of people occasioned by a global economy. The United States has historically relied upon both tests, either one of which is sufficient to establish a viable claim to citizenship.[1] To this extent, U.S. policy is more flexible than that of most countries. Combining the two tests may prove difficult. The following scenario is illustrative. Country X grants citizenship based on *jus sanguinis.* A couple from Country Y, which relies on *jus soli,* have a child while they are temporarily resident in Country X. The child would be stateless since it would qualify under neither test.

In the last fifty years the issue of statelessness has become a major concern in public international law. In the aftermath of the Second World War, territorial changes in Central and Eastern Europe led to the expulsion of millions of people from their historic homelands. The independence of India and its division into two separate states in 1947 placed additional millions on the move. In the 1960s governments of newly independent East African states expelled Indian minorities within their borders. The handover of the British Crown Colony of Hong Kong to China in 1997 left many ethnic Indian and Malaysian citizens of the colony stateless, for they were no longer British subjects nor Chinese citizens. Two years later the reversion of the Portuguese colony of Macao to China created the same problem, especially for Eurasians. The forces of nationalism and territoriality have combined to deprive ethnic and religious minorities of the citizenship they had always assumed was theirs by right of birth. Not only groups but also individuals were subject to expulsion. In 1974, the government of the Soviet Union expelled Alexander Solzhenitsyn and deprived him of his passport. The doctrine that a government could determine, without interference, who its citizens were, even at the cost of expatriation, led to tragic consequences, and international law appeared to offer no remedy.

In 1954, the United Nations sponsored a convention that defined *stateless persons* and accorded them basic rights. The convention defined a stateless person as one "... who is not considered a national by any State under the operation of its law." Article 3 required equal protection:

> The Contracting States shall apply the provisions of this Convention to stateless persons without discrimination as to race, religion or country of origin.[2]

As of 1998, fifty-six governments and the Holy See had adhered to the convention. The United States was not one of these.

Voluntary and involuntary migration has altered the traditional view of citizenship based on kinship. Governments have enacted statutes permitting the award of citizenship based on a period of residence during which the individual has shown him or herself to be a productive member of the community. The process, usually referred to as naturalization and sometimes as legitimation, requires the decision of an administrative or judicial tribunal. The criteria under municipal law vary widely. The United States requires a minimum of five years, although the period is shortened to three years in the case of the spouse of a citizen. Other governments have such rigid requirements that naturalization is limited to the very few. Switzerland is one of these.

---

[1] For U.S. laws, see Aliens and Citizenship, *Statutes at Large* 44:121 (1926); Nationality Act, ibid. 54:1137 (1940); Immigration and Nationality Act, ibid. 66:163 (1952); Immigration and Nationality Act (amendments), ibid. 79:911 (1965); Immigration and Nationality Act (amendments), ibid. 104:4978 (1990); and Immigration and Nationality Technical Corrections, ibid. 108:4305 (1994).
[2] Convention relating to the Status of Stateless Persons (September 28, 1954), 360 U.N.T.S. 130, 136.

The plight of those who find themselves expelled from the land of their birth and unable to meet the requirements for naturalization in their new homeland is an issue in human rights law. The International Covenant on Civil and Political Rights (1966), as described in the preceding chapter, provides in article 24 dealing with the rights of children that "[e]very child has the right to acquire a nationality." The commitment is ambiguous because it does not cover those who, through no fault of their own, have been deprived of their citizenship. If the government of a state adhering to the convention expatriates an individual, has it violated a basic human right? A broad reading of the article suggests that such a violation has indeed occurred, but no international consensus exists on this point. The right to acquire a nationality is not the same as a guarantee of a nationality. Positive international law has yet to clarify this issue.

DUAL CITIZENSHIP

In 2000, the German government introduced legislation to recognize dual citizenship (*doppelte Staatsbürgerschaft*) and in doing so took a step toward recognizing a reality which most other governments have refused to accept; namely, in those regions of the world where transnational mobility is commonplace an individual may well have two passports. The emerging concept of citizenship in the European Union suggests a regional as well as a national dimension in the definition of political obligation. Traditionally governments have only reluctantly acknowledged the existence of dual citizenship, for it contradicts the classical definition of sovereignty. How can one authority be absolute and perpetual regarding an individual when another authority can make the same claim? If both states require military service, whose uniform will a conscript wear?[3] To which government will a dual citizen have a tax liability?

Presumably the individual could resolve the difficulties associated with dual nationality by exercising a right of expatriation, that is, the renunciation of citizenship in one of the two states. The Hague Conference for the Codification of International Law (1930) asserted in the preamble to a convention on nationality ". . . that every person should have a nationality and should have one nationality only."[4] In the event of a dispute between governments regarding an individual with dual nationality, the convention stipulated in article 4:

> A State may not afford diplomatic protection to one of its nationals against a State whose nationality such a person also possesses.[5]

The principle that an individual of dual nationality could not play one government against the other is a part of customary international law, as modified by the *Esphahanian* case.[6] The claimant for restitution of lost property was an Iranian, who emigrated to the United States and became a naturalized citizen in 1958. Subsequently he

---

[3]During the First World War, U.S. citizens of Italian parentage were conscripted into the Italian army on the thesis that they were still subjects of the king of Italy (i.e., *jus sanguinis*). See 3 Hackworth 353.
[4]Convention on Certain Questions Relating to the Conflict of Nationality Laws (March–April 1930), reprinted in A.J.I.L. 24 (July 1930): 192.
[5]Ibid., 193. See also von Glahn, 152.
[6]Esphahanian, *Claimant* v. Bank Tejarat, *Respondent* (March 29, 1983), Iran-United States Claims Tribunal reprinted in 72 I.L.R. 478.

returned to work in Iran, where he established a bank account. The Iranian revolution of 1979 led to the nationalization of the bank account, and Esphahanian turned to the Iran–United States Claims Tribunal for relief. The Iranian government argued that, following article 4, the claimant was an Iranian (*jus sanguinis*) and that the United States could not represent him against his own country. The U.S. counterargument was that the "dominant and effective nationality" of the claimant was American and that he was entitled to the full protection of that citizenship. By a vote of two to one, the Tribunal accepted the U.S. position, but the issue is far from resolved. Indeed, the decision remains controversial since international law does not generally recognize the notion of a "dominant and effective" allegiance in the case of dual nationality.

TREASON

These and other considerations lead directly to the question of political loyalty. In the early Middle Ages, the word *treason,* derived from the French, simply meant "disloyalty to one's king or liege lord" and could therefore be used to punish any word or deed found objectionable by the monarch. In 1351, King Edward III promulgated a statute, which defined treason as levying war against the sovereign, counterfeiting money, conspiracy, or even adultery.[7] Mindful of the potential for abuse inherent in such a broadly defined offense, the framers of the Constitution restricted the definition of the crime to "levying war" against the United States or otherwise assisting its enemies. Moreover, the Constitution requires for conviction the testimony of two witnesses or a confession given freely in an open court.[8] Given the rigor of these standards, it is hardly surprising that there have been few convictions for treason in the history of American law. Prosecutors usually prefer the charge of espionage, for which the standards of proof are not as high.

Although infrequent, federal prosecutions for treason do illuminate the problems associated with dual citizenship. In 1952, the U.S. Supreme Court addressed the issue of dual nationality and the charge of wartime treason. Tomoya Kawakita was a U.S. citizen (*jus soli*) of Japanese parents, who traveled to Japan to complete his secondary schooling prior to the outbreak of the war in the Pacific. Hostilities between the United States and Japan prevented his return. In 1943 he attained his majority and secured civilian employment in a munitions factory, where his duties included overseeing American prisoners compelled to work there. Threats and acts of brutality were his method. After the cessation of hostilities Kawakita applied for an American passport and returned to the United States, where he was recognized by a former prisoner. Pending investigation, he was charged with treason and convicted in a federal jury trial. His attorneys then petitioned the U.S. Supreme Court for a writ of certiorari, arguing that after 1943 he had considered himself a citizen of Japan (*jus sanguinis*) and had, for example, accepted a Japanese passport for a visit to China.

---

[7]Frederick Pollock and Frederic William Maitland, *The History of English Law* (Cambridge: At the University Press, 1895), 501–507. See also 11 *Halsbury's Laws of England,* 478.
[8]Constitution, art. III (3). The standard of two witnesses was derived from English law. See Henry John Stephen, *New Commentaries on the Laws of England* (London: Butterworth, 1841–1845; reprint New York: Garland Publishing, 1979), 4:426.

In a split decision of five to three (with one abstention), the Court upheld the conviction. Writing for the majority, Justice William O. Douglas argued that Kawakita had never renounced his U.S. citizenship during the critical period from 1943 to 1945, and that his duties in a munitions factory gave "aid and comfort" to the enemy during a time of war.[9] Douglas drew upon the treason statute of Edward III to the effect that actions which embolden the enemy are a form of treasonable conduct, and he dismissed Kawakita's contention that during the war he had expatriated himself. "Fair-weather citizenship," wrote Douglas, is not a tenable doctrine. Three members of the Court dissented, saying that in Kawakita's mind he had accepted Japanese citizenship and was, therefore, not guilty of treason. The difficulty in making such a determination is obvious. If citizenship is a state of mind, under what circumstances can an individual exercise a personal right of expatriation? The immigration laws of the United States have always recognized the right of an individual to transfer allegiance from one state to another, and that fact alone raises questions about the nature of treason.

All too often, the combined pressures of public hysteria and political expediency distort the legal process in the matter of treason, as the following two cases illustrate. The first is the treason trial and conviction of "Tokyo Rose" in postwar California. Iva Ikuko Toguri D'Aquino was a U.S. citizen (*jus soli*), who visited Japan before war broke out in the Pacific. Through the good offices of a neutral legation in Tokyo she sought to return to the United States but was refused the necessary travel documents. To earn a living she accepted employment with Radio Tokyo as one of a dozen or so English-speaking female announcers, who read announcements and introduced musical selections in broadcasts beamed to American forces in the Pacific. Using the name "Ann" and sometimes "Orphan Ann," D'Aquino would play recordings and offer brief commentary. Court records indicated that the Japanese security police kept her under surveillance, and she was not regarded as politically reliable. The nom de guerre "Tokyo Rose" was a general reference used by American servicemen for all the women broadcasters. At war's end she worked as an interpreter for the U.S. Army. Pursuant to an investigation by the Army Counterintelligence Corps (CIC), she was detained for a year in Japan and then repatriated to stand trial on a charge of treason. A federal court in San Francisco found her guilty of treason in 1949 and sentenced her to ten years. The Ninth Circuit Court of Appeals upheld the conviction.[10]

D'Aquino was released in 1955 and immediately began to work for her rehabilitation. The California state legislature recommended that she receive a pardon;[11] even the foreman of the jury, which convicted her, had second thoughts. On his last day in office President Gerald R. Ford quietly pardoned her, but a presidential pardon does not resolve lingering questions. Is being a disc jockey for a wartime foe tantamount to treason? Why were others in the same position not indicted? Was D'Aquino afforded due process during her interrogation by military authorities? Ultimately, the answers to these and related questions will have to come from the framers of the Constitution, who

---

[9]*Kawakita v. United States,* 343 U.S. 717, 730–736 (1952).

[10]*D'Aquino v. United States,* 192 F. 2nd 338 (1951). The appeal was a veritable textbook on constitutional law involving as it did such issues as detention for a year without trial, the authority of the military to arrest a civilian for treason, the use of hearsay evidence, and misrepresentation by military authorities as to the defendant's legal rights.

[11]" 'Tokyo Rose' Pardoned," *New York Times,* 20 January 1977, A1, 8.

prudently restricted the charge of treason so that it could not serve the cause of demagoguery.

The second "case" demonstrated the primacy of expediency over principle in interpreting the nature of treason. In 1942, Guillermo Francisco was a citizen of the Commonwealth of the Philippines, then a dependency of the United States. As an officer in the Philippine constabulary and a member of a politically prominent family, he was awarded a commission with the rank of colonel in the U.S. Army. When the Japanese army overran the Philippines, Francisco found himself confined under harsh conditions as a prisoner of war (POW), and he accepted a Japanese offer to change sides. As a collaborator the now-General Francisco organized a paramilitary force, which hunted down guerrillas and escaped POWs. In the literal sense he waged war against the United States. With the end of hostilities U.S. military authorities briefly detained him, but President Truman directed that no Filipino should be tried for treason, even those who had militarily collaborated with the Japanese. The reason for this exculpatory policy was that the Truman administration needed the support of the oligarchical families to reestablish its control over the Philippines, and a trial of General Francisco along with other socially prominent collaborators might have triggered anti-Americanism.[12] A comparison with the D'Aquino case is almost redundant, for her offense only touched upon the constitutional definition of treason, whereas Francisco did "levy war" against the United States. Is treason a political or legal concept?

ASYLUM

In the Middle Ages an individual could seek sanctuary in a church—a practice which established the belief that one could by reaching a given place be secure from arbitrary authority. Customary international law recognizes the right of a government to grant asylum to those fleeing persecution. A principle of the common law of humankind evolved into conventional law in 1951, when the United Nations opened for signature a multilateral treaty on refugees, including the right of asylum.[13] In 1967, a modified and expanded version of the convention, entitled a "protocol," appeared and attracted the adherence of 132 states, plus the Holy See.[14] The United States adhered to the protocol a year later, and in 1980 Congress enacted implementing legislation.[15]

The norms having been established, their efficacy required testing, which was not long in coming in the form of a judicial decision. In September 1991, Jean Bertrand Aristide, the elected president of Haiti, was forced into exile by a military coup d'état. This event increased the already significant flow of refugees from Haiti to the southeastern United States. The "boat people" landed in Florida and claimed asylum as victims of political persecution. As early as 1981, the United States and Haiti had agreed on a policy whereby the U.S. Coast Guard could interdict refugees on the high seas and return them to Haiti. Three Presidents—Ronald Reagan, George Bush, and William Clinton—endorsed the policy of interdiction and repatriation. Human rights organiza-

---

[12]David Joel Steinberg, *Philippine Collaboration in World War II* (Ann Arbor, MI.: University of Michigan Press, 1967), p. 157.
[13]Convention Relating to the Status of Refugees (July 28, 1951), 19 U.S.T. 6259.
[14]Protocol Relating to the Status of Refugees (January 31, 1967), 19 U.S.T. 6223.
[15]Refugee Act of 1980 (March 17, 1980), 94 Stat. 102.

tions insisted that the arrangement did not provide for adequate screening of refugees to identify those whose lives might be in danger if sent home. Considerations of universal human rights led to the initiation of a federal suit, the purpose of which was to end interdiction and allow each refugee a full hearing by officials of the Immigration and Naturalization Service (INS). On appeal the case went in 1993 to the U.S. Supreme Court, where a majority decided to uphold the policy of the executive branch. A lone dissenter presented a counterargument. Setting aside for the moment the voting outcome, a review of the arguments illustrates the complexity of the asylum issue.

The petitioner (i.e., human rights organizations) argued that the intent of conventional and statutory law was to shield the individual refugee from the power of a tyrannical government. The evaluation of each case on a person-by-person basis was essential. The site of the evaluation, whether inside or outside the territory of the United States, was not a definitive consideration. It is the spirit of international refugee law which mattered. The decision hinged upon the interpretation of the Convention Relating to the Status of Refugees (1951) as incorporated into the subsequent protocol (1967). Article 33(1) states:

> No Contracting State shall expel or return (*refouler*) a refugee in any manner whatsoever to the frontiers of territories where his life of freedom would be threatened on account of his race, religion, nationality, membership of a particular social group or political opinion.

Since both the English and French texts are equally authentic, the interpretation of the French word *refouler* is critical. Refouler encompasses a broad range of dictionary meanings, but the word must be defined within the context of the treaty. Articles 32 and 33 of the convention make a distinction between *expulsion* and *return,* equating refouler with the latter. The petitioner insisted that the Haitian refugees were being expelled, but the majority of the Supreme Court focused on the notion that they were being returned. The Refugee Act of 1980 makes a distinction between being deported and returned, and the opinion stressed the difference in meaning. Specifically the Supreme Court interpreted *refoulement* (the act of sending refugees back) as a "defensive act."[16] At one point the opinion referred to the program of interdiction as a "naval blockade."[17]

Justice Harry A. Blackmun dissented and defended the thesis that the international and municipal law protecting refugees served a general humanitarian purpose, which the United States was obligated to observe. The dissent raised a fundamental question in the study of international law: Should interpretations of universal norms depend upon legal formalism or on an humanitarian view of the law? International law, especially in the field of human rights, must accommodate a diversity of cultural traditions. For that reason the law is often general, leaving open, for example, the meaning of *refouler.* National courts are at liberty to apply a restrictive interpretation to a general prescriptive statement about asylum, and since the end of the Cold War many European governments have moved in this direction. In the bipolar world of confrontation between the United States and the Soviet Union, refugees were often a political asset,

---

[16]*Sale v. Haitian Centers Council,* 509 U.S. 155, 181, 192 n. 4 (1993).
[17]Ibid., 187. The expression is infelicitous because an earlier Supreme Court (1861) had determined that a blockade is an act of war.

and asylum was readily granted those fleeing a totalitarian system. In a world system dominated by economic considerations, refugees are viewed as an administrative problem with the result that the formerly generous approach to asylum has all but been abandoned.

The case of Cardinal Joszef Mindszenty of Hungary is illustrative of changing attitudes toward asylum. In October 1956, the Soviet army suppressed a popular uprising in Hungary, but not until political prisoners had been freed. One of these was Cardinal Mindszenty, who was then granted diplomatic asylum in the U.S. legation in Budapest, where he remained until 1971, when Hungarian authorities permitted him to leave the country for exile in Austria. For fifteen years the Cardinal had lived in an apartment on the premises of a diplomatic mission, and his case attracted media attention throughout the West.[18] Diplomatic asylum of this character is almost an anachronism. Although some embassies may open their doors to persons fleeing revolutionary turmoil, their stay would be brief.

ALIENS

Closely related to the right of asylum is the responsibility of a government for aliens within its territory. In Chapter 3, the issues associated with the application of international law within the state were introduced, and this discussion builds upon the thesis that a government has a responsibility toward aliens within its jurisdiction. The operative doctrine is that of due diligence, which requires that the government afford the same protection to aliens as is available to citizens. Certain restrictions may apply with regard to the ownership of property, but the procedural rights associated with due process must be observed except in time of war or a national emergency. For his or her part, the individual is obligated to obey the laws of the host state and to be a productive member of the community. Duties in this regard do not include military service, service on a jury, or the holding of a public office. In sum, the alien must demonstrate obedience, but allegiance in terms of political obligation is reserved for the home country. In this regard the distinction between obedience and allegiance may be critical, as evidenced by the preceding discussion of treason.

A series of cases decided by a binational commission in the 1920s developed the meaning of due diligence as a rule of international law. In 1923, the United States and Mexico had concluded an agreement providing for the establishment of a commission that met in Washington to decide claims " . . . in accordance with the principles of international law, justice and equity." The presidents of Mexico and the United States each appointed a member and then agreed on a third member, who would chair the meetings. The commission's brief was one of settling claims of citizens of the United States against Mexico " . . . except those arising from acts incident to the recent revolutions."[19] The exclusion of claims resulting from insurrection is a regional principle associated with Latin American international law and would not be binding on non-Hemispheric states. The purpose was to deny an outside power the pretext for armed intervention as had often been the case in the states of the Caribbean.

---

[18]*Keesing's Contemporary Archives,* 18 (October 23–30, 1971), 24888A.
[19]General Claims Convention (September 8, 1923), 9 Bevans 935, 936. See also A. H. Fellers, *Mexican Claims Commissions, 1923–1934* (New York: The Macmillan Co., 1935).

In 1926, the commission applied the principle of due diligence in a series of decisions. The first was the claim of Pauline Neer to the effect that Mexican authorities had failed to demonstrate due diligence in the apprehension and punishment of the murderers of her husband, an American mining engineer in the state of Durango. The Mexican and neutral members of the commission voted to disallow the claim, arguing that the requirements of Mexican law had been met. An investigative magistrate had examined the evidence, and authorities arrested the alleged perpetrators. A lack of evidence, however, led to their release, and there the case was closed. In a lengthy dissent the American member raised a key question: Is justice under international law dependent upon the formal fulfillment of the procedures of municipal law? In this instance the dissenter insisted that international law demands adherence to standards of justice which may well surpass those of municipal law. As a consequence the American member concluded that the Neer case represented a failure to provide the justice and equity demanded by the general claims agreement between the United States and Mexico.[20]

The second case also centered on a claim of a denial of justice. The murder victim was Byron Janes, who like Neer was an American mining engineer in Mexico. In this instance eyewitnesses positively identified the murderer as Pedro Carbajal, a former employee at the mine. Although the *comisario* of police was notified within five minutes of the shooting, he delayed organizing a mounted posse for almost an hour and later reported no trace of Carbajal, who had fled on foot. Reports circulated that Carbajal was at a nearby ranch, and that he had even returned to the scene of the crime. Apart from interviewing witnesses, the authorities took no action. Laura Janes, wife of the deceased, filed a claim with the commission, in which she argued that the dilatory tactics of the *comisario* constituted a denial of justice. The commission found that the executive authorities had failed to meet the standard of due diligence and in a unanimous decision awarded compensation to the widow. The American member wrote the following in a separate opinion:

> International law is a law for the conduct of nations grounded on the general assent of the nations of the world. The law is therefore, of course, the same for all members of the family of nations. Obviously it can only be modified by the same processes by which it is formulated, namely, by general assent of the nations. It does not seem possible to conceive of a situation in which a single nation could by a municipal enactment denying a right of redress, relieve itself from making compensation for failure to observe a rule of international law.

Accordingly, the member concluded that the claimants had suffered "*moral* damage" and were entitled to redress irrespective of the laws governing police procedures at the El Tigre mine, the crime scene.[21]

---

[20]*The United States of America on Behalf of L.F.H. Neer and Pauline E. Neer v. The United Mexican States* (October 15, 1926), *Opinions of the Commissioners under the Convention concluded September 8, 1923* (Washington, D.C.: U.S. Government Printing Office, 1927), 71–80. Hereafter *Opinions of the Commissioners.*

[21]*The United States of America on Behalf of Laura M. B. Janes v. The United Mexican States* (November 16, 1926), *Opinions of the Commissioners,* 109, 131.

The third case grew out of an incident all too common on international frontiers—a cross boundary shooting. Early in 1922, Walter Swinney, a young American, was trapping from a rowboat on a branch of the Rio Grande, which formed the boundary between Mexico and the United States. Two Mexican customs officials observed him and, suspecting him to be a smuggler, summoned him to approach their side of the river. According to their statements, Swinney attempted to row back to the American shore. Whereupon they fired a warning shot. He allegedly returned fire, and they shot a second time mortally wounding him. The two officials then placed themselves at the disposal of Mexican officials in the town of Nuevo Laredo. Although they were initially arrested, the officials were soon released without ever being placed on trial. The public prosecutor took the position that the officials had opened fire in the line of duty, and he closed the case without hearing the evidence of two Americans who witnessed the shooting. Moreover, an inspection of Swinney's pistol by the American consul and others showed that it was not fired and cast doubt on the Mexican claim that the officials returned fire in self-defense. Nor was there any evidence to show that Swinney was a smuggler or behaving in a suspicious manner. The commission concluded that the shooting was reckless and awarded compensation to Swinney's parents. The findings of the commission contained the following doleful conclusion:

> Human life in these parts, on both sides, seems not to be appraised so highly as international standards prescribe.[22]

Due diligence required that both executive and judicial officers of the respondent government not only meet the standards of their national municipal code but also conform to international norms of humanity and justice.

In terms of American law, the Fourteenth Amendment (1868) is the constitutional guarantee of the protection of due diligence to be afforded aliens traveling or residing in the United States. The commitment to due process and to equal protection bars discrimination against aliens. Chapter 3 described state laws that attempted to restrict the right of aliens to own property, attend public schools, or engage in selected commercial pursuits. Federal authority progressively eliminated these restrictions in an effort to realize the amendment's goals. Although the need to maintain public order, especially in time of an emergency, may necessitate the imposition of restrictions, such as those imposed on enemy aliens during World War II, the principle of nondiscriminatory treatment of aliens remains a norm of international law.

THE CALVO CLAUSE

Carlos Calvo (1824–1904) was an Argentine diplomat and legal scholar, who published one of the first comprehensive texts on international law in the modern period.[23] Latin American governments resented the interference of external powers in support of Eu-

---

[22]*The United States of America on Behalf of J.W. and N.L. Swinney v. The United Mexican States* (November 16, 1926), *Opinions of the Commissioners,* 131, 133.

[23]*Derecho internacional: teórico y práctico de Europa y América* (International law: theory and practice in Europe and America) (Paris: D'Amyot Librairie Diplomatique, 1868).

ropean and North American business interests in Central America and the Caribbean; and Calvo articulated a doctrine that quickly became part of regional international law. As it came to be called, the Calvo clause encompassed two interrelated ideas: (a) a reaffirmation of the sovereignty and territorial integrity of the Latin American republics, and (b) a refusal to accord aliens greater legal protection than was available to citizens of the country in question.[24] The proposition that an alien had to rely on the same local remedies as the citizen was subject to the qualification of diplomatic intercession on the part of the alien and ultimately arbitration as noted previously in the Mexican-American claims commission. Despite these limitations, the Calvo clause initiated a development which ultimately achieved universal status.

In 1902 to 1903, naval units of Great Britain, Germany, and Italy blockaded the coast of Venezuela in an effort to compel that government to meet its financial obligations. On December 29, 1902, Luis Drago, the foreign minister of Argentina, in a note addressed to Secretary of State John Hay insisted that force not be used to secure the repayment of loans.[25] Hay responded positively on February 17, 1903, but added that arbitration under the auspices of a neutral party remained a possibility. Combining the Calvo clause and the Drago doctrine provides a developing society with a degree of protection needed to secure its independence. At an international law conference convened in 1907 in The Hague, Latin American delegates lobbied for the adoption of a multilateral treaty designed to codify the work of Calvo and Drago into conventional law. The effort was a success, and what is sometimes known as the Porter treaty (named after Horace Porter, the U.S. delegate) was adopted. Article 1 stipulated:

> The Contracting Powers agree not to have recourse to armed force for the recovery of contract debts claimed from the Government of one country by the Government of another as being due to its nationals.[26]

The case of a Texas-based dredging company working in Mexico reveals the working of the Calvo clause and related Drago doctrine. In 1914, U.S. troops occupied Veracruz in a show of force directed against the regime of General Huerta, as discussed in Chapter 5. Against this background of confrontation and armed intervention, the North American Dredging Company instituted proceedings before the claims commission of the United States and Mexico for restitution, alleging a violation by Mexican authorities of a contract for harbor improvement. The Mexican commissioner referred to the Calvo clause, by which the company voluntarily alienated its right to appeal to its own government for protection. Instead the contractor was obligated to limit an appeal to the judicial process open to citizens of Mexico. The commission found that the contractor had not exhausted these local remedies and disallowed the complaint, but not until it conducted a detailed examination of the Calvo clause.

Specifically, the commission noted that while an individual may commit him or herself not to seek diplomatic protection, such a limitation may not be said to affect the right

---

[24] 5 Hackworth 635. Also see Donald R. Shea, *The Calvo Clause: A Problem of Inter-American and International Law Diplomacy* (Minneapolis: University of Minnesota Press, 1955), p. 19.
[25] F.R.U.S. (1903) 1: 1–5.
[26] Convention Respecting the Limitation of the Employment of Force for the Recovery of Contract Debts (October 18, 1907), 2 Malloy 2248, 2254.

of a government to seek redress for wrongs done its citizens. The right of an individual to enter into a contract must be balanced against the duty of a government to represent the interests of its citizens. The commission succinctly stated the matter as follows:

> The present stage of international law imposes upon every international tribunal the solemn duty of seeking for a proper and adequate balance between the sovereign right of national jurisdiction, on the one hand, and the sovereign right of national protection of citizens on the other.[27]

In 1873, Hamilton Fish, secretary of state in the Grant administration, made clear his government's position, when he stated:

> The rule of the law of nations is that the Government which refuses to repair the damage committed by its citizens or subjects, to punish the guilty parties or give them up for that purpose, may be regarded as virtually a sharer in the injury and as responsible therefor.[28]

Fish's view is suggestive of the distinction between subject and object status in international law, as developed in Chapter 4. As a true subject of international law, a state may demand redress for injuries done its citizens. Again, a decision of the claims commission is instructive. Mexican federal troops arrested Harry Roberts, a U.S. citizen, on May 5, 1922, and detained him under harsh conditions for nineteen months until he was formally charged with being a member of an outlaw band. A subsequent trial did not take place. The commission determined that although Mexican authorities had ample reason to arrest Roberts, the prolonged pretrial detention and the conditions which accompanied it were unwarranted. By a unanimous vote it directed that the Mexican government pay compensation.[29] The United States did not contest the right of judicial officers in Mexico to indict Roberts. Rather the argument was that the general legal norm of a speedy trial was not observed, and this circumstance constituted a lapse of due diligence on the part of local authorities. Due diligence may, however, be an elusive concept. Is it an impingement on the sovereignty of a state or a valid appeal for the protection of rights of aliens? The question remains open and can only be decided on a case-by-case basis.

Topics for Discussion

1. Distinguish between *jus sanguinis* and *jus soli*. Which standard(s) does the United States apply? How might a conflict of laws involving these doctrines lead to a condition of statelessness?
2. The constitutional definition of treason, which is based on medieval English law, appears clear, but the application may be arbitrary in the event of an individual with dual nationality. Is the historic standard of allegiance to one and only one

---

[27]The United States of America on Behalf of the North American Dredging Company of Texas v. The United Mexican States (March 31, 1926), *Opinions of the Commissioners,* 21, 23.
[28]Secretary of state to the U.S. minister in Mexico (August 15, 1873), reprinted in 6 Moore 655.
[29]The United States of America on Behalf of Harry Roberts v. The United Mexican States (November 2, 1926), *Opinions of the Commissioners,* 100–106.

sovereign realistic in a world characterized by the increasing mobility of people? Or is treason, like the classic definition of sovereignty, a notion that has been overtaken by events?

3. Asylum is a universally recognized right, yet European and North American governments are moving to restrict that right. In terms of humanitarian international law what should be the standards of asylum?

4. Governments of Latin America have historically protested the interference of the U.S. and European powers in their affairs, yet violations of human rights may justifiably occasion such interference. Where should the line be drawn between the sovereign integrity of a state and the obligation *erga omnes* to treat aliens with due diligence?

CHAPTER 9

Jurisdiction

The global economy challenges the role of the territorial state, whose sovereignty was based on the assumption of impermeability. The transnational nature of commercial and social communication erodes borders and with them the traditional notion of citizenship. Individuals may well find themselves subject to the will of one or more governments, or two governments may compete for exclusive jurisdiction over an individual. With respect to juridical persons, such as multinational corporations or banks, the issue is more complex, for the nature of their operations makes them subject to the municipal codes of several states. International law must confront the reality that rules developed for a fragmented international system may no longer be useful in an age of interdependence.

Jurisdiction may either be personal or territorial. Citizenship forges a bond of allegiance to the state, and the individual is bound by it regardless. Conversely, territorial jurisdiction is limited to the sovereign realm of the state, including merchant vessels and commercial aircraft. The ice floe murder case of 1971 reveals the intricacy of a claim of jurisdiction which a government may advance. Working as an employee of a defense research laboratory, Mario Escamilla was stationed at an arctic weather station situated on an island of glacial ice. Following an argument with a fellow worker, Escamilla shot and killed him. A U.S. district court in Alexandria, Virginia, tried the case, and Escamilla was convicted of involuntary manslaughter. The verdict was appealed, and an appellate court did order a new trial, largely because of instructions given—or not given—to the jury.[1]

The issues in international law are twofold. Was the ice floe part of the territory of the United States? If not, did courts of the United States still have jurisdiction because Escamilla was an American citizen? In 1948, an act of Congress defined the "United States" in a territorial sense as including ". . . all places and waters, continental or insular, subject to the jurisdiction of the United States."[2] A subsequent section further developed the definition to encompass:

> Any island, rock, or key containing deposits of guano, which may, at the discretion of the President, be considered as appertaining to the United States.[3]

The definition is all-inclusive, and in the trial of Escamilla the prosecutor asserted that the statute did include, by implication, ice islands although they were not specifically mentioned. The difficulty with this argument and a point not addressed at the trial was

---

[1] *U.S. v. Escamilla,* 467 F. 2d 341 (1972).
[2] Title 18, U.S.C., sec. 5: United States defined (June 25, 1948), Statutes at Large 62:685.
[3] Ibid., sec. 7(4).

that Canada also claimed the same ice floe and could have asserted its jurisdiction over the matter.[4] The law relied upon by the prosecution did not recognize a counterclaim based on Canadian sovereignty. The question of situs and with it jurisdiction remained unresolved. The second question addressed the implications of Escamilla's citizenship. Assuming that U.S. title to the ice floe was doubtful, was Escamilla still subject to U.S. law? The response was that a citizen of the United States remains subject to the U.S. code wherever he or she goes.

The implications of the doctrine that an individual remains an allegiant of a state and subject to its laws raises complex issues, as demonstrated by the case of William Joyce, who was convicted of treason by a British court in 1945. Joyce was born in 1906 of naturalized parents in the state of New York, thereby qualifying him for U.S. citizenship under both *jus sanguinis* and *jus soli*. After a stay in Ireland, he lived in England from 1921 to 1939. Shortly before the outbreak of war in Europe he applied for and received a British passport, which enabled him to visit Germany. In Berlin he accepted employment as an announcer on radio broadcasts beamed to Britain. At no time did he renounce the allegiance implicit in the passport. At war's end, British authorities placed him under arrest on a charge of treason. His subsequent trial and conviction hinged upon the passport, which guaranteed the protection of the Crown. The prosecution argued that protection and allegiance are correlative. By accepting the passport, Joyce had expressed his allegiance to Great Britain, and his action in giving aid and comfort to the enemy during wartime constituted treason.[5]

EXTRADITION

Asserting jurisdiction over an individual abroad is quite often complicated, for the process of extradition itself has a number of pitfalls. Extradition is a process whereby a government requests another to surrender a person who has committed a crime either in the requesting state or against a citizen of that state. Bilateral treaties govern the process, and no lawmaking convention has yet to be drafted. Consequently, variations in procedure exist, but customary international law has established accepted guidelines for the process. The extradition treaty between Mexico and the United States (1978) provides an illustration.[6] The treaty opens with a reciprocal commitment to extradite persons charged with offenses in the requesting state, subject to exceptions and qualifications, and these are critical. If the person sought is a national of the requesting government, the procedure is straightforward. Should the person not be a national of the requesting party, that government must make a convincing case to the effect. The lack of equivalency of penalties for the commission of a given crime, for example, homicide, may also impede the completion of the process of extradition. In general, if the government of the requested state, after reviewing the evidence, is convinced

---

[4]F. M. Auburn, "International Law and Sea-Ice Jurisdiction in the Arctic Ocean (Based on *U.S. v. Escamilla*)," *International and Comparative Law Quarterly* 22 (July 1973): 552–557.
[5]*R. v. Joyce,* Court of Criminal Appeal, 2 All England Law Reports 673–678 (1945) and *William Joyce v. Director of Public Prosecutions,* House of Lords, 31 The Criminal Appeal Reports 57–105 (1946).
[6]Extradition Treaty between the United States of America and the United Mexican States (May 4, 1978), 31 U.S.T. 5061.

that a crime, as interpreted by its own laws, has been committed, the alleged offender will be extradited.

Article 5 of the treaty recognizes the exception of a political offense:

> Extradition shall not be granted when the offense for which it is requested is political or of a political character.

A political offense is an act undertaken as part of a organized movement whose purpose it is to seize political power.[7] Even here an exception applies in the form of the *attentat* clause, which identifies an attempt on the life of a head of government as an extraditable offense irrespective of the political motive. Finally, the growing recognition of the need for concerted action against those who commit crimes against humanity imposes a requirement that they be extradited to stand trial before an international tribunal.

The political offense exception is, however, often a subjective issue to be determined by political rather than judicial authority. The following three cases reveal the judgmental character of a ruling on whether an offense is political and therefore not extraditable. In 1979, a bomb exploded in Tiberias, a city under Israeli governance. Two people suffered mortal wounds and others were seriously injured. Abu Eain, the alleged perpetrator, was later apprehended in the United States, and the government of Israel requested his extradition based on a bilateral treaty similar to that of the United States and Mexico. Eain argued in federal court that he was a member of the Palestine Liberation Organization (PLO), and that whatever actions he had undertaken were political in character; that is, he acted as a part of an organized movement attempting to seize power. He further charged that Israeli authorities were seeking his extradition not for the bombing, but for undisclosed purposes. An appellate court ruled that the evidence established probable cause of his participation in the bombing, and that he should be extradited. The final decision lay, however, with the secretary of state, who had two months within which to decide.[8]

The second case involved the Irish Republican Army (IRA). Joseph Patrick Thomas Doherty was a member of the IRA underground in Northern Ireland. During a fire fight in Belfast in 1981, a British officer was mortally wounded, and fleeing a charge of murder Doherty sought to escape to the United States, where he was apprehended. The British government applied for his extradition, and a federal district court heard the case. After reviewing the evidence, the court determined that the political exception clause would apply because Doherty was a member of an organization engaged in an overt effort to seize political power. Consequently, the request for extradition was denied.[9] In 1986, a parallel case arose when the British government again requested the extradition of a suspected member of the IRA, who had allegedly participated in bombings in England. The accused was a U.S. citizen named Quinn of Irish background. In part because of his American citizenship, the court was skeptical of his claim to the protection of the political exception clause under the guise of being an Irish nationalist. In

---

[7]Von Glahn, 230–235.
[8]*Eain v. Wilkes,* Seventh Circuit (1981) reprinted in 79 I.L.R. 439, 458.
[9]*In re Extradition of Doherty,* District Court, Southern District, New York (1984), reprinted in 79 I.L.R. 475.

this instance, the request for extradition was granted.[10] The foregoing cases underline the subjective nature of the political exception clause. A court in New York (Doherty) may honor it, and another in California (Quinn) may not. Under the circumstances one may speak less of a rule than of a general precept which may or may not apply.

UNIVERSAL JURISDICTION

As noted in Chapter 1, the U.S. Supreme Court under the leadership of John Marshall viewed piracy as an offense against the law of nations and recognized the duty of the United States to combat this form of international criminal activity, wherever it occurred. The concept of crimes against humanity developed out of unparalleled acts of genocide during the Second World War with the understanding that those who perpetrated such offenses would be subject to prosecution by any government which apprehended them, much in the same way as pirates.[11] The *Filartiga* and *Pinochet* cases discussed in Chapter 2 are representative of the point. The principle of universal jurisdiction draws upon the concept of *erga omnes* in the sense that every government has a duty to pursue and punish international criminals. Antiterrorism legislation incorporates the doctrine of universality into U.S. law, in that acts of violence designed to coerce or intimidate anywhere in the world are punishable in the courts of the United States.[12] Similarly, U.S. law calls for the prosecution of war crimes wherever they may occur.[13]

The case of John Demjanuk (litigated 1981–1993) illustrates the application of universality to establish the jurisdiction of the court, and it reveals the problems inherent in this doctrine. Demjanuk was a retired Ohio automobile worker, who had immigrated in 1952 from the Ukraine. In 1955, he became a U.S. citizen. Subsequent investigation into his background created the suspicion that he might have been a guard at a concentration camp during the latter part of World War II, and the government of Israel sought to extradite and try him as a war criminal. The U.S. Department of Justice revoked his citizenship in 1981, and four years later he was extradited to Israel. Although an Israeli trial court sentenced him to death, the verdict was appealed, and in 1993 the Supreme Court of Israel vacated the sentence. Demjanuk then returned to the United States.[14] Appellate tribunals in Israel and the United States reviewed the record and concluded that the evidence was insufficient to sustain the extradition and conviction.

The Demjanuk case teaches that the principle of universality, while a valid one, must be applied with caution. In the aftermath of internal and international wars following the end of the Cold War in 1989, the international community has sought to develop the means of bringing war criminals to justice. One approach involves the creation of special tribunals first for Yugoslavia and later for Rwanda, and another requires that national courts prosecute the offenders under their municipal codes. The

---

[10]*Quinn v. Robinson,* Ninth Circuit (1986), reprinted in 79 I.L.R. 490.
[11]Brownlie, 308; and von Glahn, 256.
[12]Antiterrorism Act of 1990 (November 5, 1990), 104 Stat. 2250.
[13]War Crimes Act of 1996 amended (November 26, 1977), 111 Stat. 2436.
[14]*Demjanuk v. Petrovsky,* Sixth Circuit (1985), reprinted in 79 I.L.R. 535. See also Stephen Labaton, "Judges Assail U.S. Handling of Demjanuk," *New York Times,* 18 November 1993, A1, A16.

goal of equal protection favors the former approach, for a single court operating on the basis of international consensus is better able to protect itself from the pressures that often accompany the trials of those accused of war crimes.

MINIMUM STANDARDS OF JUSTICE

The process of extradition raises the delicate issue of reconciling two discrete legal systems, and in trying to do so human rights may suffer. In one system a given offense may be a misdemeanor and in another a capital crime. The possession of certain types of narcotics is an example, as evidenced by the laws of the Netherlands and Saudi Arabia on the same subject. Does a government incur an obligation to honor a request for extradition even in the event of a disparity in legal codes? An innovative approach recommends making a qualitative distinction between those human rights which are so fundamental that they must be observed irrespective of the circumstances and those of lesser importance which may be restricted.[15] Such fundamental rights include the right to life, to individual dignity and well-being, and to freedom from persecution. A second tier includes those rights which may be abridged only in time of war or national emergency. Those would include freedom of movement and residence as the imposition of censorship. Typically, an individual charged with espionage might not be tried in open court for fear of disclosing state secrets. A third and final tier of rights which might be curtailed are those necessary for the maintenance of public order. An example would be the right to privacy. As the following cases indicate, the administration of different tiers of human rights is not as simple as might appear at first blush.

The first case was that of Jens Soering, a German national and an undergraduate student at an American university. Soering fled the United States to escape prosecution by the Commonwealth of Virginia on a charge of capital murder. Subsequently British police apprehended Soering, and the United States applied for his extradition. Soering then appealed to the European Court of Human Rights (ECHR),[16] arguing that the European Convention on Human Rights in Protocol 6 (1989) outlawed capital punishment. The court upheld the appeal and blocked the extradition order on the grounds that capital punishment was violative of European standards of human rights.[17]

The case involved an unsuccessful attempt to reconcile the national codes of Germany, Great Britain, and the United States against the background of European human rights law. From the beginning the obstacles appeared insurmountable unless authorities in Virginia entered into a prior agreement that they would not ask for the death penalty, which they declined to do. The constitutional question was one of states' rights, and the issue in international law one of human rights. The ECHR carefully considered both arguments and determined that the latter must outweigh the former. In this instance of competing objectives, a rule of proportionality must apply. Compromising on the sentence would have meant clearance for extradition and a trial, but the prosecution was not ready to compromise.

---

[15]John Dugard and Christine Van den Wyngaert, "Reconciling Extradition with Human Rights," *American Journal of International Law* 92 (April 1998): 187, 210.

[16]The ECHR is an appellate court charged with hearing appeals based on alleged violations of the European Convention of Human Rights. For the text of Protocol 6, see 22 I.L.M. 538.

[17]*Soering case: Extradition of German National from the United Kingdom* (July 7, 1989), ECHR, reprinted in 28 I.L.M. 1063.

In the Netherlands first a trial and then an appellate court heard a case similar to *Soering*. A U.S. soldier was being held by the Dutch police prior to extradition on a charge of murdering his wife, also an American, at a military base in Holland. The case was governed by an agreement between the United States and the Netherlands providing that such crimes would be tried by a court martial acting under American military law, which introduced the possibility of the death penalty. Dutch courts were caught between two competing claims. The first was a status of forces agreement (SOFA) with the United States requiring extradition, and the second a commitment to the European norm of banning capital punishment. Again the rule of proportionality applied. This time the military prosecutor accepted an obligation not to ask for the death penalty, and the accused was extradited.[18]

During 1991, judicial authorities in Canada received a request for the extradition to California of an accused murderer. Again the question of capital punishment arose, for Canadian law has abolished the death penalty. In this instance geography played a key role, in that Canadian officials did not want their country to become a haven for fleeing felons from the United States, but that concern was tempered by the belief that the state should not take a life. A compromise in the form of a pledge by the prosecutor not to ask the jury for the death penalty relieved the situation, and the accused was extradited.[19] The application of the rule of proportionality enabled the two governments to pursue a prudent policy within the framework of good law. In sum, extradition remains a legal question to be resolved against a background of diplomacy.

ABDUCTION

In the event that extradition is not feasible, governments often resort to abduction to bring those accused of crimes to trial. In 1960, Israeli agents kidnapped Adolf Eichmann in Buenos Aires, so that he could be placed on trial for crimes against humanity perpetrated during World War II. As conclusive as was the evidence in this case, the government of Argentina protested the covert violation of its territorial sovereignty and lodged a formal complaint against Israel with the United Nations. While the Security Council in no way condoned the crimes of the accused, it declared that the government of Israel should make "appropriate reparation" to Argentina and asserted with regard to abduction:

> . . . that acts such as that under consideration, which affect the sovereignty of a member state and therefore cause international friction, may, if repeated, endanger international peace and security.[20]

The foreign minister of Israel expressed regret for the violation of Argentine law, but insisted that the unique character of the situation justified exceptional methods. The Israeli riposte rested on the assumption that a resort to extradition proceedings might well have

---

[18]*Netherlands v. Short* (January 26 to March 30, 1990), Court of Appeal, The Hague, reprinted in 29 I.L.M. 1375.

[19]*Ng v. Canada* (September 26, 1991), Supreme Court of Canada, reprinted in 98 I.L.R. 473, 479.

[20]"Security Council Acts on Argentina's Complaint Against Israel," *United Nations Review* 7 (June 23, 1960): 15. Publicists also debated the legitimacy of abduction, see the letters of Erich Fromm and E. A. Halevi to the *New York Times,* 17 June 1960, 30.

proven ineffective, which raises the notion of feasibility. Is a government obligated to adhere to the rules of law when they are unavailing?[21] The issue remained unresolved.

The dictum of the Security Council has in the last decade come under the scrutiny of courts in the United States. Combating international drug trafficking requires undercover operations abroad, and these often lead to the kidnapping of suspected felons from countries where these individuals have sought an apparently safe haven. Although judicial rulings vary on the use of abduction, the trend in American jurisprudence is to recognize the jurisdiction of a court irrespective of the manner in which the defendant was brought before it. The case cited is usually that of Frederick Ker, an alleged embezzler who had fled to Peru from Illinois in the 1880s. The U.S. Department of State arranged for extradition, and an operative of a detective agency was provided with a warrant and sent to Lima. Ignoring the extradition papers in his pocket, the agent abducted Ker and forcibly placed him on a ship bound for the United States. Ker petitioned the U.S. Supreme Court for his release arguing that kidnapping is an unlawful act and therefore a violation of the principle of due process. Rejecting his petition, the Court ruled that the manner in which he was brought to Illinois was not a mitigating circumstance, and that judicial authorities of that state were entitled to place him on trial, abduction notwithstanding.[22] Significantly, the U.S. government had not authorized the seizure of Ker by a detective, but had intended to rely upon the established procedure of extradition. Sixty-six years later the U.S. Supreme Court ruled on a case of abduction from one state to another and in doing so explicitly upheld the earlier ruling, giving rise to the *Ker-Frisbie* doctrine of refusing to invalidate a conviction because of the forcible seizure of the accused in another state.[23]

It is notable that in one instance a federal court called the decision in *Ker* into question. The decision involved, however, not only abduction but also the admission of evidence secured without benefit of a warrant. Francisco Toscanino, a citizen of Italy but resident in Uruguay, was suspected by U.S. law enforcement agencies of being a drug trafficker. American agents seized him in Montevideo and forcibly took him over the border to Brazil, where he was subjected to three weeks of hostile interrogation characterized by mental and physical duress. Eventually he was flown to the United States, placed on trial, and convicted in 1973 of violating federal laws on narcotics. Toscanino instituted an appeal based on a denial of the constitutional right of due process as evidenced not only by the kidnapping and detention, but also by the use of wiretap evidence acquired in Uruguay without the benefit of a warrant or equivalent authorization. The appellate court acknowledged these arguments and remanded the case to a lower court review and revision. The precedent of implied toleration of abduction set in *Ker* was deemed inconsistent with due process.[24] Despite the apparent reversal of *Ker,* the appellate court appears to have been less influenced by the issue of abduction than by the three weeks of "physical torture" in Brazil.

In a 1991 decision a federal appellate court again dealt a blow to the thesis that abduction, while not desirable, was permissible. Federal agents forcibly seized Rene Martin

---

[21] Georg Schwarzenberger, *International Law and Order* (New York: Praeger Publishers, 1971), pp. 240–241.

[22] *Ker v. Illinois,* 119 U.S. 436, 444 (1886).

[23] *Frisbie, Warden v. Collins,* 342 U.S. 519 (1952).

[24] *U.S. v. Toscanino,* Second Circuit (1974), 500 F. 2nd 267, 275.

Verdugo-Urquidez in Mexico, so that he could be tried in the United States for drug trafficking. The government of Mexico lodged an official protest against the violation of its territorial sovereignty, and a court of appeals ruled that the 1978 extradition treaty with Mexico prohibited government-authorized kidnapping. Presumably the ruling in *Ker* did not apply, because the detective who seized him was not authorized to take such action. The indictment was dismissed, and the defendant returned to Mexico.[25] The interposition of the government of Mexico proved decisive. By comparison, the government of Italy did not seek to intercede on behalf of Toscanino. One may speculate on the possible effect of a protest from the Italian embassy in Washington over the abduction of an Italian from Uruguay to the United States via Brazil.

In 1992, the U.S. Supreme Court addressed the issue of abduction in the case of Humberto Alvarez-Machain, a Mexican physician implicated in the torture and murder of a U.S. Drug Enforcement Administration (DEA) agent and his pilot. Unidentified parties had spirited Alvarez-Machain out of Mexico to California, where DEA agents arrested him. A U.S. court concluded that the manner of his arrest violated the extradition treaty with Mexico and ordered him repatriated. The Ninth Circuit Court of Appeals upheld this interpretation of the treaty, as it had a year earlier in the *Verdugo-Urquidez* case. The government then appealed to the Supreme Court, which by a six-to-three vote reversed the appellate court and ruled that although the act of abduction might be in violation of general principles of international law, the treaty itself did not prohibit such an act if necessity required it. Three members of the Supreme Court joined in a dissent based on the premise that the extradition treaty implicitly forbade the kind of covert operation which led to the defendant's arrest.[26]

The foregoing overview of case law reveals an absence of a clear-cut response to the question of whether abduction is permissible within the framework of international law. One school of thought insists that if it is not forbidden, it is permitted. The counterargument is that the extradition treaties, indeed all treaties, must be interpreted not only in terms of their literal text but also against the background of their overall purpose, which is to ensure amicable relations among states. Justice Story put the matter succinctly in a case involving the seizure of a French ship—The *Apollon*—berthed in the Spanish province of Florida by U.S. customs officers. The captain of the vessel intended to off-load his cargo, so that it could surreptitiously be brought into the United States. American agents preempted the supposed smuggling effort by entering Florida and taking control of the ship. Story denounced the seizure as an affront to Spain and pointed out that American officials had no authority to enforce their revenue code in foreign territory. He stated explicitly:

> The laws of no nation can justly extend beyond its own territories, except so far as regards its own citizens.[27]

Until the modern period Story's dictum stood unchallenged, but the rise of transnational terrorism has occasioned rethinking on the matter. The forcible seizure of terrorists overseas may have become a necessity occasioned by the need for self-defense.[28] The impermeability of the territorial state may no longer be taken for granted.

[25]*U.S. v. Rene Martin Verdugo-Urquidez,* Ninth Circuit (1991), 939 F. 2nd 1341, 1352.
[26]*U.S. v. Alvarez-Machain,* 504 U.S. 655 (1992).
[27]The *Apollon,* 22 U.S. (9 Wheaton) 362, 370 (1824).
[28]Arlen Specter, "How to Make Terrorists Think Twice," *New York Times,* 22 May 1986, A31.

A HIERARCHY OF CLAIMS

Jurisdiction in the struggle against transnational criminality has the appearance of a web of sometimes contradictory decisions, yet an overview of these precedents identifies three levels of state responsibility. (1) The premier claim to jurisdiction is held by the government in whose territory the act occurred. (2) The government whose citizens have suffered loss of life or injury may assert jurisdiction. (3) The government which captures and detains felons may place them on trial, as customary international law dictates in the case of pirates.

Two cases—the *Achille Lauro* and Pan American Flight 103—demonstrate the interplay of these claims. On October 7–9, 1985, four Palestinian Arabs, in an act of piracy, seized control of the Italian cruise liner, *S.S. Achille Lauro,* which was on route from Alexandria to Port Said at the entrance to the Suez Canal. Sailing first to Syrian waters, the ship then returned to Egypt, where the pirates were taken into custody by local authorities. Subsequently Syrian officials disclosed that they had recovered the body of an American citizen, who had been murdered during the hijacking. Lacking knowledge of the murder and in accordance with an agreement to release hostages on board the ship, the Egyptian government authorized the departure of the hijackers by air for Tunisia. The flight was, however, diverted by U.S. carrier-based aircraft to a base in Sicily, where Italian authorities arrested the hijackers and placed them on trial in Genoa, the *Achille Lauro*'s home port. The four were convicted and imprisoned. In terms of the aforementioned criteria for establishing jurisdiction, Italy had the strongest claim because the offense took place on an Italian-flag vessel; the United States possessed the right to prosecute those who had murdered a citizen;[29] and Egypt might have arrested the four pirates when the ship returned to Port Said although such action would have placed at risk the lives of the passengers and crew.

On December 21, 1988, a bomb exploded on Pan American Flight 103 over Lockerbie, Scotland, killing all 270 on board. Investigators identified two Libyan nationals and former members of that country's service as the probable perpetrators. The two were eventually extradited from Libya to stand trial in a Scottish court, which convened in the Netherlands.[30] In this tragic incident, an international convention sponsored by the United Nations in 1971 provided a basis for determining jurisdiction.[31] Essentially three rules apply to international public air transport. The first is the principle of territoriality, under which the government in whose airspace the offense occurred has the responsibility to act. The second is the government under whose flag the aircraft operates, and the third are the authorities in the state where the aircraft lands after having survived an attempt at sabotage. In the case of Flight 103, both Scotland for the United Kingdom and the United States possessed jurisdiction, but the extradition agreement with Libya resolved the potential conflict of interest by stipulating a trial before a Scottish court.

---

[29]Covey T. Oliver et al., *The International Legal System: Cases and Materials,* 4th ed. (Westbury, NY: The Foundation Press, 1995), p. 183.
[30]"Trial and Error," *New Republic* (May 15, 2000): 11.
[31]Convention for the Suppression of Unlawful Acts against the Safety of Civil Aviation (September 23, 1971), 24 U.S.T. 568.

VESSELS

Warships and other public vessels represent the sovereign integrity of the flag state, whether they are on the high seas or visiting a foreign port. Jurisdiction in this instance is not an issue, but clarity in the matter of private vessels is another matter. In 1887, the U.S. Supreme Court confronted the issue of jurisdiction over a crime committed on board a merchant vessel. A Belgian freighter was docked at a New Jersey port when one of the crew—Joseph Wildenhus— assaulted and mortally wounded another sailor. Local authorities arrested Wildenhus and charged him with homicide, whereupon the Belgian consul applied for a writ of habeas corpus,[32] calling for Wildenhus's release on the thesis that the crime involved only Belgians and took place on a Belgian-flag vessel. A treaty concluded by the United States and Belgium in 1880 gave their respective consular officers jurisdiction over crimes committed aboard ship unless these ". . . disturb tranquility and public order."[33] In his opinion, Chief Justice Morrison R. Waite noted that "felonious homicide" is indeed a threat to the community. *Wildenhus* established the precedent of local control whereby port authorities would make the determination regarding "tranquility and public order." In most instances, such as jumping ship, the flag state's laws are applied.

The decision of the Permanent Court of International Justice (PCIJ) in the *Lotus* case (1928) placed the question of jurisdiction within the broader context of the nature of international law. In 1926, the French steamer *Lotus* was cruising in international waters off the coast of Turkey and collided with a Turkish vessel. Eight Turkish seamen perished, although an additional ten were rescued by the *Lotus,* which then proceeded to Constantinople (Istanbul). The watch officer of the *Lotus,* Lieutenant Demons, was detained by Turkish authorities and ultimately convicted on a charge of manslaughter. The government of France protested and filed a claim before the PCIJ, alleging that the Turkish court lacked jurisdiction over a collision on the high seas, and that French law would provide a remedy for actions regarding a French vessel.

The PCIJ was evenly divided, so its president had to break the deadlock with a casting vote. The result was a decision in support of the Turkish interpretation. Although the United Nations Convention on the High Seas (1958) reversed the PCIJ and endorsed the French position,[34] the legal theory relied upon by the PCIJ remains instructive. In support of the Turkish contention that its courts possessed jurisdiction over events on the *Lotus,* the PCIJ stated:

> It would be contrary to general international law to demand that a State should have to find a permissive rule of that law in every case over which it claimed jurisdiction before its courts.

* * *

> The Court therefore concludes that, since the offence produced its effects on the Turkish ship, no rule of international exists prohibiting the Turkish

---

[32]*Habeas corpus* is a Latin expression meaning "You have the body."
[33]Rights, Privileges, and Immunities of Consular Officers (March 9, 1880), 5 Bevans 494, 497.
[34]Convention on the High Seas (April 29, 1958), 13 U.S.T. 2312, 2315.

authorities from taking proceedings against Demons because of the fact that he was on board the French ship.[35]

In essence, what is not prohibited by international law is permitted. The PCIJ's ruling reflects the political reality of a decentralized international system dominated by sovereign states

EXTRATERRITORIALITY

There remains the question of reconciling divergent legal norms and procedures. In the nineteenth century, the major powers solved the problem by establishing a system of capitulations—bilateral treaties whereby jurisdiction, especially in criminal cases, over Europeans and North Americans in Africa and Asia was exclusively reserved to the consuls of the home country. Local courts could not place foreigners protected by capitulations on trial. In 1844, the United States and China concluded a FCN treaty, which gave U.S. consuls jurisdiction over Americans charged with crimes committed in those areas of China open to foreigners.[36] Pursuant to the treaty, a U.S. court for China heard cases involving American citizens.[37] The arrangement was an affront to the national sensibilities of the Chinese, and in an effort to improve Sino-American relations it was discontinued in 1943[38] after a century of operation. The Ottoman Empire provides a parallel example of extraterritorial courts, which functioned until terminated in 1923. Over time these institutions proved to be a political liability, and the practice of insisting upon capitulations has lapsed.

During the Cold War confrontation between the United States and the Soviet Union, the stationing of armed forces abroad became commonplace. The United States has concluded bilateral SOFAs with Asian and European governments. In 1956, the United States and Greece concluded a prototypical SOFA containing the following provision:

> The Greek authorities, recognizing that it is the primary responsibility of the United States authorities to maintain good order and discipline where persons subject to United States military law are concerned, will, upon the request of the United States, waive their primary right to exercise jurisdiction . . . , except when they determine that it is of particular importance that jurisdiction be exercised by the Greek authorities.[39]

The foregoing clause does not award to a foreign power the exclusive jurisdiction of a capitulation, but the wording is close enough to touch upon national sensibilities. To many citizens of the host countries, SOFAs are an unwelcome reminder of an era of spheres of influence dominated by imperial powers.

In an international system increasingly dominated by commercial objectives, the imposition of economic sanctions, either multilateral or bilateral, may serve to enforce international law, especially against those states known to harbor terrorists. In 1992, the

---

[35]*The Lotus* Case, PCIJ: Fourth Annual Report, Series E, No. 4 (June 15, 1927–June 15, 1928), 166, 171, 173.
[36]Peace, Amity, and Commerce (July 3, 1844), 6 Bevans 647, 654.
[37]2 Hackworth 184.
[38]Relinquishment of Extraterritorial Rights (January 11, 1943), 6 Bevans 739.
[39]Status of United States Forces in Greece (September 7, 1956), 7 U.S.T. 2555, 2558.

United Nations Security Council resolved to impose trade sanctions on Libya in retaliation for its involvement with those suspected of carrying out the bombing of Pan American Flight 103. Over time, the effect of the sanctions gradually eroded until by 1999 only Great Britain and the United States stayed the course of enforcement. Bilateral sanctions are even more difficult to impose because of the complex legal situation of multinational corporations. President Jimmy Carter resorted to economic sanctions on Iran in response to the seizure of the U.S. embassy in Teheran in November 1979.[40] Indifference on the part of other governments, especially Pakistan, weakened the effect of the policy. Moreover other governments are usually unwilling to allow American subsidiaries chartered to do business in their countries to participate in sanctions even though a presidential executive order has put them in place. In the 1980s, Western European governments argued that American companies licensed by them were subject to their trade regulations and not those of the United States.[41] Extraterritorial jurisdiction appears to have little effect on world commerce and banking. Money laundering by criminal cartels and corrupt officials is representative of the problem. The United States and other members of the Group of 7[42] have previously attempted to use quiet diplomacy in dealing with countries known to be safe havens for ill-gotten money, but in early 2000, the major economic powers shifted to a policy of disclosure by naming some fifteen countries that shield suspicious assets.[43] Whether such publicity will have a deterrent effect on money laundering remains an open question.

TERRORISM

Political violence threatens the existence of an international system based on law, and combating terrorism may require preemptive action abroad. Both U.S. law and practice treat terrorism as a sequence of indiscriminate acts of violence dangerous to human life.[44] The U.S. Department of Justice possesses the statutory authority to prosecute those who commit terrorist acts against American citizens abroad. This assertion of extraterritorial jurisdiction led in 1998 to the indictment of Osama bin Laden, a citizen of Saudi Arabia, on charges of criminal conspiracy in the bombing of two U.S. embassies in East Africa. The indictment grew out of a broad grant of authority giving the prosecutorial power of U.S. attorneys a global reach.[45]

---

[40]The national emergency was declared on November 14, 1979, in accordance with the National Emergencies Act (September 14, 1976), 90 Stat. 1255. President Reagan continued this policy, see *Public Papers of the Presidents: Ronald Reagan, 1985* (Washington: U.S. Government Printing Office, 1988), 2:1329.

[41]International Trade Administration, U.S. Department of Commerce, *Orders to U.S. Foreign Subsidiaries in France, Italy, the Federal Republic of Germany and the United Kingdom concerning the Denial of Export Privileges for Soviet Gas Pipeline Equipment* (September 9, 1982) reprinted in 21 ILM 1098.

[42]Canada, France, Germany, Great Britain, Italy, and Japan.

[43]The Bahamas, the Cayman Islands, the Cook Islands, Dominica, Israel, Lebanon, Liechtenstein, the Marshall Islands, Nauru, Niue, Panama, the Philippines, Russia, St. Kitts and Nevis, and St. Vincent and the Grenadines as listed in Joseph Kahn, "15 Countries Names as Potential Money Laundering Havens," *New York Times,* 23 June 2000, A4.

[44]Antiterrorism Act (November 5, 1990), 104 Stat. 2250.

[45]Benjamin Weiser, "Saudi Is Indicted in Bomb Attacks on U.S. Embassies," *New York Times,* 5 November 1998, A1. See also Terrorist Acts Abroad against United States Nationals (November 18, 1988), 102 Stat. 4404.

Other governments have also followed the American precedent. In 1999, Chinese authorities seized Wu Man, a resident of Hong Kong, in Thailand and brought him to China on a charge of transnational criminal activity. The accused is the holder of a British overseas passport, which guarantees consular protection. British authorities protested that they had not been notified, but the Chinese government stated that it has the right to arrest Chinese people anywhere. The presumption is that *jus sanguinis* creates a bond of indelible allegiance, which no Chinese may forsake.[46] In this instance the assertion of extraterritorial jurisdiction rests upon a theory of permanent citizenship and a concomitant denial of dual nationality. Most governments permit a renunciation of citizenship, and many accept, albeit tacitly, dual citizenship. The Chinese practice appears somewhat archaic in this regard. By comparison the underpinning of U.S. law on extraterritorial jurisdiction over terrorist or other criminal acts rests not upon citizenship, but rather on the act itself. The distinction is fundamental.

THE INTERNET

The internet symbolizes the age of communication, yet the advent of the information super highway has taken place without a concomitant development in international law. National legal codes govern e-commerce and the type of material available from home pages, but the internet is worldwide, and no international convention governs this activity.[47] National courts may protect the rights of consumers, who order goods on the internet, but a more serious problem is the political propaganda of violence. In 2000, the Office for the Protection of the Constitution, Federal Republic of Germany, reported that extremist groups have established 330 home pages, of which 130 are in Europe and 200 in North America. The messages often encompass ethnic hate and advocate the use of force to achieve political goals. In some instances detailed instructions regarding, for example, the building of lethal devices are available. The technique of using the net to publicize a list of political opponents marked as targets of violence is in place. German law bans racist propaganda and the use of symbols associated with racism; U.S. law does not. The First Amendment (1791) to the U.S. Constitution protects freedom of speech and of the press, including online journals. By comparison the German criminal code mandates a term of imprisonment of three to five years for the use of graphics and text that in the United States fall within the category of protected speech.[48]

The international legal issues surrounding the internet invariably hinge on the question of jurisdiction. If a U.S. citizen with a home page in North America violates the German criminal code regarding the use of racist graphics and text, can that person be prosecuted in a German court? Yes, but the offense is not extraditable because the act is not a crime in the United States. Again, the remedy is a lawmaking convention establishing international standards governing the internet. The European Union (EU) is moving in the direction of establishing a regional body of law on the subject, but that

---

[46]Rahul Jacob, "UK and China Agree to Disagree," *Financial Times,* 9 December 1999, 6.
[47]Jean Eaglesham, "Web of Confusion," *Financial Times,* 9 September 1999, 13.
[48]*Rechtsextremistische Aktivitäten im Internet* (Right-wing extremist activities in the internet), Office for the Protection of the Constitution, Federal Republic of Germany. (www.verfassungsschutz.de/renetz/rechts), 24 June 2000. For an analysis of the impact of the internet on political communication, see Richard Davis and Diana Owen, *New Media and American Politics* (New York: Oxford University Press, 1998), pp. 116–130.

does not solve the German government's problem of websites in North America. Only a universal approach will prove satisfactory. The internet implicitly raises questions regarding the traditional theory of sovereignty, as expressed by Justice Story in the *Apollon* affair. Story's view was that of the impermeability of the state, and he denied the right of U.S. customs officers to enforce their revenue code on Spanish territory. The internet has changed the concept of an international boundary. Frontiers are porous and no longer capable of sustaining the traditional theory of sovereignty. State responsibility has come to apply not only to human rights and to the environment, but also to international communications.

Topics for Discussion

1. Customary international law stresses the sovereign equality of states in the belief that each is supreme in its own territory and over its own citizens. Contemporary world politics challenges that thesis through the development of transnational patterns of communication and commerce. How can the traditional theory of sovereign jurisdiction be reconciled with the emerging international system?

2. Extradition involves a request by one government to another to deliver up a fleeing felon for trial. What reasons may a requested government offer for a deniai of an extradition request?

3. Government-sanctioned abduction for purposes of a criminal prosecution takes place more often than diplomats like to admit. What are the international legal ramifications of abduction? Is the policy of the United States consistent on this matter?

4. The claim of extraterritorial jurisdiction may depend upon the political obligation of citizenship, particularly through *jus sanguinis*. As an issue of human rights law, should the community of states recognize the right of an individual to renounce his or her citizenship and embrace a new one, thereby negating the jurisdictional claim of the former sovereign?

CHAPTER 10

Dispute Resolution

The judgment in the *Lotus* case hinged on the sovereign authority of the Turkish government to take those actions not prohibited by international law. The French government sought to defend its maritime sovereignty, and both parties turned to the court established by the League of Nations to adjudicate disputes. The judicial process is one of seven methods provided by international law for the resolution of disputes. The others are bilateral negotiations, good offices, mediation, inquiry, conciliation, and arbitration. In their totality these methods assure compliance with the rules of international law. The concept of compliance raises the issue of consent on the part of individual governments. The Austinian theory of international law posited the need for a government to give its prior consent to a rule of international law before being obligated to observe it. By comparison, the opinions authored by Marshall and Story in the early decades of the U.S. Supreme Court presumed that the new republic was from its inception bound by the law of nations. The progressive development of institutionalized means of dispute resolution lends credence to the latter interpretation.

NEGOTIATION

Negotiation is the least structured of the seven methods. The process is informal, and a third party does not play a role. The essence of negotiation is compromise, and political considerations may often be paramount although the question may be couched in legal terms. In 1934, President Lázaro Cárdenas of Mexico nationalized the properties of American and British oil companies in his country. Washington and London responded by seeking a resolution through a process of negotiations.[1] These continued until 1941 when the need to secure Mexican support for the Allied war effort engendered Anglo-American concessions, which under other circumstances would not have been possible. Direct negotiation has the advantage of simplicity and confidentiality, but it lacks a prior commitment to reach a settlement. The bilateral talks may continue interminably until they result in little more than political theater. Nevertheless, negotiation is the first and indispensable step in the process of dispute resolution.

GOOD OFFICES

At this stage a third party enters the scene, albeit in a restricted role. Good offices involves an effort by a disinterested government to bring the contending parties together usually by facilitating communication and providing a secure conference site. Starting in late 1971, Henry A. Kissinger, then the national security adviser in the Nixon administration,

---

[1]General Claims Commission Protocol (April 24, 1934), 9 Bevans 1008–1013.

began a dialogue with Le Duc Tho, the North Vietnamese representative, at a chateau outside of Paris. Although the French foreign ministry did not participate in the discussions, it did make the necessary arrangements and thereby contributed significantly to the talks leading to a cease-fire agreement.[2] Good offices may entail a political risk for the third party, for a failure of the bilateral negotiations may well lead to a diplomatic embarrassment. In a parliamentary system of government the foreign minister would be exposed to searching questions from the opposition. Therefore good offices should only be entered into when the government in question enjoys firm political support and is reasonably certain of success. Otherwise a government may find that it has undercut its international prestige.

International organizations may provide good offices without running a political risk. Starting in 1975, the United Nations Security Council authorized the secretary-general to undertake a mission of good offices aimed at restoring the political unity of the divided Republic of Cyprus.[3] Successive secretaries-general have undertaken this mission, which requires them to submit a semiannual report on the Cyprus question to the Security Council. In February 1998, tensions in the Persian Gulf had reached a point at which Anglo-American military action against Iraq seemed imminent. The Security Council authorized Secretary-General Kofi Annan to undertake a good offices mission to Baghdad, where he succeeded in de-escalating the crisis. An international civil servant can draw upon the prestige of the intergovernmental organization (IGO) he or she represents without running the risk of compromising national honor. IGOs are uniquely suited for the task of good offices.

MEDIATION

The dividing line between good offices and mediation is so indistinct that the two methods are often linked. The Annan mission to Iraq implied some measure of mediation. Nevertheless mediation is a step beyond good offices because a third party is at the conference table and is able to intervene in the discussion by proposing a settlement of the contentious issue. At the first Hague Conference (1899) twenty-six states' parties concluded a multilateral treaty, which defined mediation as follows:

> The part of the mediator consists in reconciling the opposing claims and appeasing the feelings of resentment which may have arisen between the States at variance.

And further:

> Good offices and mediation, either at the request of the parties are variance, or on the initiative of Powers strangers to the dispute, have exclusively the character of advice and never have binding force.[4]

The Treaty of Portsmouth, New Hampshire (1905), which ended the Russo-Japanese War, offers an example of mediation. The Japanese and Russian delegates entered the

[2]Henry A. Kissinger, *White House Years* (Boston: Little, Brown, 1979), pp. 1163, 1462–1463.
[3]United Nations, Security Council, *Official Records,* Resolution 367 (March 12, 1975) reprinted in Necati Ertekün, *The Cyprus Dispute* (Nicosia: K. Rustem and Brother, 1984), pp. 254–255.
[4]Pacific Settlement of Disputes: First Hague Conference (July 29, 1899), 1 Bevans 230, 235.

peace conference with two sets of instructions—those covering issues on which no concessions could be made as opposed to those open to bargaining. President Theodore Roosevelt served as mediator, although much of the credit for the mediation should go to Secretary of State Elihu Root. Japan had gained the upper hand on land and at sea, and her government presumed the understanding of the American president—a confidence which was not misplaced. The Russian government, weakened by a revolution, viewed mediation as an acceptable means of ending the conflict. The political requirements for mediation were in place, and in the space of a few weeks the treaty of peace was in place.[5] The successful outcome of the mediation was marred by the inability of the mediator to appease "the feelings of resentment" resulting from the war. Eventually both states that were party to the treaty expressed criticism of it, and the mediator was held to blame. A prudent head of government should reflect carefully before opting for the role of mediator. The plaudits are transitory.

COMMISSION OF INQUIRY

A commission of inquiry presents an opportunity for a speedy and authoritative resolution of a dispute. Notably the commission is an ad hoc body established after a violation of international law has occurred. The findings of the commission are subject to review by the two contending governments, and normally the emphasis is on cobbling together an acceptable solution to the dispute rather than rendering a legal judgment. Within the framework of international law the commission seeks a political solution. In this regard the work of the commission is preceded by a detailed international agreement governing the procedure to be followed. At this stage either of the governments engaged in the dispute may impose limitations on what the commission may do. Members of the commission include representatives of the two governments involved as well as those of disinterested powers. After the commission has delivered its report, it disbands.

The Dogger Bank incident of 1904 offers a useful case study. During the Russo-Japanese War, the Baltic fleet of the Russian navy sortied and proceeded through the North Sea en route to Asian waters. One night off the coast of England, the Russian squadron encountered unidentified vessels and opened fire. The targets turned out to be British fishing boats, one of which was sunk with a loss of two lives. The first step in resolving the resultant dispute was the negotiation of an Anglo-Russian treaty providing for a commission of inquiry and establishing the terms of its operation. Specially, the treaty stated:

> The Commission shall inquire into and report on all the circumstances relative to the North Sea incident, and particularly on the questions as to where the responsibility lies and the degree of blame attaching to the subjects of the two high contracting parties, or to the subjects of other countries in the event of their responsibility being established by the inquiry.[6]

---

[5]J. A. White, "Portsmouth 1905: Peace or Truce?" *Journal of Peace Research,* 6 (1969): 359, 363.
[6]North Sea Convention (November 25, 1904) reprinted in F. E. Smith and N. W. Sibley, *International Law as Interpreted during the Russo-Japanese War* (Boston: Boston Book Co., 1905), p. 284.

The commission found that the Russian flotilla action in firing upon British trawlers violated international law, and the Imperial Russian government paid compensation to Great Britain.[7] The British government had espoused the claims of the individuals who had suffered in the incident, the reason being that individuals do not have standing. Only a government could then make a claim against another government.

In 1907, forty-four state delegations convened a second Hague Conference and reissued, in a slightly revised form, a multilateral convention defining the role of inquiry:

> International commissions of inquiry are constituted by special agreement between the parties in dispute. The inquiry convention defines the facts to be examined; it determines the mode and the time in which the commission is to be formed and the extent of the powers of the commissioners.[8]

Notably, the diplomatic measures agreed upon at the two Hague Conferences recognized that mediation and inquiry did not apply to those questions involving either the national honor or the vital interests of the signatory powers.

The 1907 convention provided a framework for the Netherlands and Germany to resolve a dispute through inquiry in the aftermath of the First World War. In 1916, the Dutch steamship, *Tubantia,* sank in the North Sea, and indications were that she had been torpedoed by a German submarine. After prolonged negotiations, the Netherlands and Germany agreed in 1921 to refer the matter to a commission of inquiry, which consisted of five members, two appointed by the states involved in the dispute and three by the neutral powers of Denmark, Sweden, and Switzerland. The commission concluded that an exploding torpedo did sink the *Tubantia,* but recognized the possibility that the torpedo may have been aimed at another target. As a result of the report Germany paid compensation to the Netherlands.[9]

Under the auspices of the League of Nations inquiry gained a multilateral character, which meant that its utilization was no longer dependent upon a bilateral agreement between the two contending governments. The international community could now implement this method on its own initiative. On October 19, 1925, hostilities broke out on the border between Greece and Bulgaria, and ten days later the League of Nations authorized the formation of a commission of inquiry to ascertain the facts and fix responsibility for the incident. In the meantime both parties were called upon to observe a cease-fire. The commission consisted of diplomats and military officers from France, Great Britain, Italy, the Netherlands, and Sweden. Within a month the commission completed an on-site investigation combined with official interviews in Athens and Sofia. The report recommended the payment of compensation by Greece to Bulgaria, a recommendation accepted by the League and the two governments party to the dispute.[10]

---

[7]George Grafton Wilson, *Handbook of International Law,* 3rd ed. (St. Paul, MN: West Publishing Company, 1939), pp. 230–231.

[8]Pacific Settlement of International Disputes: Second Hague Conference (October 18, 1907), 1 Bevans 577, 587. See also Manley O. Hudson, "Hague Conferences," *Encyclopedia of the Social Sciences* (New York: Macmillan Co., 1932) 7: 242–244.

[9]United Nations, General Assembly, Twentieth Session, 1965, Sixth Committee, 1 May 1964, *Report of the Secretary-General on Methods of Fact-Finding* (A/5694), 6–7.

[10]Ibid., 17.

A more controversial inquiry by the League of Nations involved the Japanese occupation of Manchuria, a province of northeastern China, on September 18–19, 1931. The Chinese representative at the League called for action to preserve the peace, and under League pressure the Japanese delegate agreed to the formation of a commission of inquiry. The commission drew its five members from France, Germany, Great Britain, Italy, and the United States. Lord Lytton, the British representative, chaired the proceedings. After a year of investigative work, the commission submitted an exhaustive report on the historical background of the Manchurian crisis and the Japanese military action.[11] Based on the report, the debate in the League was sympathetic to China, and Japan withdrew from the League as a result. The Japanese charged the Lytton commission with bias, which underlines the need for a successful inquiry to be preceded by a reciprocal commitment on the part of both parties to accept the outcome. Such was the case with the Dogger Bank affair and the *Tubantia* investigation. Conversely, the imposition of an inquiry upon a reluctant government will have adverse diplomatic results.

CONCILIATION

Conciliation broadens the purview of inquiry and enhances the process with a defined structure. Under the terms of inquiry an international organization or the involved states will act after the fact to establish a fact-finding body. Conciliation has the advantage of committing governments in advance to the acceptance of the work of a commission and thereby imposing a "cooling-off" period, usually of a year, during which a practical solution can be determined. Initially conciliation grew out of bilateral treaties, such as those negotiated by William Jennings Bryan, secretary of state from 1913 to 1915. The Bryan treaties followed a standard formula, which entailed the appointment of a five-member commission charged with first investigating the factual background of a dispute and then recommending remedial measures to ensure an amicable solution.[12] The object was to bring about a positive outcome of those disputes not impinging upon national honor or vital interests.

Bryan negotiated twenty treaties of conciliation, one of the first of which was the prototypical treaty with Great Britain. The bilateral agreement established the rules of conciliation as follows:

> The High Contracting Parties agree that all disputes between them, of every nature whatsoever, other than disputes the settlement of which is provided for and in fact achieved under existing agreements between the High Contracting Parties, shall, when diplomatic methods of adjustment have failed, be referred for investigation and report to a permanent International Commission, to be constituted in the manner prescribed in the next succeeding article; and they agree not to declare war or begin hostilities during such investigation and before the report is submitted.
>
> The International Commission shall be composed of five members, to be appointed as follows: One member shall be chosen from each country, by the

---

[11]Ibid., 17–18.

[12]Elmer Plischke (ed.), *Contemporary U.S. Foreign Policy: Documents and Commentary* (New York: Greenwood Press, 1991), pp. 362–363.

Government thereof; one member shall be chosen by each Government from some third country; the fifth member shall be chosen by common agreement between the two Governments, it being understood that he shall not be a citizen of either country.[13]

The foregoing provisions defined the essence of conciliation as a process requiring a prior commitment to an amicable settlement through a committee previously assembled for that purpose. Typically, the duration of the appointment remained open with the result that commissions gradually disappeared as their members retired and were not replaced. Bilateral conciliation agreements served a symbolic purpose in reducing the potential for armed conflict, but their practical application was limited. For the most part the Bryan treaties and their counterparts have fallen into abeyance.

As was the case with inquiry, conciliation, too, developed a multilateral dimension. In 1928, the League of Nations sponsored a convention obligating states parties to institute conciliation procedures based on permanent commissions to be formed within six months of adhering to the treaty.[14] The United Nations revived the idea of conciliation in 1990, when it opened for signature a revised and elaborated set of rules. These included a pledge of secrecy on the part of the commissioners and a requirement that they convene at the headquarters of the United Nations in New York.[15] Regional organizations have also sought to institutionalize conciliation. For example, the Conference on Security and Co-operation in Europe (CSCE) included in its final act of 1975 a provision requiring the thirty-five states parties to employ amicable means of dispute resolution.[16] Subsequently, the CSCE produced a report focusing on conciliation and detailing in precise terms the procedures to be followed. The report assessed the comparative advantages of a three- as opposed to a five-member commission and concluded that the traditional preference for five members offered a guarantee of an equitable solution to the problem.[17] Nevertheless the CSCE procedures remain only a "draft." Whether conciliation, either in its bilateral or multilateral form, has fulfilled its expectations is doubtful. Once thought to possess great potential, conciliation eventually disappointed its early advocates.[18]

ARBITRATION

In 1840, William Ladd, a New England farmer, wrote a pamphlet for the newly formed American Peace Society in which he called for the formation of a tribunal capable of resolving disputes among nations. War, he argued, would then become obsolete as an

---

[13]Advancement of Peace (September 15, 1914), 12 Bevans 370, 371.
[14]General Act for the Pacific Settlement of International Disputes (September 26, 1928), 93 L.N.T.S. 343.
[15]*Draft Rules for the Concilation of Disputes between States* (November 28, 1990), reprinted in 30 I.L.M. 231, 238–240.
[16]U.S. Department of State, *Conference on Security and Co-operation in Europe: Final Act* (Helsinki, 1975), Publication 8826 (August 1975), 79–80.
[17]*Report of the CSCE Meeting of Experts on Peaceful Settlement of Disputes* (February 8, 1991), reprinted in 30 I.L.M. 384.
[18]Manley O. Hudson, *International Tribunals: Past and Future* (Washington, D.C.: Brookings Institution, 1944), 229.

instrument of statecraft.[19] Although Ladd did not envision the formation of a permanent world court, he did advocate the formation of arbitral tribunals, that is, special courts created to resolve such issues as might arise between governments, and he sought to apply this method to Anglo-American relations. While mediation and conciliation involve compromise based as much on political considerations as on law, arbitration is a legal process carried out by a tribunal created for that purpose. In terms of functional specificity, arbitration represents an advance over the other forms of dispute resolution, and Ladd's objective was the institutionalization of those measures supporting the cause of peace.

The *Alabama* claims (1871) set a precedent for a successful arbitration. During the American Civil War, the Confederate navy adopted a strategy of raiding enemy commerce. Warships assigned to this task roamed the oceans in search of merchant vessels flying the enemy flag and destroyed them. The *Alabama* was a Confederate raider, and before its destruction off the coast of France it captured and sank some forty merchantmen of the United States. The *Alabama* had been constructed at a shipyard in Liverpool, England, and after being launched it sailed to the Canary Islands, where its armaments were added and a Confederate naval officer took command. After the war's end, the United States charged Great Britain with a violation of the international law of neutrality for having constructed the raider and enabling it to put to sea. The damage done by the *Alabama* and other Confederate raiders was considerable, and the United States claimed damages from Great Britain. The two governments agreed to an arbitration and signed a *compromis,* which is a prior commitment to accept the judgment of the arbitral tribunal. The *compromis* also defines the structure within which the arbitration will take place and identifies the procedure for an appeal, if appropriate, from the arbitral award. In the instance of the *Alabama* claims, the two parties agreed to an arbitral tribunal composed of representatives from Italy (chair), Brazil, and Switzerland, who would convene in Geneva.

The United States opened with the legal argument that the Civil War was an internal conflict and lacked an international character. The British declaration of neutrality in May 1861 was therefore unwarranted and constituted an act of intervention in the affairs of a friendly state. The forces of secession were at war with the United States, and necessity required the suppression by force of the effort to dissolve the Union. The assistance rendered by British commercial interests to the cause of the Confederacy, specifically the *Alabama* and other raiders, was violative of international law, and compensation for damages was due.[20] The British case rested on two legal facts. First, President Abraham Lincoln had declared a naval blockade of southern ports and authorized the seizure of contraband on the high seas. Second, a blockade being an act of war, Great Britain and later France were within their rights to issue declarations of neutrality. Such declarations did not constitute intervention in an internal conflict because the naval strategy of the United States gave the war an international

---

[19]Denna Frank Fleming, *The United States and the World Court* (Garden City, N.Y.: Doubleday, Doran and Co., 1945), p. 17. See also John Hemmenway, *Memoir of William Ladd* (Boston: American Peace Society, 1872).

[20]United States, *The Argument at Geneva* (New York: D. Appleton and Co., 1873), pp. 7–16.

dimension.[21] Although the tribunal awarded damages to the United States, contemporary international law favors the British interpretation that a civil war is indeed an international responsibility. Since 1996, the province of Chechnya in the Russian Federation has been the scene of intermittent warfare, and President Clinton took a public stand on the need for a negotiated settlement rather than a war of attrition.[22] The 1871 position of the United States that international law requires a passive policy of silence in an internal war has given way to the belief that the international community has an obligation to isolate such conflicts and bring them to a close, which was essentially the public goal of Anglo-French diplomacy during the Civil War.

The flexibility of procedure in an arbitration is a principal advantage of the process. In the *Alabama* claims arbitration, a tribunal convened, and both sides made formal presentations. In 1872, Great Britain and the United States agreed to arbitrate a boundary dispute. An 1846 Anglo-American treaty settled the "Oregon question" but failed to delimit the maritime boundary between the province of British Columbia and the state of Washington. The line ran through the Juan de Fuca Strait, but the presence of numerous islands in this waterway made locating the exact position of the boundary a contentious issue. The two governments invited Wilhelm I, emperor of Germany, to serve as arbitrator. He agreed and referred the matter to three specialists in international law, two of whom were serving justices on high courts. They rendered an expert opinion, which the emperor endorsed as the final settlement.[23] In this instance the procedure called for an exchange of written arguments to be evaluated by a disinterested committee of experts. The arrangement was practical and cost effective. The arbitration contributed a new concept to international law, that of the *thalweg* or most navigable channel. The maritime boundary between two adjacent states should henceforth follow the *thalweg* rather than the principle of equidistance. In 1905, the U.S. Supreme Court relied upon the concept of the *thalweg* in settling a boundary dispute between the states of Louisiana and Mississippi, as discussed in Chapter 3. Russia and China resolved a long-standing riparian boundary problem in 1986 by agreeing to accept the *thalweg*. The judgment of Wilhelm I provided a precedent that continues to govern international boundary law. Arbitrations are ad hoc arrangements, but they contribute to the development of international law.

The success of arbitration requires a prior commitment growing out of a political understanding between the two states. A complementarity of interests enabled the United States and Great Britain to collaborate in the arbitration of war claims or a territorial problem. The arbitral commission created by Iran and the United States for the reciprocal settlement of claims provides an example of a failed arbitration, although one which was touted at its inception in 1981 as a major advance in international law. On November 4, 1979, Iranian militants occupied the premises of the U.S. embassy in Teheran, an event which began a year of captivity for American diplomatic and consular personnel. President Carter responded ten days later by imposing economic sanctions

---

[21]Great Britain, *The Case of Great Britain as Laid before the Tribunal of Arbitration Convened at Geneva* (Washington, D.C.: Government Printing Office, 1872; reprint Millwood, N.Y.: Kraus Reprint Co., 1978), 1: 7–18.

[22]Judy Dempsey, "Clinton calls for political solution in Chechnya," *Financial Times,* 3 November 1999, 1.

[23]John Bassett Moore, *International Arbitrations to which the United States Has Been a Party* (Washington, D.C.: Government Printing Office, 1898), 1: 219, 228–235.

on Iran. These included freezing of Iranian bank accounts in the United States.[24] Through the good offices of the Popular Republic of Algeria, the hostages were released on January 19, 1981. The agreements which brought about the release were collectively referred to as the Algiers Declarations, and they encompassed a procedure designed to bring about a settlement of the financial claims of each party to the dispute. The Iran–United States Claims Tribunal consisted of nine members, three appointed by each government and the remaining three selected on the basis of mutual agreement. The tribunal convened in The Hague on May 18, 1981, and after some procedural wrangling began its work. The first two years resolved none of the major issues, such as the return to Iran of the property of the deposed shah, and two of the judges resigned.[25]

A unique feature of the tribunal was its adherence to the arbitration rules of the United Nations Commission on International Trade Law (UNCITRAL).[26] The UNCITRAL rules were developed as a model law that could be enacted into national commercial codes. France, Canada, and Cyprus are among the states which have adopted the rules with little or no modification,[27] but neither Iran nor the United States had enacted counterpart legislation. The tribunal was therefore engaged in an experimental application of a model law, and that circumstance combined with the underlying political difficulties complicated the task. The lesson learned is that arbitration works best when the issue is well defined, and the states parties enjoy a political relationship which enables them to set their own rules to resolve the issue.[28] The essence of arbitration is the freedom to act without being encumbered by rules that may be inappropriate to the situation. The League of Nations sponsored in 1928 a General Act of Arbitration, but the reservations imposed by states adhering to the treaty eviscerated its effect.[29] Some have proposed a revised general treaty on the model designed by the League, but repetition of that experiment would probably have the same result. In an age of standardization, arbitration allows for a procedure that recognizes the diversity of states. The advantages in law and diplomacy are considerable.

ADJUDICATION

Of the seven methods of dispute resolution, adjudication before an established tribunal is the most highly structured. Although the ideal of an international court capable of resolving disputes among governments has roots in medieval European thought, the first such tribunal was not established until 1920, when the League of Nations created the

---

[24]The president acted under the authority granted him by the International Emergency Economic Powers Act (December 28, 1977), 91 Stat. 1626.

[25]George H. Aldrich, *The Jurisprudence of the Iran–United States Claims Tribunal* (Oxford: Clarendon Press, 1996), pp. 2–19. For the text of the constitutive agreements, see pp. 541–551. The records of the *Tribunal* are available in the series *Iran–United States Claims Tribunal Reports,* ed. Ruth Pogany (Cambridge: At the University Press, 1983–1996).

[26]Aida B. Avanessian, *Iran–United States Claims Tribunal in Action* (London: Graham & Trotman, 1993), pp. 3–5.

[27]Howard M. Holtzmann and Joseph E. Neuhaus, *A Guide to the UNCITRAL Model Law on International Commercial Arbitration* (Boston: Kluwer Law and Taxation Publishers, 1988), pp. v–vii.

[28]Louis B. Sohn, "International Arbitration in Historical Perspective: Past and Present," in *International Arbitration: Past and Prospects* (Boston: Martinus Nijhoff Publishers, 1990), p. 17.

[29]For the text of reservations, see United Nations, *Multilateral Treaties Deposited with the Secretary-General: Status as of 31 December 1997* (ST/LEG/SER.E/16), 997–1000.

Permanent Court of International Justice (PCIJ).[30] The PCIJ functioned until 1940 and was replaced seven years later by the International Court of Justice (ICJ), one of the major components of the United Nations system.[31] Adjudication raises a question which does not arise with reference to the other methods of dispute resolution, namely, the distinction between those issues that are justiciable and those that are not. International law recognizes the role of *vital interests* in the conduct of state policy. The rights of a state to exist, to preserve its independence, to defend its territorial integrity, and to uphold its sovereignty fall within the meaning of vital interests, which do not lend themselves to adjudication.[32] Indeed the advocate of realpolitik would insist that vital interests represent a positive moral goal, which those entrusted with power must serve.[33] The opposing point of view rests on the assumption that without mandatory adjudication of disputes, violence in the international system will continue unabated. The experience of the PCIJ and ICJ highlights these contending approaches.

As organized in 1920, the League of Nations consisted of two principal bodies—the Council and the Assembly. The former served as a steering committee dominated by the major powers,[34] and the latter comprised all the states party to the Covenant of the League. Both the Council and the Assembly had to concur in the election of the judges on the PCIJ. The fifteen judges each served a term of nine years, with one-third being renewed every three years, so that the PCIJ was a continuing body.[35] In contentious cases in which one party had a judge on the PCIJ and the other did not, the rules provided for the appointment of an ad hoc judge, so that both parties would be represented during the proceedings. Today's ICJ has the same basic structure.

The competence assigned to the PCIJ encompassed four types of cases:

    a. Interpretation of a treaty,
    b. Any question of customary or conventional international law,
    c. Such factual questions as would indicate a violation of international law, and
    d. Determination of reparations.[36]

The ICJ has the same purview. Although the formulation is precise, its application is not always straightforward because finding the borderline between justiciable and nonjusticiable questions poses a challenge. The PCIJ avoided controversy by embracing a policy of judicial restraint. Yet even with a limited docket the PCIJ rendered decisions of precedential value. Japan, Russia, and the United States did not join the PCIJ, but twenty-nine other states did accept the optional clause of the statute and with it a

---

[30]The PCIJ and its successor under the United Nations are often referred to as the "world court." Although the expression is technically inaccurate, it is expressive of the function of the tribunal. See Brownlie, p. 709.

[31]Lawrence Ziring, Robert Riggs, and Jack Plano, *The United Nations: International Organization and World Politics,* 3rd ed. (New York: Harcourt College Publishers, 2000), 220–228.

[32]Kelsen and Tucker, pp. 71–80.

[33]Hans J. Morgenthau, "The Mainsprings of American Foreign Policy: The National Interest vs. Moral Abstractions," *The American Political Science Review* 44 (December 1950): 833, 854.

[34]Initially the permanent members of the Council were France, Great Britain, Italy, and Japan. Germany joined the League of Nations and received a permanent seat on the Council in 1926. The United States, too, would have been a permanent member, but the Senate rejected the treaty in 1920.

[35]Although the United States, despite the efforts of President Calvin Coolidge, did not become a member of the PCIJ, two of its citizens (Manley O. Hudson and John Bassett Moore) served as justices.

[36]Statute for the Permanent Court of International Justice (December 16, 1920), 6 L.N.T.S. 391, 403.

commitment to adjudicate those disputes so intractable that they could not be resolved through diplomacy.[37] One of these states was Nicaragua—a fact of significance for a judgment rendered by the ICJ in 1984.

In addition to the *Lotus* case, two other decisions by the PCIJ merit attention. The first concerned the *Mavrommatis Concessions* (1924). In 1914, authorities of the Ottoman Empire granted M. Mavrommatis, a Greek national, a concession to supply water and electricity to the city of Jerusalem. With the end of the First World War the province of Palestine became a mandate administered by Great Britain under the League of Nations, and Mavrommatis sought to reclaim his rights under the initial concession. In this matter he was represented by the government of Greece, for the PCIJ could accept complaints only from true subjects of international law, that is, states. The British government was the respondent. The PCIJ upheld Mavrommatis's claim although it did not award him the compensation, which he sought. The decision established two principles, whose validity remains current. The first is that a claimant must satisfy all local remedies before turning to the PCIJ. Specially, the government bringing the case must demonstrate that a diplomatic solution is out of the question. The second is that a government may at its discretion espouse the claim of a private citizen, but it is not obligated to do so. The decision to turn to the PCIJ may well be influenced by political rather than legal considerations.[38] The ICJ affirmed the second point in 1964 in a case involving the rights of Belgian shareholders in a company providing electricity in Spain.[39]

A second decision involving individual property rights threatened by state action was long neglected but has recently returned to prominence. The political outcome of the First World War saw the rebirth of the Polish state, which had lost its sovereignty during the dynastic wars of the eighteenth century. Territories formerly governed by Austria, Germany, and Russia were combined to create the Polish Republic. As in the case of the *Mavrommatis Concessions,* the question arose as to the property rights of owners who were not citizens of the new state. In 1919, the Polish government expropriated a German-owned chemical factory at Chorzow as part of the peace settlement of that year. The German government challenged the expropriation without compensation to the shareholders and turned to the PCIJ for relief. In its ruling, the court concluded:

> It is a principle of international law that the reparation of a wrong may consist in an indemnity corresponding to the damage which nationals of the injured State have suffered as a result of the act which is contrary to international law.[40]

The PCIJ also noted that although Germany and Poland had previously agreed to arbitrate their disputes, such an agreement did not preclude a recourse to adjudication by one party or the other. The precedent set in decision on the factory at Chorzow applies

---

[37]Forest L. Grieves, *Supranationalism and International Adjudication* (Urbana, IL: University of Illinois Press, 1969), pp. 66–67.
[38]*The Mavrommatis Palestine Concessions: Collection of Judgments* (Greece v. Great Britain), PCIJ, Series A, No. 2 (1924), 7, 13–15.
[39]*Barcelona, Traction, Light and Powers Company* (Belgium v. Spain), 1964 ICJ Reports 6.
[40]*Case Concerning the Factory at Chorzow: Collection of Judgments,* PCIJ, Series A, No. 17 (1928), 27.

currently in countries whose governments have, as a result of revolutionary change, expropriated real property owned by foreigners. The resumption of normal diplomatic and trade relations between Cuba and the United States will involve a review of the Chorzow doctrine as it applies to American-owned properties in the island republic.

In 1946, the ICJ came into being with a structure and competence that mirrored the PCIJ.[41] Like its predecessor, the ICJ consists of fifteen justices elected for a term of nine years. One-third are elected every three years, so that the court is a continuing body. Ad hoc justices are allowed on the same basis as in the PCIJ. The election of a judge requires the approval of a majority of the two deliberative units of the United Nations— the Security Council and the General Assembly. As a matter of practice, the five permanent members of the Security Council are invariably represented on the ICJ.[42] The ten remaining justices are chosen from various legal cultures in order to achieve a diversity of points of view. The competence of the ICJ parallels that of the PCIJ. Article 36(3) of the United Nations Charter represents an innovation, in that it authorizes the Security Council to refer a dispute to the ICJ, and the Security Council did so once in a case involving the right of innocent passage through an international strait.[43] Although the ICJ normally meets in a plenary session (*en banc*), a chamber of five justices may hear a case if the governments party to the dispute give their prior consent. The use of a panel is often the preferred choice in a boundary dispute.

The outputs of the ICJ fall roughly into three categories: judgments, orders, and advisory opinions. In a contentious proceeding between two governments, known as the applicant and respondent, the judgment may, for example resolve a territorial dispute. Each government opens with a memorial, a book-length statement setting forth its arguments. The presentation of the case, or pleadings, may also involve the direct examination of witnesses. Once the ICJ has examined the evidence, it issues a judgment based on the merits of the case. Official records distinguish between pleadings and merits. Before the ICJ can hear a case, it may, as a matter of necessity, issue orders for interim measures (often referred to as provisional measures) designed to prevent further damage to one of the states party to the dispute. Such preliminary steps allow both sides to prepare and present their memorials. The PCIJ introduced the practice of advisory opinions, and the ICJ has further developed it. The Security Council, the General Assembly, or a specialized agency of the United Nations may request an advisory opinion on a point of law. In 1996, the ICJ responded to a request from the General Assembly and the World Health Organization for an advisory opinion on the use of nuclear weapons.[44] Through advisory opinions the ICJ may serve to legitimize decisions of the Security Council and to that extent they may exercise a political effect.[45] In this regard a much-needed reform would authorize the secretary-general of the United Nations to

---

[41]For a comprehensive view of the Statute of the International Court of Justice and related documents, see Shabtai Rosenne (ed.), *Documents on the International Court of Justice* (Boston and Dordrecht: Martinus Nijhoff, 1991).

[42]The permanent members of the Security Council are China, France, Great Britain, Russia, and the United States.

[43]*The Corfu Channel Case* (Great Britain v. Albania), 1949 ICJ Reports.

[44]*Advisory Opinion on the Legality of the Threat or Use of Nuclear Weapons* (July 8, 1996), International Court of Justice reprinted in 35 I.L.M. 809.

[45]Jose E. Alvarez, "Judging the Security Council," 90 *American Journal of International Law* (January 1996): 1, 4.

turn to the ICJ for an advisory opinion on an issue for which he or she is responsible.[46] Presently, the Security Council and the General Assembly show little interest in such a grant of authority to the secretary-general.

The record of the ICJ indicates that its principal contributions are in the resolution of territorial questions or the interpretation of treaties. A premier example is a 1951 decision in a dispute between Great Britain and Norway over the delimitation of maritime boundaries. Starting in 1935, the Norwegian government had delimited an exclusive fisheries zone through the means of drawing a straight baseline along the coast. The British government applied in 1949 to the ICJ for relief arguing that the Norwegian decrees enclosed vast stretches of the oceans and unlawfully restricted the freedom of the seas. (The *Mortensen* case of 1906 also involved a restricted fishing zone, as described in Chapter 2.) Counsel for Norway responded that well-established historic rights enabled his government to limit the presence of foreign fishing vessels in coastal waters, and that the decrees were in accordance with customary international law. In its judgment the ICJ found in favor of Norway and established the principle that the point from which the breadth of the territorial sea is measured could be an artificial line drawn in such a manner as to follow the general configuration of the coast. The court not only emphasized geographic factors, but also took into account the economic interests of the coastal state. The judgment stated:

> Finally, there is one consideration not to be overlooked, the scope of which
> extends beyond purely geographical factors: that of certain economic
> interests peculiar to a region, the reality and importance of which are clearly
> evidenced by long usage.[47]

Other governments were quick to utilize this precedent, and it became part of the United Nations–sponsored Convention on the Law of the Sea in 1982.

A second and more controversial judgment grew out of a complaint in 1984 on the part of Nicaragua against the United States. In the summer of 1979, the Sandinistas—a revolutionary movement—overthrew the military dictatorship in Nicaragua. Starting in 1981, the Reagan administration opted for a policy of destabilizing the Sandinista government on the thesis that it represented a threat to the security of the region. There followed a period of neither peace nor war, but rather what one author has termed "intermediacy."[48] The United States supported the forays into Nicaragua of a guerrilla army based in neighboring Honduras and engaged in a campaign of political warfare against the Sandinistas. In a contentious proceeding, the Nicaraguan government turned to the ICJ and submitted a memorial to the effect that the actions of the United States constituted an act of aggression in violation of the Charter of the United Nations and of regional guarantees of the sovereignty and territorial integrity of Latin American states.

In the first phase of the case, the ICJ had to determine whether it possessed jurisdiction over the matter. In its memorial, Nicaragua made reference to a resolution dated

---

[46]Boutros Boutros-Ghali, "Global Leadership After the Cold War," 75 *Foreign Affairs* (March/April 1996): 86, 90.
[47]*Fisheries Case: Judgment* (Great Britain v. Norway), 1951 ICJ Reports, 118, 133.
[48]Philip C. Jessup, "Should International Law Recognize an Intermediate Status between Peace and War?" 48 *American Journal of International Law* (January 1954): 98.

September 24, 1929, in which the Nicaraguan Congress had declared its adherence to the Statute of the PCIJ. Under the Statute of the ICJ, adherence to the League Court automatically carried over to the ICJ. The difficulty, as pointed out in the counter-memorial of the United States, was that the archives of the League of Nations in Geneva contained no record of the Nicaraguan declaration, which had purportedly been transmitted by telegram. Nevertheless, the ICJ ruled that the intent of Nicaragua to join the PCIJ in 1929 sufficed. Nicaragua also referred to a bilateral treaty of amity with the United States whereby both signatories agreed:

> Any dispute between the Parties as to the interpretation or application of the present Treaty, not satisfactorily adjusted by diplomacy, shall be submitted to the International Court of Justice, unless the Parties agree to settlement by some other pacific means.[49]

The twofold argument of a multilateral and a bilateral international agreement led the ICJ to conclude that Nicaragua was indeed bound by the optional clause of its statute; that is, failing a diplomatic solution, a dispute is to be submitted to adjudication by the court.[50]

The second phase of the case focused on the merits of Nicaragua's application. Although the United States refused to participate in this phase, it did advance the argument that the right of collective self-defense embodied in, for example, the Charter of the United Nations (article 51) and the Rio Treaty on Mutual Assistance[51] provided a basis in international law for intervention on the side of the forces combating the Sandinista regime. The ICJ determined that a government may not invoke a multilateral treaty to justify a plea of self-defense without offering supporting evidence. An appeal to the rule of necessity does not suffice. In the end, the ICJ was critical of both sides, but a majority held that the action of the United States was contrary to its treaty obligations.

As noted at the beginning of the discussion of adjudication, the debate over whether a question is truly justiciable must be answered early in the proceedings. After a review of the contending arguments, the ICJ concluded:

> There can be no doubt that the issues of the use of force and collective self-defense raised in the present proceedings are issues which are regulated both by customary international law and by treaties, in particular the United Nations Charter.[52]

The outcome of the ICJ ruling on Nicaragua's application was the termination in 1985 by the United States of its acceptance of compulsory jurisdiction under the optional clause of the court's statute.[53] Arguing that the ICJ had departed from its statute by endeavoring to rule on a political dispute involving the vital interests of the United States,

---

[49]Treaty of Friendship, Commerce and Navigation (January 21, 1956), 9 U.S.T. 449, 467. The United States terminated the treaty on May 1, 1986, after giving prior notice of one year.

[50]*Case Concerning Military and Paramilitary Activities in and against Nicaragua: Jurisdiction of the Court and Admissibility of the Application* (Nicaragua v. United States), 1984 ICJ Reports, 392, 413.

[51]Inter-American Treaty of Reciprocal Assistance (September 2, 1947), 4 Bevans 589.

[52]*Case Concerning Military and Paramilitary Activities in and against Nicaragua: Merits* (Nicaragua v. United States), 1986 ICJ Reports, 16, 27.

[53]"U.S. Terminates Acceptance of ICJ Compulsory Jurisdiction, 7 October 1985," 86 *Department of State Bulletin* (January 1986): 67.

Secretary of State George Shultz concluded that his government would only accept the jurisdiction of the ICJ based on the mutual consent of both states party to the dispute. Congressional hearings revealed the controversial nature of this decision, in that members of the international law community viewed it as weakening the development of world law.[54] The problem of what issue is justicable as opposed to political remains a matter of debate. Less than one-third of the members of the United Nations adhere to the optional clause and recognize the obligation of compulsory jurisdiction. Most governments reserve to themselves the right to decide when and if adjudication is an appropriate modality for resolving a dispute. The ICJ itself has subsequently moved toward a position of restraint in its 1999 decision to not accept the application of Yugoslavia condemning NATO allies for the use of force in Kosovo and Serbia a year earlier.[55] In rejecting this application the ICJ was at pains to defer to the political organs of the United Nations. Two points of view have emerged. The first argues that the function of the court is secondary to the Security Council. Trying to recast strategic confrontations between states in legal terms is counterproductive.[56] The counterargument places the court on an equal plane with the Security Council and suggests that the ICJ actively map out its own sphere of competence.[57] The second thesis is attractive, but in a world of realpolitik, judicial restraint is a more prudent policy.

A REGIONAL COURT

Inspired by the commitment of the Hague Conferences of 1899 and 1907 to the pacific settlement of disputes, Costa Rica, El Salvador, Guatemala, Honduras, and Nicaragua agreed in 1907 to establish the Central American Court of Justice. Each government appointed a justice for a term of five years—a decision required the concurrence of, at least, three judges. The competence of the court covered (a) disputes among the member states, (b) complaints of individuals against a government other than their own, and (c) international questions, including those involving outside powers.[58] Delays in appointing justices combined with procedural problems made the court a short-lived experiment. The court rendered its final and perhaps most precedential decision in 1917, when it established a legal regime of partnership among El Salvador, Honduras, and Nicaragua over the Gulf of Fonseca. The government of El Salvador brought the complaint in response to the conclusion of a treaty between Nicaragua and the United

---

[54]See particularly the statement by Burns H. Weston in U.S., Congress, House of Representatives, Committee on Foreign Affairs, *U.S. Decision to Withdraw from the International Court of Justice: Hearing before the Subcommittee on Human Rights and International Organizations,* 99th Cong., 1st sess., 1985, 92–109.

[55]*Case Concerning the Legality of the Use of Force: Jurisdiction and Admissibility* (Yugoslavia v. Belgium) 2 June 1999, reprinted in 38 I.L.M., 950, 961.

[56]For an explication of the argument in favor of the primacy of the political organs of the United Nations, see Harry H. Almond, Jr., "The *Military Activities Case:* New Perspectives on the International Court of Justice and Global Public Order," 21 *The International Lawyer* (Winter 1987): 195, 208. On September 26, 1991, the court ordered the discontinuance of the case. See "Current Developments," 86 *American Journal of International Law* (January 1992): 173–174.

[57]For an activist interpretation of the court's role, see Thomas M. Franck, "The 'Powers of Appreciation': Who is the Ultimate Guardian of UN Legality?" 86 *American Journal of International Law* (July 1992): 519, 521.

[58]Antonio Sanchez de Bustamante, *The World Court,* trans. Elizabeth F. Read (New York: Macmillan Co., 1926), pp. 68–77.

States whereby the latter could establish naval bases on the gulf.[59] Supported by Honduras, El Salvador argued that the gulf was a shared responsibility, and that Nicaragua was not entitled to lease naval bases without the prior approval of the other republics. The court upheld this interpretation.[60] The idea of a multistate condominium over a body of adjacent waters continues to merit attention.

Mediation is the preferred method of resolving disputes in Latin America, as indicated by two Hemispheric conventions concluded in 1936.[61] In combination the treaties required a cooling-off period, the formation of mixed commissions, and a mediatory role on the part of third parties. Nevertheless armed conflicts continue to occur, one of the most serious of which was a frontier war between Ecuador and Peru in early 1995. Ecuador's size would have doubled if its claim to Peruvian territory would have been granted. The forces of the two countries clashed on the frontier. Argentina, Brazil, Chile, and the United States collaborated to mediate a cease-fire, but the truce failed to resolve the conflicting claims.[62] The episode illustrates the fragility of pledges to seek peaceful solutions to international disputes even in an area characterized by a high level of cultural homogeneity and elite complementarity. International law provides seven frameworks within which governments can work toward a peaceful resolution of their disputes, but political will remains a precondition for success. Without the will, the legal machinery will remain inert.

Topics for Discussion

1. What are the seven modalities of dispute resolution? How do they compare with reference to the changing ratio of political to legal considerations?
2. What is the doctrine of vital interests? Should international law limit itself only to "justiciable" disputes? If so, how should these be defined?
3. What is the role of a mediatory power? Should it concentrate on developing the overlapping interests between the contending governments, or should it use mediation to advance its own foreign-policy agenda?
4. Most governments, including the United States since 1985, do not accept the optional clause of the Statute of the International Court of Justice, which constitutes a prior obligation to adjudicate disputes within the framework of international law. Should all members of the United Nations be required as a condition of membership to adhere to the optional clause? What would be the consequences of such a requirement for the ICJ?

---

[59]Bryan-Chamorro Treaty (August 5, 1914), 3 Bevans-Redmond 2740.
[60]*The Republic of El Salvador v. the Republic of Nicaragua* (March 9, 1917), Central American Court of Justice, reprinted in *American Journal of International Law* 11 (July 1917), 674, 730.
[61]Prevention of Controversies: Inter-American (December 23, 1936), 3 Bevans 357, and Good Offices and Mediation: Inter-American (December 23, 1936), 3 Bevans 362. The United States was a party to both conventions.
[62]"Peru, Ecuador Sign Truce," *Facts on File,* 23 February 1995, 114–115.

CHAPTER 11

Territory

Disputes among governments more often than not arise from overlapping territorial claims. The largest single category of cases heard by the ICJ concerns land and maritime boundary problems. Territory is linked to sovereignty, and it is not surprising a government will go to great lengths to defend its title to a frontier village or to a distant island. Prestige is the essence of a successful foreign policy, and territorial integrity is the hallmark of a state's prestige. Even in an era characterized by the erosion of the legal significance of international borders, the boundary marker continues to possess an emotional attraction which the forces of supranationalism cannot overcome. Customary international law recognizes five basic methods of acquiring title to territory: (a) discovery and occupation, (b) forces of nature, (c) acquisitive prescription, (d) cession, and (e) conquest.[1] State practice varies with each of these methods. For example, the United States has historically questioned the validity of prescriptive rights established over time as opposed to a formal transfer of title. Yet each method has played a role in the history of international boundary disputes.

DISCOVERY AND OCCUPATION

At the end of the fifteenth century, Portuguese and Spanish mariners engaged in a race to claim for their respective sovereigns lands in what Europeans viewed as the "new world." The threat of war between the two strongest naval powers of the period was imminent, but Pope Alexander VI interceded and mediated a solution based on an artificial maritime boundary represented by a meridian or longitudinal line running through the South Atlantic. After lengthy negotiations, emissaries of Portugal and Spain concluded the Treaty of Tordesillas in 1494, whereby the forty-ninth meridian west of Greenwich became the boundary between Portuguese territory on the east and Spanish territory on the west.[2] The line runs through present-day Brazil and explains that country's Portuguese heritage. During the Anglo-Argentine War of 1982 over the Falkland/Malvinas Islands, the government of Argentina cited the treaty as part of its legal argument that the contested islands were a part of its historic territory. Painstaking historical research is often critical in establishing title to territory.

Discovery alone is, however, insufficient to buttress a territorial title. The claimant state must demonstrate effective and continuous occupation. Evidence of occupation consists of the administration of laws, the provision of public services, and the maintenance of security. The discovery of an uncharted island must be followed by the establishment of

---

[1]Malanczuk, pp. 147–151, and von Glahn, pp. 297–303.
[2]Treaty between Spain and Portugal concluded at Tordesillas (June 7, 1494) reprinted in *European Treaties Bearing on the History of the United States and Its Dependencies to 1648,* ed. Frances Gardiner Davenport (Washington, D.C.: Carnegie Institution, 1917), pp. 93–100.

viable public authority. Governments may resort to issuing postage stamps or performing other nominal acts, but these do not suffice. An international tribunal investigating the claim of one state vis-à-vis another will invariably study the history of governmental administration in the area concerned.

FORCES OF NATURE

Rivers often form boundaries between states. The Amur, Congo, Rhine, and Rio Grande provide examples, but rivers constantly alter their course through the operation of natural forces. Riparian boundaries are always in motion, much to the consternation of legal purists. The three basic forces are accretion, erosion, and avulsion. Rising waters in the spring cause accretion (i.e., a buildup of soil on one country's side of the river and erosion on the other country's bank). As long as the changes are gradual and imperceptible, both parties acknowledge a slight shift in the boundary. If this principle were not applied, governments would spend large sums conducting annual surveys, with minimal benefits. Avulsion is, by contrast, sudden and perceptible, a case in point being a flood causing a river to change its course. In such an instance the customary rule is that the boundary remains fixed with the result that an enclave of national territory may form on the other side of the river boundary. Alternatively, a binational boundary commission may simply agree to an amended line following the river's new course.[3] In the context of these issues, potamology (the scientific study of rivers) sets the rules for boundary making.

While these principles may appear abstract, their application has a profound effect on the populations involved. In 1906, the small town of Rio Rico was on the north side of the Rio Grande River and consequently situated in the United States. Then the river flooded and changed its course, so that the town found itself situated on the south side and therefore a part of Mexico. The Rio Ricans disputed the change, but in 1976 a judge of the U.S. Immigration and Naturalization Service ruled that since the United States had exercised no jurisdiction over the town since 1906, it had become Mexican territory.[4] The river changed its course and with it the citizenship of the people of Rio Rico.

PRESCRIPTION

The concept of acquisitive prescription derives its meaning from civil law, which recognizes title to land based on continuous control and usage over a period of time, say ten years. The same concept applies in international law. A government may acquire title to territory by fulfilling three requirements.[5] First, the state advancing an argument based on prescription must demonstrate a public display of sovereign control manifested in, for example, the collection of revenue, operation of schools, issuance of licences, conducting a census, and maintenance of law and order. The exercise of governmental powers must be actual and not nominal. This test is similar to that associated with discovery, but with a major difference. Discovery involves the acquisition of title to uncharted and

---

[3]Treaty to Resolve Pending Boundary Differences and Maintain the Rio Grande and Colorado as the International Boundary: United States and Mexico (November 23, 1970), 23 U.S.T. 371, 383.
[4]"Citizenship Claim of Border Resident Rejected by Judge," *New York Times,* 2 December 1976, 29.
[5]2 Whiteman, pp. 1062–1066.

unclaimed territory, usually referred to as *res nullius* or land belonging to no one. Prescription refers to the transfer of title from one sovereign to another, for prescriptive rights must always be asserted against a counter claimant.

The second test is that of acquiescence. Other powers having an historic claim to the territory must defer to the government in control. Misunderstanding exists in the belief that silence alone may mean acquiescence, yet customary international law is unclear on this point. Normally the power which acquiesces does so with a public gesture, such as observing the maritime regulations or revenue laws of the current sovereign. Closely linked to acquiescence is the doctrine of estoppel.[6] The two concepts differ somewhat although their practical effect regarding prescriptive rights is the same. As noted, acquiescence means the absence of a challenge and usually an act of implied recognition of the other state's sovereignty. Estoppel covers an official statement by a government to the effect that it has no territorial claim to the area under consideration. In 1933, the PCIJ developed the notion of estoppel and good faith in a territorial dispute between Denmark and Norway. During a meeting in 1919, the Danish ambassador informed the Norwegian minister for foreign affairs that his government had no claim to the Spitsbergen Islands and asked the minister if Norway would reciprocate by terminating its rights in Greenland. Subsequently, the minister made an oral commitment to this effect. When Norway later sought to press its claims in Greenland, Denmark invoked the doctrine of estoppel by pointing out that it had taken the minister's assurances in good faith. Norway was by its own action estopped or precluded from insisting upon territorial rights in Greenland.[7]

The third test requires a demonstration of sovereignty over time, but how much time? The question defies a clear-cut answer. In the Rio Rico decision, the United States took the position that it had alienated its rights by failing to exercise jurisdiction over the community for a period of seventy years. Other precedents suggest a shorter length of time. In 1903, Great Britain and the United States agreed to submit a dispute concerning the boundary between Alaska and British Columbia to an arbitral tribunal. The resolution of the issue required, in part, the satisfaction of the third test. The United States had purchased Alaska in 1867 and had established its new administration based on what were thought to be Russian claims vis-à-vis adjacent Canadian territory. The question is whether the contested territory, in this instance the area around the coastal inlet known as the Lynn Canal, had been lawfully transferred from Russian to American sovereignty. Or had American military authorities assumed too much and inadvertently extended their control over lands belonging to Canada? The United States argued that:

> Upon the purchase of Alaska by the United States in 1867, the officers of the United States took formal possession, with appropriate ceremonies, of the territory at the head of the Lynn Canal.... From that time until the present the United States has retained that possession, and has performed the duties and exercised the powers of sovereignty there.
>
> For certainly more than twenty years after that, there was not a suggestion from the British Government that the possession was not rightful. In the

---

[6]Brownlie, p. 158; and Malanczuk, p. 154.
[7]*Legal Status of Eastern Greenland: Judgment* (Denmark v. Norway), PCIJ, Series E, No. 9 (1933), 141, 144.

meantime, the Naval and Military officers of the United States governed the Indians who lived at heads of the inlets.[8]

The tribunal interpreted this historical record as an indication of acquiescence on the part of Great Britain, and the award favored the United States.

The obverse of prescription is abandonment, a process whereby a government relinquishes its claim to territory, often without realizing it. Following the war with Spain in 1898, the United States acquired by treaty of peace the Philippine Islands. On a tour of inspection in 1906, General Leonard Wood, the regional military governor, sought to visit the island of Palmas (Miangas) located in an area in which the Philippines and the then Dutch East Indies (today Indonesia) overlap in a series of small islands. To his astonishment the governor saw the Dutch flag flying over what he presumed to be a U.S. possession. Diplomatic exchanges failed to resolve the question of title, and the two governments agreed to a *compromis* (1925) providing for arbitration by Professor Max Huber of Switzerland. Both sides prepared extensive memoranda detailing the historical and legal arguments for their claims. The arbitrator received these and then reached a decision in favor of the Netherlands. The United States had based its argument on the principle of discovery by Spanish explorers and insisted that it had inherited that title by virtue of the treaty of peace. The Netherlands countered by pointing out that since the eighteenth century the island had been under Dutch administration, and Spain had acquiesced. The jural fact of effective and continuous sovereign jurisdiction over the island proved decisive. The presumed title of the United States was neither absolute (irrefutable based on discovery) nor inchoate (imperfect because of nonexistent Spanish administration).[9]

The concept of intertemporal law undergirded the decision, and the arbitration represents the point at which this standard became a means of assessing territorial claims, albeit a somewhat disputed standard.[10] Intertemporal law refers to a theory under which the validity of a territorial claim is evaluated not on the basis of present-day rules of law, but rather in terms of the law as it existed (or is assumed to have existed) at the time the claim was initiated. Judge Huber determined that the principle of title by discovery was not a rule of law when Spanish mariners first visited the island of Palmas in the early 1600s. Consequently the United States could not rely on a legal argument which did not exist when the first Europeans reached the island. The application of intertemporal law means that a government must search historical records to determine what the rules were at the inception of the claim.[11] The task is difficult, and the results are invariably indeterminate.

Intertemporal law proved a pivotal factor in a decision of the ICJ regarding territory. The first concerned a dispute in 1953 between Great Britain and France over two island groups, little more than rocky outcroppings in the English Channel. The two governments submitted the case to the ICJ, which ruled in favor of Great Britain.[12] Each

---

[8]*The Alaska Boundary Case* (United States v. Great Britain), 1903 reprinted in 15 R.I.A.A., 534.

[9]*The Island of Palmas Case* (United States v. Netherlands), 1928 reprinted in Bishop, 400–405. For the *compromis* see 10 Bevans 81.

[10]Philip C. Jessup, "The Palmas Island Arbitration," *American Journal of International Law* 22 (October 1928), 735, 739.

[11]1 Hackworth 393; Shaw, 346–347.

[12]*The Minquiers and Ecrehos Case: Judgment* (Great Britain v. France), 1953 ICJ Reports, 72.

side presented its argument in terms of the historical record as interpreted on the basis of intertemporal law. The historical account began with the Norman Conquest (1066) and traced various decrees, both secular and ecclesiastical, regarding jurisdiction over the islands. The attempt to confirm a critical date from which sovereignty could be traced failed to provide unequivocal results.[13] Did the title of the king of France lapse in 1204 because of a failure to enforce decrees? Did an English abbey hold the Ecrehos by right of feudal tenure from the king of England? Unraveling these and related questions to identify a critical date verifying English or French sovereignty was a frustrating task, and the ICJ's decision reflected a best estimate given the often conflicting medieval records.

In the decisions on the Island of Palmas and on the Channel Islands, an underlying question was when the United States, in the former instance, and France, in the latter, had abandoned their respective claims. The legal history of these territories did not provide a specific date of abandonment, so the international jurist is left with the problem of trying to determine when the prescriptive rights of the new sovereign took effect. The following two cases indicate the complexity of that problem. The first concerns Clipperton Island, an uninhabited point of land some 670 miles southwest of Mexico. In 1858, a French naval officer cruised the island and laid claim to it for France. Thirty-nine years later the crew of a Mexican gunboat raised their flag on the island and proclaimed it to be Mexican territory based on the papal award in the Treaty of Tordesillas (1494). France protested, and both parties agreed to an arbitration under the auspices of King Victor Emmanuel III of Italy, who decided in favor of France.[14] The arbitrator acknowledged the claim of Spain and then Mexico derived from discovery, but insisted that the French naval expedition and repeated statements by the French government demonstrated the exercise of sovereignty even though the island was uninhabited. Again the welter of historical claims and the absence of a critical date make the award appear capricious. The case emphasizes, however, the salient point that the argument for prescriptive rights invariably does not include a point in time when they become incontrovertibly valid. In the instance of Clipperton Island, the history of French jurisdiction spanned scarcely forty years, yet the arbitrator found that to be sufficient.

The second illustration of abandonment is emotionally freighted and therefore still subject to debate. The Treaty of Guadalupe Hidalgo (1848) concluded the war between Mexico and the United States and established the land boundaries between the two countries. At the time maritime boundaries received little attention, and the treaty left these questions open.[15] Off the coast of California near San Diego are eight small islands about whose status the 1848 treaty is silent. Over time the United States extended its jurisdiction over what has become known as the Northern Archipelago, although no critical date for the establishment of sovereignty was proclaimed. First in 1894 and again

---

[13]Gerald Fitzmaurice, "Disputed Claims to Territory (The Case of the Minquiers and the Ecrehos): The 'Critical Date,' " in 32 *The British Year Book of International Law, 1955–56* (London: Oxford University Press, 1957), pp. 20, 33.

[14]*Sovereignty over Clipperton Island: Arbitral Award* (January 28, 1931) reprinted in 26 *American Journal of International Law* (April 1932), 390.

[15]Boundary questions between the United States and Mexico appear to have a life of their own. See Treaty on Maritime Boundaries (May 4, 1978) in Marian Lloyd Nash, *Digest of United States Practice in International Law 1978,* U.S. Department of State (Washington, D.C.: U.S. Government Printing Office, 1980), pp. 946–948.

in 1944, the Mexican government sponsored academic commissions to determine whether the United States was in unlawful occupation of its national territory. Both studies raised doubts regarding the prescriptive rights of the United States, but the Mexican Ministry of Foreign Affairs did not lodge a protest with the U.S. Department of State. The absence of a diplomatic demarche leads to the conclusion that Mexico has no intention of asserting its historic rights to the islands.[16] Through silence Mexico has acquiesced to the U.S. claim.

Silence was not the rule in the negotiations between Mexico and the United States over "El Chamizal"—an area of 600 acres between El Paso, Texas, and Ciudad Juárez, Chihuahua. Negotiations over this area began in 1911, when representatives of the two governments sought to establish the true position of the Rio Grande at the time it became an international boundary. The project proved impossible because repeated flooding had caused the river to change its course. In 1963, Mexico and the United States agreed to the construction of a canal designed to control the river, and the plan called for the retrocession to Mexico of two-thirds of the tract.[17] Whatever prescriptive rights the United States possessed in the Chamizal were waived in the interests of amity. Constructing a canal to fix the course of a river boundary is, however, a solution that only a few governments can afford. In most instances the forces of nature triumph over the efforts of boundary commissioners to apply principles of international law to their work.

CESSION

Voluntary cession avoids the ambiguity associated with such methods as discovery or prescription. Both parties agree to a transfer of title to territory usually against political concessions or payment. Three such territorial cessions were critical in U.S. history. President Thomas Jefferson negotiated the purchase of Louisiana from France in 1803 for $15 million.[18] The Gadsden treaty of 1853 provided for the purchase by the United States of territory from Mexico. In exchange for $10 million and specified political concessions the territory changed hands.[19] Such a treaty usually contains political clauses resolving latent issues, and to that extent the instrument is a commitment to amity and the peaceful settlement of disputes. Similarly in 1867, the United States purchased Alaska (Russian America) from the Czar's government for a reported $7.2 million.[20] The agreement specified that the two sides would appoint agents who would carry out the formal exchange of territory, including the handover of military installations.

A treaty arranging for the peaceful cession of territory and with it an affirmation of friendly relations should (a) define the new international boundary in precise cartographical terms, (b) specify the preconditions required to secure the transfer, (c) indicate

---

[16]Jorge A. Vargas, "California's Offshore Islands: Is the 'Northern Archipelago' a Subject for International Law or Political Rhetoric?," 12 *Loyola of Los Angeles International and Comparative Law Journal* (1990), 687, 721.

[17]Convention on the Solution of the Problem of the Chamizal (August 29, 1963), 15 U.S.T. 21, 23. For the background of the negotiations, see 3 Whiteman 680.

[18]Cession of Louisiana (April 30, 1803), 7 Bevans 812.

[19]Gadsden Treaty (December 30, 1853), 9 Bevans 812.

[20]Cession of Alaska (March 30, 1867), 11 Bevans 1216. Some question exists as to whether all of the money was actually paid. See Benjamin Platt Thomas, *Russo-American Relations, 1815–1867* (Baltimore: The Johns Hopkins Press, 1930), pp. 156–162.

the procedures which will accomplish the handover of territory, (d) describe any residual rights which the former sovereign may retain, and (e) set a date on which the law of the former sovereign will be replaced by that of the new government. Such an agreement is of necessity technical, and its language must be precise. The Warsaw treaty resolving differences between the Federal Republic of Germany and the People's Republic of Poland in 1971 failed to meet the aforementioned test of draftsmanship. The bilateral agreement did recognize Poland's western frontier as delimited by Great Britain, the Soviet Union, and the United States at the Potsdam Conference (1945) as no longer subject to change. This boundary decision brought with it a problem in international law because the reconciliation treaty did not specify the date on which German sovereignty ceased, and Polish sovereignty began.[21] Was the transfer of territory effective at the end of the Second World War or with the conclusion of the Warsaw treaty? The answer is speculative, and oversights of this nature may engender more problems than they resolve.

CONQUEST

One of the founders of political geography, Friedrich Ratzel of the University of Leipzig, wrote:

> The majority of wars, about which the history of the last two thousand years teaches us, were wars for land. Rome waged wars of expansion against its neighbors and sent in colonists to secure with the plow and defend with the sword conquered territories. In the nineteenth century wars inspired by nationalism sought to liberate peoples, to overcome fragmentation, and to round out national territories.[22]

Writing at the same time, Frederick Jackson Turner of the University of Wisconsin, posited the thesis that the westward movement provided the stimulus for the development of American democracy.[23] Expansionist wars are a fact of realpolitik, and international law faces the daunting task of trying to reconcile this international reality with the need to create a stable world order.

To what degree, then, can conquest be considered a legitimate basis of title to territory? Until the adoption of the Covenant of the League of Nations (1920) the question scarcely arose, for war was a political and not a legal problem. The Covenant made the waging of an aggressive war an offense against the international community and called upon all members of the League to contain the aggressor. In 1931, the Japanese army advanced from Korea and occupied Manchuria, the northeastern province of China. The League responded by organizing a commission of inquiry under Lord Lytton. Although not a member of the league, the United States participated and joined in the Lytton commission's report that the Japanese action was contrary to the principles of the

---

[21] Warsaw Treaty Concerning Basis for Normalizing Relations (November 18, 1970), reprinted in 10 I.L.M. 127.
[22] Friedrich Ratzel, *Politische Geographie* (Political geography) (Munich: R. Oldenbourg, 1903), p. 94.
[23] Frederick Jackson Turner, *The Frontier in American History* (New York: Henry Holt and Co., 1958), pp. 243–268.

Covenant. Accordingly, Secretary of State Henry Stimson sent identical notes to the governments of China and Japan, in which he denied recognition to the de facto situation created in Manchuria by unilateral Japanese action. Military conquest does not create a basis for the lawful transfer of title to territory. Quincy Wright wrote in a commentary on the Stimson note that its significance in the development of international law could scarcely be overestimated.[24] The essence of this evaluation is that the use of military force to acquire new territory is no longer a revisionist policy to be contained by the workings of the balance-of-power system, but rather a legal issue. The path entered on to here would lead after the Second World War to the trials of major war criminals on a charge of committing a crime against peace.

While the theory is impressive, its application in practice is often judgmental. The Middle East provides an example. The state of Israel came into being in 1948 in the course of a war dividing the former British dependency of Palestine between Israeli and Arab forces. The cease-fire line separating Israel from Jordan was a provisional border, but was it an internationally recognized boundary? In June 1967, Israeli forces occupied the West Bank of the Jordan River as well as the historic district of Jerusalem, both of which areas were under Jordanian administration. The government of Jordan insisted that its territorial integrity had been violated and invoked the principle of nonrecognition embodied in the Stimson doctrine. Israel countered with the argument that the 1948 armistice had not resolved the issue of a legal border and therefore the occupied areas or parts of them could be annexed. On June 27, 1967, the Israeli parliament enacted bills extending Israeli laws and administration throughout Jerusalem. A day later President Johnson issued a statement to the effect that the United States did not recognize unilateral changes in the status of the city, essentially a restatement of the Stimson doctrine.[25] The United Nations General Assembly adopted a similar position the following month.[26] The powers continued to regard Jerusalem as a *corpus separatum* (an entity governed by a special international regime). After prolonged diplomatic bargaining, the United Nations Security Council adopted a resolution calling for the withdrawal of Israeli forces from territories recently occupied.[27]

The questions of Jerusalem and of the West Bank remain open as indicated by the ongoing peace process begun in Madrid in 1991. International law offers two possible explanations. The first is the theory of *uti possidetis* (as you possess it), which establishes title to territory based on the line of military demarcation. In this instance Israel would assert its possession of the territories seized in 1967 on the ground that they were in dispute and therefore open to incorporation, albeit by armed force. The countervailing theory is that of *status quo ante bellum* (the situation as it existed before the

---

[24]Quincy Wright, "The Stimson Note of January 7, 1932," *American Journal of International Law* 26 (April 1932): 342. See also Robert Langer, *Seizure of Territory: The Stimson Doctrine and Related Principles in Legal Theory and Diplomatic Practice* (Princeton: Princeton University Press, 1947).

[25]"White House Statement: June 28, 1967," *Department of State Bulletin* 57 (July 17, 1967): 60.

[26]United Nations, General Assembly, Resolution 2253 (July 4, 1967), reprinted in *Department of State Bulletin* 57 (July 24, 1967): 113.

[27]United Nations, Security Council, Resolution 242, S/RES/242 (November 22, 1967), reprinted in *UN Monthly Chronicle* 4 (December 1967): 19–20. Despite the Cold War representatives of the United States and the Soviet Union both voted in support of the resolution.

outbreak of war). Jordan would support this interpretation and insist that the 1948 armistice line could not be altered except by a formal treaty. Accordingly, Israel's presence in the occupied territories was that of a military government temporarily imposed on a foreign community. Legal title to the territories in question remained Jordanian. Legal formalism eventually gave way to pragmatic diplomacy, and Israel and Jordan concluded a treaty of peace in 1994.[28] Georg Schwarzenberger summarized the labyrinth of issues surrounding title to territory in the former province of Palestine by suggesting that students of international law content themselves with the enumeration of rights and wrongs on both sides without trying to ascribe justice to one party or the other.[29] The advice is well taken.

The international boundary between Iraq and Kuwait presents an equally complex case of contending titles to territory. Modern Iraq grew out of three separate provinces of the Ottoman Empire, which the British army organized as a single entity after the occupation of Baghdad during the First World War. Dependency on Great Britain lasted until 1932, when Iraq joined the League of Nations as a sovereign member. Kuwait was a British protectorate from 1897 to 1961, and during that period it became a center for the production of oil. The international boundary between Iraq and Kuwait remained undefined, and such Kuwaiti practices as slant drilling across the border into Iraq exacerbated the tension between the two states. In August 1990, Iraqi forces occupied the disputed frontier zone and then all of Kuwait, and the following January a coalition led by the United States waged a successful war to expel Iraq from Kuwait. A part of the cease-fire agreement stipulated that the boundary commission sponsored by the United Nations would demarcate the international border. Iraq and Kuwait each appointed a member to the commission, and the United Nations secretary-general chose three independent experts, one of whom would serve as the leader of the group.[30] The commission studied each sector of the frontier and placed markers (pillars) to establish the exact location of the boundary. Had this project been undertaken in the 1960s, it would have contributed to a reduction of tension between the two states. A scientific demarcation of a boundary invariably contributes to friendly relations, and indeterminate borders are a source of friction.

These case studies indicate that conquest alone does not serve to guarantee title to territory. The conclusion of a treaty of peace resolving outstanding political questions, including territorial disputes, is the final and definitive act. Nevertheless, care must be taken to ensure attention to detail. The absence of a critical date in the German–Polish Warsaw treaty is a potentially troublesome oversight. It is at this stage that creative diplomacy plays a key role. Working within the framework of customary international law, diplomats can draw upon the five methods to construct a settlement, which involves a political agreement with legal consequences. In understanding territorial questions, one should bear in mind that the political precedes the legal.

---

[28]Treaty of Peace between the State of Israel and the Hashemite Kingdom of Jordan (October 26, 1994), reprinted in 34 I.L.M. 46.

[29]Georg Schwarzenberger, *International Law and Order* (New York: Praeger Publishers, 1971), pp. 280–281.

[30]For a documentary history of the work of the Iraq–Kuwait boundary commission, see *Demarcation of the International Boundary between the State of Kuwait and the Republic of Iraq by the United Nations* (Kuwait: Center for Research and Studies on Kuwait, 1994).

EVIDENCE

Contentious cases involving territory lend themselves to resolution either through arbitration or adjudication. The parties engage in extensive research to prepare memoranda (arbitration) or memorials (adjudication) in support of their claims. In this context, history becomes a study of geography over time, and the supporting documents reflect that interpretation.

Exhibits prepared for an arbitral tribunal or for the ICJ follow a standard format and include the following: (a) statutes and treaties, (b) administrative documents such as tax receipts, diplomas, or licenses, (c) census rolls, (d) statements of international organizations, and (e) maps and charts. The last of these items is a subject of some debate, in that one body of thought insists that cartographic evidence is inconclusive and of little value.[31] Yet the record of litigation gives evidence to the contrary. The memorandum prepared by the United States for the island of Palmas arbitration certified that nearly 1,000 maps published between 1599 and 1898 were examined, and the case for the United States depended in large measure on a cartographic history of the island.[32] In 1982, Canada and the United States agreed to litigate a dispute over the maritime boundary in the Gulf of Maine before a chamber of the ICJ. In its memorial the United States presented a four-page summary of the history of hydrography in the gulf, making specific reference to charts published in 1718 and 1797.[33] Canada responded with a counter-memorial covering the history of official and private charting of the gulf from 1610 forward.[34] Four of the five judges of the chamber found the Canadian argument, buttressed as it was by research on maps and charts of the area, to be persuasive. In litigation before international tribunals scholarship has its rewards.

Maps portray geographical facts, and invariably they make a political statement. Governments advancing territorial claims will use historical as well as modern maps, and international tribunals attach weight to this evidence.[35] Both official and unofficial maps possess evidentiary value, as do accounts written by explorers and others with a knowledge of the area in question.[36] The customary rules of evidence applicable to maps suggest four principles. The first is that quantity triumphs over quality. Tribunals assess cartographic evidence from the standpoint of whether it establishes a trend to the effect that public perception over time shows the region in dispute as part of a particular state. In 1927, the Privy Council of Great Britain was called upon to resolve a question concerning

---

[31]Durward V. Sandifer, *Evidence before International Tribunals,* rev. ed. (Charlottesville: University of Virginia Press, 1975).

[32]*The Island of Palmas Arbitration: Memorandum of the United States of America,* n.d. (Washington, D.C.: Government Printing Office, 1925), 25. The United States also relied upon cartographic evidence in the arbitration with Great Britain over the boundary of Alaska (1903). See U.S. Congress, Senate Document 162, 58th Cong., 2nd sess., *Alaskan Boundary Tribunal: United States Atlas* (Washington, D.C.: Government Printing Office, 1904).

[33]*Case Concerning Delimitation of the Maritime Boundary in the Gulf of Maine Area: Memorial Submitted by the United States of America* (September 27, 1982), International Court of Justice (unbound), 64–68.

[34]*Delimitation of the Maritime Boundary in the Gulf of Maine Area: Annexes to the Counter-Memorial Submitted by Canada* (June 28, 1983), International Court of Justice (unbound), 23–31.

[35]Charles Cheney Hyde, "Maps as Evidence in International Boundary Disputes," *American Journal of International Law* 27 (April 1933): 311, 314.

[36]Ian Brownlie, *African Boundaries: A Legal and Diplomatic Encyclopedia* (Berkeley: University of California Press, 1979), p. 5.

the Canada–Newfoundland boundary dispute in the Labrador Peninsula. Both sides relied upon maps, especially railroad maps, to support their claims. The Privy Council assessed the evidence and concluded:

> The maps here referred to, even when issued or accepted by departments of the Canadian Government, cannot be treated as admissions binding on that Government; for even if such an admission could be effectively made, the departments concerned are not shown to have had any authority to make it. But the fact that throughout a long series of years, and until the present dispute arose, all the maps issued in Canada either supported or were consistent with the claim now put forward by Newfoundland, is of some value as showing the construction put upon the Orders in Council and statutes by persons of authority and by the general public in the Dominion.[37]

The overall effect of maps on elite and mass opinion may prove critical.

The second principle is that even a map proven to be inaccurate continues to possess probative value. Writing for the U.S. Supreme Court in 1895, Justice John Marshall Harlan addressed a challenge to the eastern boundary of Texas. The line followed the course of the Red River, which had been charted by a Philadelphia mapmaker, John Melish, in 1818. The map had served as the basis for a treaty of amity between the United States and Spain in 1819 and was therefore considered definitive. Unfortunately, the Melish map had the Red River in the wrong place. The question then became one of science versus tradition. Should the boundary of Texas be corrected (with a loss of territory for the Lone Star State) in accordance with accurate geographic data? Or should the line remain the one established on the basis of a flawed map? The Court favored tradition, and Harlan accepted the original map despite its error.[38] As noted in Chapter 3, the principles of international law govern territorial disputes between the constituent members of a federation. The province of Labrador and the state of Texas are both regarded as subjects of international law in such litigation. Municipal and international law interact, and one body of law continues to inform the other.

The third principle is that judges rarely, if ever, see the original maps. The customary practice is for each side to prepare an atlas of those maps selected to support its case. Photocopies of the maps may be reduced or enlarged to suit the needs of the litigator. The use of black-and-white copies eliminates the effect of coloration and alters the impression made by a given map. Nevertheless such techniques are viewed as legitimate and are not subject to challenge. In the Alaska boundary and the Palmas Island arbitrations, the United States prepared atlases based on extensive archival research. When Chief Justice Melville Fuller wrote the opinion in the case of *Louisiana v. Mississippi* (1905), as noted in Chapter 3, the documents available to him included atlases assembled by the two contending states. In all of these instances the Louisiana atlas exerted an obvious effect on Fuller's opinion. Cartographic historians study the details of the original of a particular map, such as that done by Melish in 1818, but international lawyers seeking to define a trend rely upon copies and eschew a painstaking analysis characteristic of historical research.

---

[37] *Re Labrador Boundary,* 2 Dominion Law Reports 401, 427 (1927).
[38] *United States v. Texas,* 162 U.S. 1, 38 (1895).

The fourth principle is that maps used as evidence may depict lands and seas which do not exist, as strange as that may seem. The Hague Codification Conference (1930) sought to prepare a basis for a multilateral convention on the law of the sea with emphasis on the rules for drawing maritime boundaries. Gilbert Gidel, a French professor of international law, participated in the conference and subsequently wrote an authoritative volume on the law of the sea.[39] In this work he included diagrams of an imaginary coast showing the effect of islands on the delimitation of the seaward boundary of a state. In 1968, the state of Louisiana submitted a list of exhibits to the U.S. Supreme Court in a maritime boundary case and included the Gidel diagrams, to which Justice Potter Stewart made reference in his opinion.[40]

LAW, TERRITORY, AND CONFLICT

The progressive reduction of conflict among states is the primary goal of international law. Since territorial disputes more often than not undergird conflict, the test of international law must be its ability to resolve these without resort to armed force. In the period since the end of the Second World War the record is mixed. A signal success was the role of the International Bank for Reconstruction and Development (the World Bank) in bringing to an end in 1960 the confrontation between India and Pakistan over the division of the waters of the Indus River. The bank's good offices brought the parties together, and they assigned to the bank a continuing role as an observer to ensure compliance with their agreement.[41] The de-escalation of conflict under the auspices of an intergovernmental organization (IGO) lends support to the world order school and encourages the progressive development of international law.

In the United Nations, the Western Powers collaborated to bring about the peaceful settlement of territorial disputes on the model of the Indus River treaty, yet the breakup of European colonial empires transformed the political map and engendered many boundary problems, some ancient and others new. The status of Portuguese India was one of these. As a dominant sea power in the early 1500s, Portugal had founded commercial centers throughout Asia, among them Goa and associated territories on the western coast of India. Indian independence in 1947 left the new republic with Portuguese enclaves within its national territory, and in 1961 Indian army units occupied these vestiges of European imperialism. The United Nations Security Council attempted to pass a resolution calling for an Indian withdrawal and a negotiated solution, but some members of the Security Council, including the Soviet Union, blocked the proposal. International opinion favored the argument that because Goa was tied to India by history and culture, the use of armed force to regain national territory was permissible.[42] In this sense the action in Goa was a war of national liberation, which met with tacit approval.

---

[39]Gilbert Gidel, *Le droit international public de la mer* (The public international law of the sea) (Chateauroux: Établissements Mellotteée, 1934), 3: 633.
[40]*U.S. v. Louisiana: Appendix G, Map Exhibits and Related Materials for Brief of the State of Louisiana* (filed September 3, 1968), exhibit 58, p. 9. See also *United States v. Louisiana,* 394 U.S. 11, 24 n. 29 (1969).
[41]Indus Water Treaty (September 19, 1960), reprinted in *American Journal of International Law* 55 (July 1961): 797.
[42]Quincy Wright, "The Goa Incident," *American Journal of International Law* 56 (July 1962): 617, 619.

The Falkland/Malvinas Islands present a parallel case study. The aforementioned Treaty of Tordesillas (1494) placed this archipelago within the South American dominions of Spain. Following its war of independence (1810–1816) Argentina inherited the title to the historic lands of the Spanish crown, and these included the Islas Malvinas. Effective control eluded the islands, and they were sometimes a haven for pirates. In 1833, the British established a permanent colony and proclaimed their sovereignty over the Falkland Islands.[43] Unlike Mexico's acquiescence in the American occupation of the Northern Archipelago off the coast of California, Argentina repeatedly protested the British presence in the Islas Malvinas. Suddenly, in April 1982, Argentine army units occupied the islands in the name of recovering historic territory—the same position taken by India in the seizure of Goa. Great Britain responded with a successful military operation, and in two months the islands were again under British rule.[44] By 1992, diplomatic relations between Argentina and Great Britain had been reestablished, but the legacy of the war remained. How could two governments with a long-standing tradition of friendship fall to fighting over two remote islands in the South Atlantic? A territorial dispute touches the sensitive nerve of national pride leaving the partisans of law and diplomacy isolated and without influence. Goa and the Falkland/Malvinas Islands again remind us of the anarchic character of the international system.

Topics for Discussion

1. Under customary international law, what are the five means by which a state may acquire title to territory?
2. Outline the legal questions arising from the status of the Northern Archipelago. Why are the islands so symbolic for a Mexican patriot? How can international law contribute to a rational response to this issue?
3. What was the Stimson doctrine? How does it apply to other areas of the world?
4. Many new states lay claim to unredeemed national territory. Does international law justify the use of force in gaining control of the territory?

---

[43]For a legal and political history, see Julius Goebel, Jr., *The Struggle for the Falkland Islands* (New Haven: Yale University Press, 1927).

[44]Useful documentary collections are Raphael Perl, *The Falkland Islands Dispute in International Law and Politics* (New York: Oceana Publications, 1983); and Carlos Alberto Silva, *La politica international de la nacion Argentina* (International politics of the Argentine nation) (Buenos Aires: Ministry of the Interior, 1946).

CHAPTER 12

Law of the Sea

A legal regime of the oceans serves as an example of the necessity of international law in the relations of states. As early as 1370, the merchants and seafarers of Barcelona codified the customary law of the sea into a single code initially published under the title *Consulado del mar.*[1] The code addressed such subjects as neutrality and exerted an indirect influence on John Marshall's decision in the *Nereide* case of 1815. The scope of the law of the sea has progressively expanded to include jurisdiction, human rights, territory, and state responsibility. The United Nations Convention on the Law of the Sea (1982) is a constitution for the oceans designed for the governance of three quarters of the earth's surface. The law of the sea is important both in a substantive sense and as a case study on the development of international law.

THE LEGISLATIVE PROCESS

Codification is the process of moving from customary to conventional international law. The process is often frustratingly slow, and setbacks do occur. Nevertheless one of the major advances in international law since the founding of the United Nations has been the development of a sequence of steps through which conventional law comes into being.[2] Five phases characterize the process: (a) deliberation, (b) decision, (c) application, (d) adjudication, and (e) incorporation. The deliberative phase begins with the International Law Commission (ILC), a consultative organ of the General Assembly of the United Nations. Established in 1947 by a resolution of the General Assembly, the ILC has grown from fifteen to thirty-four members charged with the mission of examining current issues in international law and formulating draft articles for lawmaking conventions. The members are elected by the General Assembly for a term of five years and are chosen on the basis of their expertise. Meeting annually in Geneva, usually May and June, the ILC prepares a two-volume yearbook. The first part is the record of their deliberations on draft articles, which comprise the second part. The output is a set of recommendations to the General Assembly, and they are not binding on the world organization or its members. In three sessions (1952–1954) the ILC prepared papers for its yearbook on the law of the sea, thereby completing the initial phase of the legislative process.[3]

---

[1]Sometimes referred to as the "Consulate of the Sea," the code is often cited under its Italian title "Consolato del mare." See Briggs, p. 19; and Wilson, p. 399.

[2]The following discussion does not apply to humanitarian law (law of war), which is the responsibility of the International Committee of the Red Cross/Red Crescent.

[3]The U.S. Supreme Court cited an ILC study on historic bays as a definitive statement on maritime boundary delimitation. See *U.S. v. Louisiana (Alabama and Mississippi Boundary Case),* 470 U.S. 93, 102 (1984).

The ILC report goes to the General Assembly's Sixth Committee (international law), where the membership is political and it views the draft articles from that perspective.[4] The relationship between the commission and the committee lacks a clear definition.[5] Generally, the committee is entitled to provide the commission with guidance and direction in, for example, the selection of topics to be considered. Once the ILC submits its report, the committee is unlikely to insist upon any changes. In sum, the commission represents legal scholarship and the committee a political agenda. That the two have developed a stable working relationship testifies to the maturity of the deliberative process.

The decisional phase may take one of two forms. The General Assembly will either act directly or refer a complex matter to a universal international conference. Accordingly, the United Nations Conference on the Law of the Sea (UNCLOS I) assembled in Geneva in 1958 and produced three conventions. UNCLOS II followed in 1960, and delegates were unable to agree on such subjects as the breadth of the territorial sea. The General Assembly then formed the special Committee on the Peaceful Uses of the Sea-Bed and the Ocean Floor, after which a preliminary study called in 1970 for a general international conference.[6] Accordingly, UNCLOS III opened in Caracas in 1973 and completed its work at Montego Bay, Jamaica, in 1982. This time the output was a comprehensive convention consisting of 320 articles, plus annexes on such subjects as compulsory arbitration of disputes.[7] As is standard in a lawmaking treaty, a concluding article provided that the Law of the Sea (LOS) convention would enter into force one year after the number of states parties to the convention reached sixty. The requirement was fulfilled in 1994. As of December 1998, 127 governments had ratified the convention. Canada, Israel, and the United States had withheld their signatures. Among the Group of Seven (G-7)[8] only the two North American members remained aloof. All other leading industrial powers had recognized that their national interests lay in aligning themselves with a legal regime for the oceans.[9]

Application in terms of policy implementation is the next phase in the process. The convention provided for the establishment of the International Seabed Authority (ISA), which is located in Kingston, Jamaica. The ISA's mission is to allocate in an equitable fashion the right to explore and exploit the resources of the seabed and subsoil outside of national jurisdiction. The procedure involves the granting of licenses in exchange for the payment of royalties, which are shared among the states' parties to the convention. The principal reason for the refusal of the United States to adhere to

---

[4]The General Assembly divides its work among seven committees, which deal with questions of security, economics, humanitarian relief, non-self-governing territories, the budget, law, and special political questions.

[5]Herbert W. Briggs, *The International Law Commission* (Ithaca: Cornell University Press, 1965), 342–346; and United Nations, General Assembly, Res. 174, *Statute of the International Law Commission,* November 21, 1947 (A/CN.4/4), see especially art. 16 on the "Progressive Development of International Law," 4–5.

[6]"Promoting Peaceful Uses of the Sea-Bed," *Yearbook of the United Nations, 1970,* 24: 60–83.

[7]General Assembly, Draft Final Act of the Third United Nations Conference on the Law of the Sea (October 21, 1982), A/CONF. 62/121, reprinted in 21 I.L.M. 1245 (1982); and United Nations, *The Law of the Sea: Official Text of the United Nations Convention on the Law of the Sea,* E.83.V.5. Hereafter the LOS convention.

[8]Canada, France, Germany, Great Britain, Italy, Japan, Russia, and the United States.

[9]United Nations, Division for Ocean Affairs and the Law of the Sea, Office of the Legal Adviser, *Law of the Sea Bulletin,* no. 39 (1999): 1–8.

the convention is the insistence that the mining of the ocean floor should be open to everyone on a competitive basis and not subject to an international authority; yet other governments with the capability of deep-sea exploration regard the ISA's role in a positive light.

The implementation of the terms of the convention will inevitably lead to disagreements, and these require adjudication. To that end states adhering to the convention have established the International Tribunal for the Law of the Sea (ITLOS), which convenes in Hamburg, Germany. The selection of the twenty-one judges of the tribunal assures universal representation except, of course, for those states not adhering to the convention. All states parties to the convention have a treaty obligation to refer disputes to arbitration or adjudication. Normally this commitment means an application for relief to the tribunal, but nothing precludes turning to the ICJ or even to a special arbitral tribunal.

The *Saiga* case is representative of the tribunal's work. Flying the flag of the Caribbean republic of Saint Vincent and the Grenadines, the *Saiga* was a merchant vessel engaged in providing fuel for fishing boats off the coast of Guinea. Guinean officers arrested the *Saiga,* alleging that it was within their country's customs (contiguous) zone, a charge which proved difficult to sustain. The government of Saint Vincent and the Grenadines turned to the tribunal and applied for the release of the vessel and its crew. The tribunal found no evidence that the *Saiga* was indeed bunkering within the Guinean customs zone and ordered the release of the detainees and their ship, although the owners were required to provide a monetary surety against further legal proceedings.[10] The *Saiga* case reflects the maturity of the legal regime of the oceans and is indicative of the benefits of participating in it. For this reason all but a handful of governments have agreed to participate by ratifying the LOS convention.

The incorporation of international law into municipal law is the final phase of the process. Incorporation consists of the means through which the rules of international law become the standards for administrative and judicial decisions of national authorities. The *Mortensen* case discussed in Chapter 2 hinged on the question of whether Parliament had recognized as binding customary rules of international law regarding the delimitation of the territorial sea. The court concluded that these rules lacked judicial effect because they had never been incorporated into Scottish law. Incorporation is the touchstone that tests the efficacy of international law. Ratification of a treaty by a government is usually the means of incorporation, for most constitutions stipulate that a ratified treaty is the law of the land.

Incorporation may, however, come about through more indirect methods. One of these is an executive order or proclamation, whereby articles of a treaty are given legal effect without accepting the complete document. State practice is the conscious adherence to the norms of international law in the administration of policy, and through such state practice a government may complete the process of incorporation. President Reagan issued two proclamations incorporating provisions of the LOS convention into

---

[10]*The M/V Saiga* (Saint Vincent and the Grenadines v. Guinea), International Tribunal for the Law of the Sea (December 4, 1997), reprinted in 37 I.L.M. 360, 375–376. Also see Barbara Kwiatkowska, "Inauguration of the ITLOS Jurisprudence: The Saint Vincent and Grenadines v. Guinea *M/V Saiga* Cases," *Ocean Development and International Law* 30 (1999): 43, 48.

federal practice.[11] In the first proclamation (1983) the United States laid claim to an exclusive economic zone (EEZ) covering coastal waters to a distance of 200 nautical miles. Article 57 of the convention provides states parties the right to establish an EEZ of this magnitude, and the Reagan administration took advantage of that provision. The second proclamation (1988) extended the breadth of the territorial sea from the Jeffersonian standard (Chapter 1) of three to twelve nautical miles. Broadening the belt of adjacent waters under the sovereign jurisdiction of the United States was allowable under article 3 of the convention. Neither proclamation, however, made reference to the convention itself, but simply took advantage of its provisions, the argument being that the convention represents customary international law and the benefits bestowed by it are open to all states. The counterargument is that international law embodies both rights and duties, and claiming the first requires accepting the second. An alternative means of incorporation without ratification is a joint resolution of Congress. Legislation to enact the 1988 proclamation on the territorial sea was introduced. It passed the House of Representatives but was pigeonholed in the Senate. In sum, presidential proclamations or an act of Congress can achieve what normally would be done through treaty ratification.

OCEAN LAW

UNCLOS III completed the arduous and often frustrating task of formulating a legal regime for the oceans. Six geographic zones define the law of the sea: (a) interior waters, (b) the territorial sea, (c) the contiguous zone, (d) the exclusive economic zone, (e) the continental shelf, and (f) the high seas. In each zone the rules vary in accordance with the principle that sovereignty and distance have an inverse relationship, in that zone-by-zone sovereign authority decreases until on the high seas it is limited to vessels of the flag state. A careful balance is struck between the need for the littoral state to protect its vital interests and the concept of the oceans as a common area (*res communis*) held in public trust.[12] In the history of the law of the sea the work of two publicists typifies the contest between those who favor freedom of the seas and those seeking to enclose them. In 1609, Hugo Grotius published *Mare Liberum* (freedom of the seas) in which he refuted the claims of Portugal and Spain to broad expanses of the oceans, as represented in the Treaty of Tordesillas. Grotius based his argument on the Roman law that the oceans are *communis omnium naturali jure* (natural law makes the oceans a common heritage). The rebuttal came in 1635 with the publication of *Mare Clausam* by the English jurist John Selden, who supported the right of the king to acquire sovereignty over adjacent seas.[13] The Grotius–Selden debate continues to dominate the discussion of the law of the sea. Major maritime powers struggle to defend their strategic

---

[11]Proclamation 5030: Exclusive Economic Zone (March 10, 1983) in National Archives and Records Administration, *Codification of Presidential Proclamations and Executive Orders, 1945–1989* (Washington, D.C.: Government Printing Office, n.d.), 248–249; and Proclamation 5928: Territorial Sea (December 27, 1988), ibid., 666–667.

[12]Arvid Pardo, "Ocean Space and Mankind," *Third World Quarterly* 6 (July 1984): 559, 566.

[13]Thomas Wemyss Fulton, *The Sovereignty of the Sea* (London: William Blackwood, 1911; reprint, Millwood, N.Y.: Kraus Reprint Co., 1976), pp. 338–372.

and commercial interests while small states often see the enclosure of coastal waters as the only means of national survival.

INTERIOR WATERS

The problem of interior (inland) waters appears superficially straightforward, but as noted in the discussion of the Anglo-Norwegian *Fisheries* case in Chapter 10, the fixing of a line between the high seas and interior waters is a complex exercise. In the *Louisiana Boundary* case, the U.S. Supreme Court defined the coastline as the ordinary low-water mark which separates the ocean from inland waters.[14] Yet in the *Thames Estuary Radio* case, the Court of Appeals in Great Britain applied a more expensive standard by placing the coastline at a low-tide elevation, which was defined as a "naturally formed area of drying land" above water at low tide and submerged at high tide.[15] The United States practices a restrictive policy of limiting its maritime claims by adhering to a rigorous definition of the coastline, while other states may refer to rocks and outcroppings as points along which to chart their juridical coasts.[16] The legal definition of the coastline is sufficiently broad to allow a government to lay rather expansive claims and still remain within the limits of the LOS convention.

Minimally interior waters include estuaries of rivers, bayous, and bays, but the determination of whether a body of water is a bay is complex. The LOS convention recognizes both a juridical and an historic bay. The former must pass two geometrical tests. First the closing line connecting the two headlands of the bay must not exceed twenty-four nautical miles. Second, a semicircle whose diameter is the closing line must cover more water than land.[17] If the land enclosed by the semicircle is greater than the sea, the body of water is not a juridical bay, but a mere curvature of the coast. Islands are not considered in this equation. In notational form the formula appears as:

$$Sea \geq IIr^2/2$$

The area of the sea must be equal to or greater than that of a semicircle (i.e., the area of a circle divided by two).[18]

Since land forms are continuously changing, the effect of natural forces may alter the results of the semicircle test over time. Accordingly, governments prefer the standard of a historical bay, which is supported by prescriptive rights. The uninterrupted and unchallenged exercise of sovereignty over a body of coastal water for a period to time (usually taken to be fifty years) established title to that territory even though the outline of

---

[14]See Chapter 11, *United States v. Louisiana*, 394 U.S. 14–15 (1969).

[15]See Chapter 2, *Post Office v. Estuary Radio, Ltd.,* 3 All England Law Reports 663, 675 (1967).

[16]Jonathan I. Charney, "Rocks That Cannot Sustain Human Habitation," *American Journal of International Law* 93 (October 1999): 853, 873.

[17]The semicircle test was first proposed by the U.S. delegation at the Hague Codification Conference (1930). See Aaron L. Shalowitz, *Shore and Sea Boundaries,* U.S. Coast and Geodetic Survey (Washington, D.C.: Government Printing Office, 1962), chapter 4. A detailed description of the mathematics of maritime boundary delimitation is J. Peter Bernhardt, et al., *Developing Standard Guidelines for Evaluating Straight Baselines: Limits in the Seas, No. 106,* U.S. Department of State, Bureau of Oceans and International Environmental and Scientific Affairs (Washington, D.C.: By the Department, 1987), 36–37.

[18]The formula is adapted from Modesto Seara Vázquez, *Derecho internacional público* (Public international-al law), 9th ed. (Mexico City: Editorial Porrúa, 1983), 264.

the coast may not meet the required geometrical tests. The Chesapeake Bay and Long Island Sound are examples of the application of the historic waters doctrine. In sum, the convention lays down rules, but the application of these is open to interpretation and not subject to challenge unless the claims of the coastal state are extreme.[19]

The dividing line between interior waters and the ocean is the baseline, which is the point from which the seaward limits of maritime zones are measured. Again, the convention recognizes two types of baselines with a third variation to cover the special circumstances of islands. The normal baseline follows the sinuosities of the coast, whereas the straight baseline adheres to the general outline of the coast without attempting to mirror each curvature in the tidal shore. For example, the normal baseline for the continental United States is 53,677 statute miles while the straight baseline is 4,840 miles. Similarly, the normal baseline for Louisiana is 7,721 miles as compared with 397 miles under the straight baseline rule.[20] In theory each segment of a straight baseline should be no greater than 12 nautical miles. Otherwise the coastal state would take advantage of the rule to enclose broad expanses of the sea. In practice, governments do just that. Myanmar (Burma) has a straight baseline of 222 and Ecuador 147 nautical miles. Finland has the shortest with only 8 nautical miles.[21] The LOS convention stipulates a restrictive interpretation of the rule on straight baselines and urges states parties to use the principle with the limits of self-discipline.[22] The alternative is the progressive enclosure of the oceans—a development that the LOS convention was drafted to prevent.

The effect of offshore or barrier islands on baselines is significant. The LOS convention defines an island as land capable of supporting human life. Minimally that means the availability of fresh water. Islands in this sense have their own baselines, and often the islands serve as points along which to establish a straight baseline. In this sense, barrier islands may constitute the juridical coast of a state rather than the mainland shore. Rocks and shoals do not qualify for maritime zones, but they may serve as baseline points even though they are above water only a few hours a day. Similarly artificial islands, such as platforms set up for oil or natural gas exploration, are not entitled to maritime zones although their operators may exercise jurisdiction within 500 meters of the structure. The legal significance of islands was the issue in deciding the Alaska boundary arbitration of 1903 (Chapter 11), and the question remains a key issue in the law of the sea.

Baselines usually delimit the outer seaward boundary of a state, but may also play a role in delimiting maritime boundaries between adjacent states. Equidistance is the operative principle in customary international law.[23] The boundary between Canada

---

[19]In the 1980s, the government of Libya asserted that the Gulf of Sidra was part of its national territory—a claim lacking support in either customary or conventional international law.

[20]For tabular data see U.S. Department of Commerce, Coast and Geodetic Survey, *Coastline of the United States* (Washington, D.C.: By the Department, 1948), single sheet.

[21]P. B. Beazley, "Territorial Sea Baselines," *International Hydrographic Review,* 48 (January 1971): 143, 145.

[22]W. Michael Reisman and Gayl S. Westerman, *Straight Baselines in Maritime Boundary Delimitation* (New York: St. Martin's Press, 1992), pp. 75–77; and Louis B. Sohn, "Baseline Considerations," in 1 *International Maritime Boundaries,* ed. Jonathan I. Charney and Lewis M. Alexander (Dordrecht: Martinus Nijhoff, 1993), pp. 153, 160.

[23]S. Whittemore Boggs, "Problems of Water-Boundary Definition: Median Lines and International Boundaries through Territorial Waters," *Geographical Review* 27 (July 1937): 445.

and the United States in the Great Lakes is based on a median line. The LOS convention modifies equidistance to take into account the social and economic needs of the coastal communities. The result is the development of the rule of proportionality, whereby the ocean fronted on by two or more states will be divided roughly on a ratio of the length of a country's coastline to the amount of sea allocated to it.[24] Proportionality also applies to the division of resources on the continental shelf and to the formation of fishing zones. The concept is relatively new and remains largely judgmental in its application.

TERRITORIAL SEA

Popular beliefs about the territorial seas suggest that the coastal state exercises unrestricted sovereignty over this belt of coastal waters. The reality is that the jurisdiction of the state in question is limited by natural servitudes. In this setting, a servitude is an obligation to the international maritime community. The provision of navigational aids, coastal charts, and air–sea rescue operations are the duty of a state in its territorial sea. Vessels of all states, even warships, enjoy a right of innocent passage through the territorial sea so long as they do not pose a threat to the safety and security of the coastal community. The territorial sea represents adjacent waters over which the littoral state enforces its laws within a framework of obligations *erga omnes*.

Customary international law gave the territorial sea a breadth the equivalent of the effective range of coastal artillery.[25] The drafters of the LOS convention recognized that the cannon-shot rule as it was called had long since given way to national variations, so they proposed a standard limit of twelve nautical miles, which states parties to the convention are obligated as a matter of good faith to uphold.[26] The twelve-mile limit has now entered into customary law, as evidenced by President Reagan's proclamation in 1988 that it applied to the United States. Again, the difficulty of defining the coastline comes to the fore. The problem is perennial. In 1805, the British High Court of Admiralty rendered in the case of *The Anna* a decision that set a precedent. *The Anna,* a vessel of uncertain registry but presumably American, was approaching the entrance of the Mississippi River and was seized by a British privateer—a ship commissioned to capture enemy merchantmen in time of war. Privateeering was profitable, and the captors took *The Anna* to a British prize court, which they hoped would award them the vessel and its cargo. The owners of *The Anna* contended that the ship was within the territorial waters of the United States when captured, and therefore the seizure by a British privateer was illegal. Indeed, *The Anna* was over three miles from the mainland, but it was within two miles of mud banks forming alluvial islands. Although the islands were uninhabited, the court ruled that they were U.S. territory from

---

[24]P. B. Beazley, "Developments in Maritime Delimitation," *Hydrographic Journal* 39 (January 1986): 5, 8.

[25]Cornelius van Bynkershoek, *De domino maris* (Dominion of the sea) (Leyden: 1744), in 11 *Classics of International Law,* ed. James Brown Scott (Washington, D.C.: Carnegie Endowment for International Peace, 1923), 363–365.

[26]Nigeria has ratified the LOS convention but continues to proclaim a territorial sea thirty nautical miles in breadth. Ecuador, which has not signed the convention, insists it has a territorial sea of 200 nautical miles. For a listing of maritime boundary claims, see U.S. Central Intelligence Agency, *The World Factbook 1999* (Washington, D.C.: By the Agency, 1999).

which the territorial sea was to be measured, and that the capture was unlawful. Sir William Scott stated in his opinion:

> I think that the protection of territory is to be reckoned from these islands . . . Whether they are composed of earth or solid rock, will not vary the right of dominion.[27]

The High Court of Admiralty decided a series of cases dealing with the disposition of captured ships during the same period. In one such case Justice Scott outlined the criteria for satisfying a claim of sovereignty over coastal waters when he wrote that "ancient jurisdiction" is to be proven:

> By formal acts of authority, by holding courts of conservancy of navigation, by ceremonious processions to ascertain the boundaries, in the nature of perambulations, by marked distinctions in maps and charts prepared under public inspection and control, by levying of tolls, by exclusive fisheries, by permanent and visible emblems of power there established, by the appointment of officers specially designated to that station, by stationary guardships, by records and monuments, showing that the right has always been asserted, and whenever resisted, asserted with effect. This is the natural evidence to be looked for generally.[28]

The ICJ referred to this standard as a precedent in its 1951 decision in the Anglo-Norwegian *Fisheries* case, as discussed in Chapter 10.

The solution presented in the LOS convention is that of straight baselines from which the territorial sea is to be measured. Inscribing a baseline along a mobile coast, such as the birdfoot delta of a major river system, is an ongoing task. Spring floods bring deposits of earth creating new coastal hummocks and thereby altering the baseline. To achieve stable maritime boundaries, the convention incorporated the Bangladesh principle. The delegate from Bangladesh pointed out that the delta of the Ganges River dominates his country's coastline, and seasonal changes in the alluvial plain of the delta make the establishment of a permanent baseline difficult, if not impossible. By comparison, the rocky coast of Norway would not present this problem, but any government having to contend with a major river, for example, the Amazon or the Mississippi, would be faced with the frustrating challenge of where to put the baseline. The decision in *The Anna* is instructive on this point. As an expedient, the Bangladesh principle allows a government to declare by fiat a permanent baseline irrespective of such controlling geographic features as islands.[29] In its final form, the convention incorporated the proposal as follows:

> Where because of the presence of a delta and other natural conditions the coastline is highly unstable, the appropriate points may be selected along the furthest seaward extent of the low-water line and, notwithstanding subsequent regression of the low-water line, the straight baselines shall remain effective until changed by the coastal State in accordance with this Convention.[30]

---

[27] *The Anna,* 5 Christopher Robinson's English Admiralty Reports 373, 385d (1805).
[28] *The Twee Gebroeders,* 3 ibid., 336, 347.
[29] See statement by Ambassador Rashid (Bangladesh) in 2 *Third United Nations Conference on the Law of the Sea: Official Records,* 20 June–29 August 1974 (A/CONF.62/C.2/SR.1-46), 109.
[30] LOS convention, article 7(2).

The Bangladesh principle is indicative of the nature of the law of the sea. The convention represents a major diplomatic achievement, the goal of which was to make the law of the sea essentially a technical issue. The semicircle test for a juridical bay is a case in point. Yet as the development of rules progresses, they grow less and less specific until the stage is reached at which a government can do rather much what it wants to. For example, to compute the mean low-water mark requires lunar observations over a period of eighteen years, and it stretches the limits of credibility to believe that scientific measurements to establish a tidal boundary will be made for such a long period of time. Most governments simply make an arbitrary decision that serves their national interest. The search for technical perfection may, in the final analysis, give way to *raison d'état*.

CONTIGUOUS ZONE

The *Saiga* case hinged upon the charge that the vessel had violated the Guinean contiguous zone. Although the tribunal did not sustain the charge, its deliberations made clear the complexity—even ambiguity—of the contiguous zone. The zone is a belt of water measured twenty-four nautical miles from the baseline, within which the coastal state may, if it wishes, enforce its laws regarding customs, immigration, taxation, and environmental protection. The rule of hot pursuit applies in the contiguous zone, and felons fleeing mainland authorities will find no sanctuary there. Most governments have designated contiguous zones, but these do not affect the right of innocent passage, especially in international straits.

EXCLUSIVE ECONOMIC ZONE

The exclusive economic zone (EEZ) represents a judgmental and still controversial concept. A map showing the EEZ of the United States in the Atlantic, Gulf of Mexico, and the Pacific accompanied President Reagan's proclamation of 1983.[31] The South Pacific is covered with a series of circles, each of which represents a U.S. island with its own EEZ. Other states in the Pacific were quick to enter a demurrer. The LOS convention identifies the EEZ as an area measured 200 nautical miles from the baseline within which the coastal state possesses "sovereign rights" for the purpose of exploring, utilizing, and conserving natural resources in the ocean, on the seabed, and in the subsoil. Fishing and the offshore recovery of oil qualify as activities reserved to the zonal state. Yet governments are often reluctant to acknowledge that while the convention bestows upon them exclusive rights, it also imposes duties with regard to the preservation of the marine environment and respect for the treaty rights of other states. A premise of international law is that the right of a state to act is accompanied by the duty to act responsibly. States with overlapping EEZs are now experimenting with joint economic development zones, an idea not foreseen in the convention, but one which shows promise.[32]

---

[31]U.S. Department of State, *The United States' 200 Nautical Mile Exclusive Economic Zone as Specified by Presidential Proclamation* (March 10, 1983), Perspective Projections 4947 4-83 STATE (GE), single sheet.
[32]David M. Ong, "Joint Development of Common Offshore Oil and Gas Deposits: 'Mere' State Practice or Customary International Law," *American Journal of International Law* 93 (October 1999): 771, 777.

CONTINENTAL SHELF

The LOS convention defines the continental shelf as the submarine extension of the land out to the end of the continental margin or, alternatively, to a distance of 200 nautical miles measured from the baseline, whichever is greater. For example, the continental margin of California is barely two miles in some points, yet the convention authorizes exclusive jurisdiction out to a distance equal to that of the EEZ. With reference to the continental shelf, two observations are in order. First, the fact that a coastal state does not develop the resources of this submarine area does not adversely affect its sovereign right to do so. The lack of development does not mean abandonment in the sense of a failure to exercise prescriptive rights. In this sense the continental land mass dominates the sea, and even the presence of a nearby island belonging to another state does not alter the title to the seabed and subsoil of the continental power. Second, jurisdiction over the continental shelf is limited by the treaty obligation to protect the marine environment. Economic development which may threaten that environment is unlawful.

HIGH SEAS

The LOS convention represents a triumph of Grotius's commitment to the freedom of the seas (*mare liberum*) over such efforts as the Treaty of Tordesillas to enclose the oceans. Every state, including landlocked powers, possesses the inherent right of access to the oceans for purposes of commerce, humanitarian activity, and national security. Both the Aegean Sea and the South China Sea present challenges to this position. In each instance a mainland state, Greece and China respectively, assert sovereignty over a series of islands with the presumption that each has a territorial sea. The result is the creation of a series of interlocking maritime boundaries, which have the cumulative impact of potentially pinching off arteries of maritime commerce. While neither the governments of Greece nor China have attempted such a maneuver, implicit in the legal regime of islands is a resurrection of the idea of enclosed seas (*mare clausum*).[33] Shifts in the international balance of power may well alter the convention's concept of freedom of the seas.

THE GULF OF MAINE

The relations between Canada and the United States in the Gulf of Maine are representative of many issues in the law of the sea. Initially the exploration of the continental shelf was to be a joint venture, but the pressure of politics and policy ultimately brought the dispute before a chamber of the ICJ in 1984. The ICJ had dealt with the problem of dividing the waters separating adjacent states in the *North Sea Continental Shelf Case* (Germany, Great Britain, and the Netherlands) in 1969.[34] The three states

---

[33] Andrew Wilson, *The Aegean Dispute,* International Institute for Strategic Studies, Adelphi Papers No. 105 (London: By the Institute, 1979), 23; and Richard E. Hull, "The South China Sea: Future Source of Prosperity or Conflict in South East Asia?" *Strategic Forum: Institute for National Strategic Studies* 60 (February 1996): 2–3.

[34] Louis B. Sohn and Kirsten Gustafson, *The Law of the Sea* (St. Paul: West Publishing Co., 1984), pp. 65–68.

border the North Sea, and their respective claims to maritime zones, especially the continental shelf, overlapped. Under the heading of the rule of proportionality, the ICJ determined that each country should share the resources in proportion to the length of its coastline. The court invoked this principle in the *Gulf of Maine* case. First a line of equidistance between Canada and the United States was drawn, and then the boundary was adjusted in accordance with proportionality.

The process allows the court flexibility in adjusting to specific geographical circumstances, but this very freedom of action implies that the technical rules of the law of the sea are not as fully developed as would appear at first blush. Specifically, the ICJ stated:

> There has been no systematic definition of the equitable criteria that may be taken into consideration for an international maritime delimitation, and this would in any event be difficult *a priori,* because of their highly variable adaptability to different concrete situations. Codification efforts have left this field untouched.[35]

If efforts at codification through the legislative process developed by the United Nations are incomplete, so is the guidance afforded by precedent. The *North Sea Continental Shelf* case applied the concept of proportionality in a fashion that was not followed in the *Gulf of Maine* case, leaving practitioners in the field of international law with few hard and fast rules to follow in boundary delimitation cases.[36]

JURISDICTION

The *Lotus* case (1928)[37] focused on the question of which national code obtained on a merchant vessel involved in a binational dispute. The LOS convention provides that every government has the right to charter a ship under its own flag, and that the flag state has exclusive jurisdiction aboard that vessel. A genuine link must, however, exist between the ship and the state in question. Often such a link is not readily apparent. In 1987, President Reagan initiated a policy of "reflagging" as United States vessels Kuwaiti tankers in the Persian Gulf so that they would be secure from attack. Yet U.S. law specifies:

> The term "vessel of the United States" . . . means a vessel belonging in whole or in part to the United States, or any citizen thereof, or any corporation created by or under the laws of the United States, or of any State, Territory, District, or possession thereof.[38]

The test of a genuine link is explicit and consistent with the requirements later adopted in the LOS convention. Whether Kuwaiti tankers fulfilled the statutory requirement is doubtful.

---

[35]*Case Concerning Delimitation of the Maritime Boundary in the Gulf of Maine Area* (Canada v. United States), Judgment of 12 October 1984, ICJ Reports 1984, 70. Also see 23 I.L.M. 1197.
[36]Lewis M. Alexander, ed., *The Gulf of Maine Decision: An International Discussion,* American Society of International Law, Studies in Transnational Legal Policy, No. 21 (St. Paul: West Publishing Co., 1988), 89.
[37]See Chapter 9.
[38]Crimes and Criminal Procedure (June 25, 1948), 62 Stat. 683.

With the right of exclusive jurisdiction the flag state incurs obligations. These include the maintenance of the vessel, its safe operation on the high seas, and the conduct of periodic inspections to ensure that the vessel meets international regulations regarding lifesaving and communications equipment. Some governments, notably Liberia and Panama, have a record of chartering vessels through an administrative procedure which falls short of these standards. Entrepreneurs will often seek the charter of a foreign government in order to evade labor legislation covering the wages and the working conditions of the crew. Adherence to the requirement for a genuine link would enhance fair labor standards and contribute to maritime safety. Flag states must also use their resources to combat slavery and piracy, for the slaver and the pirate remain *hostis humani generis* (universal enemies of humankind).

Maritime sovereignty is a particularly sensitive issue when public vessels, that is, warships or other ships owned and operated by a government for a noncommercial purpose, are involved. In 1970, Simas Kudirka, a Lithuanian seaman and Soviet citizen, jumped from a Russian fishing vessel onto the deck of a U.S. Coast Guard cutter. Both ships were on the high seas. Kudirka requested political asylum on the accurate thesis that the Coast Guard ship was U.S. territory. The captain of the cutter then allowed Soviet officials to return him forcibly to his ship, an act that caused a wave of protests. President Nixon ordered a review of the policy on asylum to prevent the repetition of such an event. The sovereign status of public vessels may not be compromised. Commercial vessels on the high seas are, however, subject to visit and search. A warship may stop a merchantman to check its papers. This act lawfully includes confirming the vessel's keel number, in the course of which the boarding party has an opportunity to inspect the ship.

A CONUNDRUM

The legal regime of the polar regions offers a helpful parallel in understanding the law of the sea. For example, Antarctica and the high seas are both *res communis,* part of the common heritage of nations.[39] Since 1959, an international convention opened Antarctica to scientific exploration by all governments and at the same time closed this continental land mass to both military and commercial uses. By comparison, the Arctic is subdivided into sectors by the surrounding states and is exposed to commercial exploitation.[40] One environment is pristine, and the other is open to economic development. The law of the sea reflects the same contradictory tendencies. The LOS convention is a commitment to freedom of the seas and to peaceful economic development, yet it allows for formation of EEZs that encroach on the communal nature of the oceans. Reconciling these opposing trends will be the task of the next United Nations Conference on the Law of the Sea.

---

[39]Certain governments, notably Argentina and Chile, have in the 1940s sought to establish titles to territory in Antarctica, but these lack international recognition.

[40]Christopher Joyner, "United States Legislation and the Polar Oceans," *Ocean Development and International Law* 30 (1999): 265, 281–282.

Topics for Discussion

1. The Charter of the United Nations represents a commitment to the progressive codification of international law. Describe the structure and process established by the United Nations to achieve this goal.

2. The Law of the Sea convention recognizes six maritime zones, beginning with internal (interior) waters. What are the other five? How do they differ in terms of function and measurement?

3. In delimiting a maritime boundary between adjacent states, the principles of equidistance and equity apply. Are these concepts complementary or contradictory? How can they be reconciled in an arbitral or a judicial proceeding?

4. Historically the law of the sea has been a contest between Grotius (*mare liberum*) and Selden (*mare clausum*). The issue is not yet resolved. Why would great powers favor Grotius and small states favor Selden?

CHAPTER 13

International Agreements

International agreements are the means through which states defend their rights. Agreements embody the principle of reciprocity and guarantee to each state party an advantage based on mutual and balanced obligations. Without a formal undertaking, usually in the form of a treaty, efforts to secure collaboration among governments would be futile. Because of the centrality of treaties and other forms of agreement in international law, such publicists as Grotius and Vattel devoted considerable space to them, and in the modern period the League of Nations and then the United Nations established international tribunals for the purpose of interpreting treaties. Nevertheless, treaty law has not advanced to the stage of development as, for example, the law of the sea. Disagreement exists as to the definition of a treaty, to its standing, and to the method of interpreting it. Neither customary nor conventional international law has resolved these difficulties.

THE DEFINITIONAL PROBLEM

As a result of preliminary studies by the ILC, the United Nations sponsored a conference on the law of treaties, and in 1969 the Convention on the Law of Treaties was opened for signature. The convention defined a treaty as

> . . . an international agreement concluded between States in written form and governed by international law, whether embodied in a single instrument or in two or more related instruments and whatever its particular designation.[1]

During the drafting of the final text Latin American delegates proposed amendments to the effect that a lawful treaty must reflect mutual consent and embody fairness to all parties.[2] The majority rejected such qualifications leaving open the question of unequal agreements between a powerful and a weak state. In the *Eastern Greenland* case (1933)[3] the PCIJ had ruled that an oral statement by the Norwegian foreign minister to the Danish ambassador constituted an international commitment. The convention now requires an understanding in writing. The definition also applies to instruments not designated as "treaties." A parenthetical list includes such titles as protocol, charter,

---

[1]United Nations, Convention on the Law of Treaties, 22 May 1969 (A/CONF. 39/27), reprinted in 8 I.L.M. 679 (1969).
[2]Richard D. Kearney and Robert E. Dalton, "The Treaty on Treaties," *American Journal of International Law* 64 (July 1970): 495, 502–504.
[3]Chapter 11.

agreement, concordat, or convention. Irrespective of the official terminology all such undertakings are treaties.[4]

STANDING

The traditional theory is that treaties are contracts binding two or more states.[5] The contractual notion permits treaty novation or revision only on the basis of mutual consent. The expression *pacta sunt servanda* (treaties are to be observed in good faith) is the governing principle.[6] The opposing concept is *rebus sic stantibus* (the treaty is valid so long as the conditions under which it was signed remain in effect). Newly independent states embrace the latter argument as a means of obviating imposed agreements, some of which may date from the colonial period. Major powers favor the contractual theory because it enables them to resist demands of revisionist states. Realpolitik rather than the norms of international law governs the debate between these two interpretive principles. Above all, the idea of a contract is European and finds little or no counterpart in the African or Islamic tradition.[7] In the Global South the contractual theory appears as a guise for continued European domination. Nevertheless the convention favors *pacta sunt servanda* (article 26) and places restrictions on the resort to the doctrine of *rebus sic stantibus* (article 62), but the issue remains unresolved.

Consent is a fundamental tenet of treaty law. Every treaty must incorporate reciprocal obligations into which each party has freely entered. An imposed or octroyed treaty has no standing, for the use of force to secure acceptance of a treaty violates the commitment to sovereign equality.[8] A radical change in the fundamental circumstances governing the conclusion of a treaty will provide a basis for its termination. During the Russian Civil War (1918–1922) the government in Moscow concluded treaties of friendship with neighboring states in an effort to secure its frontiers. These treaties often contained clauses allowing Russian troops to cross the border in pursuit of guerrilla forces. Persia (modern Iran) concluded such a treaty authorizing the incursion of Russian forces into its territory.[9] The unequal nature of the treaty sparked nationalist resentment, and the seizure of power in Teheran by an Islamic party led to the abrupt denunciation of the treaty on the grounds that the new government was no longer within the Russian sphere of influence.[10] The Soviet Union made no response, leaving open the question of whether it still regarded the treaty as valid. Under the contractual theory the treaty could not be abrogated without the consent of both parties, but in this instance

---

[4]The legal vocabulary of some languages may, however, make a distinction. For example, the German word for treaty (*vertrag*) implies greater significance than an agreement (*abkommen*). A peace agreement would be a treaty, whereas an agreement would suffice for a territorial dispute.

[5]Lauterpacht's Oppenheim, 791.

[6]Von Glahn, 477.

[7]Evangelos Raftopoulos, *The Inadequacy of the Contractual Analogy in the Law of Treaties* (Athens: Hellenic Institute of International and Foreign Law, 1990), pp. 124–147.

[8]United Nations, General Assembly, Final Act of the United Nations Conference on the Law of Treaties, 23 May 1969 (A/CONF. 39/26), reprinted in 8 I.L.M. 728, 733 (1969).

[9]Treaty of Friendship (February 26, 1921), 9 L.N.T.S. 384 . Terminated by Iran on November 5, 1979.

[10]W. Michael Reisman, "Termination of the USSR's Treaty Right of Intervention in Iran," *American Journal of International Law* 74 (January 1980): 144, 149.

a revolutionary upheaval sufficed to bring about the change. In sum the comparison of a treaty to a contract is overdrawn, for the interest of the states' parties will always supersede the literal text of the agreement.

INTERPRETATION

In 1972, the United States and the Soviet Union agreed to an arms control treaty limiting the number of antiballistic missile (ABM) systems each side could deploy.[11] Nearly three decades later the United States sought to develop a National Missile Defense capable of intercepting and destroying incoming missiles. Moscow protested that the new system violated the intent of the ABM treaty, and Washington countered that the treaty did not preclude the development of new technology. The question became one of interpretation to which there are two schools of thought. The first focuses on the original intent of the negotiators as revealed in the text of the treaty as well as those preparatory documents (*travaux préparatoires*) which led to the final act. Shared expectations must precede any amendment to a treaty.[12] The second is the teleological approach, which stresses the ultimate goal of a treaty rather than its literal text.[13] In this instance an international tribunal or even the states parties to the agreement may interpret its terms in light of the overall objectives of the negotiators. The Russian position on the ABM treaty reflects the second approach by arguing that whatever innovations in technology may occur, the goal of the treaty was to limit the deployment of missile defense systems.

In 1976, the ICJ moved, albeit hesitantly, toward the teleological position. The issue was a dispute between Greece and Turkey over the continental shelf of the Aegean Sea. The Treaty of Lausanne (1923) restored peace between the two countries and provided that the islands of the Aegean would be Greek national territory.[14] Understandably for the time, the treaty made no mention of the continental shelf, for the question of whether islands possess title to adjacent submerged lands would not evoke general interest for another thirty years. In the summer of 1975, a Turkish oceanographic research ship, the *Sismik,* undertook exploratory work in the Aegean. The Turkish government argued that the continental shelf was an extension of its Anatolian territory and therefore under Turkish sovereignty. The Greek government countered with the teleological argument that the 1923 treaty implied its sovereignty over the submerged lands around the islands of the Aegean. Diplomatic protests proved unavailing, and Greece turned to the ICJ, which adopted the teleological approach. The ICJ ruled that Greece has sovereign and exclusive rights over the submerged lands of the Aegean.[15] Although the ICJ's determination regarding the purport of the Treaty of Lausanne is a precedent, most governments favor the more restrictive approach of original intent.

---

[11]Limitation of Anti-Ballistic Missile Systems (May 26, 1972), 23 U.S.T. 3435.
[12]Myres S. McDougal et al., *The Interpretation of Agreements and World Public Order: Principles of Content and Procedure* (New Haven: Yale University Press, 1967), pp. 83–94.
[13]Brownlie, 637–638.
[14]Treaty of Lausanne (July 24, 1923), 28 L.N.T.S. 12.
[15]*Aegean Continental Shelf Case* (Greece v. Turkey), Order: September 11, 1976, ICJ Reports 1978, reprinted in 15 I.L.M. 985. Also see Shaw, 346–347.

TREATY PROCESS

The steps in the process of formulating a treaty require examination because of the legal ramifications associated with the different phases: (a) negotiation, (b) paragraphing, (c) signature, (d) ratification, (e) proclamation, and (f) implementation. The process begins with negotiation between plenipotentiaries, and two questions arise. Are the negotiators lawfully entitled to represent their governments? Do they remain within their instructions? In 1903, the newly independent Republic of Panama and the United States negotiated a treaty authorizing the construction of a transoceanic canal.[16] The announced representative for Panama was Philippe Bunau Varilla, a French engineer, whose diplomatic credentials were clouded, yet the treaty was concluded. Similarly, President Thomas Jefferson had instructed his commissioners in Paris to negotiate for the purchase of New Orleans. Instead they arranged to buy all of French Louisiana, despite their more limited instructions. Good faith is the guiding rule in these matters. Each side extends to the other the courtesy of assuming that credentials and instructions are in order. If questions arise later, they do not justify a challenge lawfulness of the negotiations.

Paragraphing, sometimes termed initialing, is the next step. As the negotiations proceed, the representatives of the parties customarily initial each paragraph as it is completed. The purpose of paragraphing is to mark the progress of the work. The negotiators' initials do not imply a legal or political obligation. The operative principle is that *nothing is agreed to until everything is agreed to.* During the summer of 2000, President Clinton hosted representatives of Israel and the Palestinian Authority at a retreat in Maryland. Although the two parties were in accord on a number of points, some questions remained open, and the talks ended in a stalemate.

Signature is the third phase. At this juncture heads of government or their designated representatives sign the treaty and commit themselves to bringing the agreement to fruition. Signature alone does not, however, create a legal obligation. The treaty is not yet in force although elements of it may be incorporated into state practice by decree, as was the case with the Reagan proclamations on the law of the sea. The definitive phase is ratification, whereby a government declares to the international community that the treaty has passed the test of its constitutional acceptance procedures. Normally the procedure requires the deposit of an instrument of ratification with the United Nations secretary-general, for the text of the agreement is then published in the *United Nations Treaty Series* (*UNTS*). The U.S. Constitution requires that the Senate approve a treaty by a two-thirds majority prior to ratification. Most political systems also presuppose legislative approval. In Germany, the Bundestag (the lower house of the parliament representing political parties) must approve a treaty, and if that agreement affects the rights of member states, the Bundesrat (upper house representing the states) must concur.[17] Similarly, under the republican constitution of 1948 the Italian government is obligated to seek the approval of both chambers of parliament if the treaty is political,

---

[16]Isthmian Canal Convention (November 18, 1903), 10 Bevans 663.
[17]Jochen Frowein and Michael J. Hahn, "The Participation of the Parliament in the Treaty Process in the Federal Republic of Germany," in *Parliamentary Participation in the Making and Operation of Treaties: A Comparative Study,* ed. Stefan Riesenfeld and Frederick M. Abbott (Dordrecht: Martinus Nijhoff, 1994), 61–63.

involves a transfer of territory, or requires supplementary legislation, for example, changes in criminal law.[18]

A constitutional and representative government frowns upon secret agreements made by the executive without the concurrence of the legislature, but the pace of ratification is often frustrating to an impatient public. A classic example is the Geneva Protocol (1925), which banned the first use of chemical weapons on the battlefield. The administration of President Calvin Coolidge adhered to the treaty, and President Gerald Ford ratified it fifty years later.[19] Ratification will often depend upon the acceptance of reservations or amendments. The former do not involve a change in the agreed text, but provide an interpretation of the treaty. The Connally[20] reservation, which governed the adherence of the United States to the Statute of the ICJ in 1947, excluded internal disputes from the court's jurisdiction. The British government adhered to the statute with the reservation that it would accept adjudication only of disputes that developed after 1945. The use of reservations is a common practice although the proposed Comprehensive Test Ban Treaty (CTBT) specifically prohibits them.[21] Amending the text of a multilateral convention is impractical. Conditional approval depends upon reservations.[22] The ban on reservations limited the constitutional role of the Senate and may have contributed to that body's rejection of the CTBT in 1999.

A reservation to a treaty must, according to the convention, be confirmed at the time of ratification. The restriction means that a government may not adhere to a multilateral convention and subsequently announce that it did so with reservations. Ratification places a time limit on reservations. The legal obligations imposed by a treaty do not change, but a reservation will alter the way in which those obligations are put into effect. The United Nations secretary-general lists all reservations in the *UNTS* so that they become part of the public history of the treaty. Governments inclined to make reservations should bear in mind that they do so under the principle of reciprocity. If one party can make a reservation, other states parties to the agreement can as well. In certain cases a reservation may not be practical as, for example, in the instance of a treaty of peace imposing a duty to pay reparations. Moreover, treaties designed to protect fundamental human rights do not readily lend themselves to reservations. The Convention on the Prevention and Punishment of the Crime of Genocide (1948) does not comport with reservations because the treaty represents an effort by the states parties to uphold the rule of law.[23] With regard to human rights the assumption is that the interests of a particular state are subordinate to that of the international community. For a government to impose a reservation would run counter to the purpose of a convention designed to

---

[18]Giovanni Bognetti, "The Role of the Italian Parliament in the Treaty-Making Process," ibid., 89–107.

[19]Protocol for the Prohibition of the Use in War of Asphyxiating, Poisonous or Other Gases, and of Bacteriological Methods of Warfare (April 10, 1925), 26 U.S.T. 571. President Ford deposited the instrument of ratification on April 10, 1975.

[20]Senator Tom Connally of Texas served as the Chair of the Senate Foreign Relations Committee, which reviews a treaty before it is reported to the floor for a vote.

[21]Comprehensive Nuclear Test-Ban Treaty (Washington, D.C.: Government Printing Office, 1998), 35.

[22]United States, Congress, 98th Cong., 2nd sess., Senate, Committee on Foreign Relations, *Treaties and Other International Agreements: The Role of the United States Senate,* committee print 98-205, ed. Ellen C. Collier, Congressional Research Service (Washington, D.C.: Government Printing Office, 1986), 109–112. Hereafter cited as Collier, *Treaties and Other International Agreements.*

[23]Frank Horn, *Reservations and Interpretative Declarations to Multilateral Treaties* (Amsterdam: North-Holland, 1988), 37–45 and 135–155.

create a legal norm. Nevertheless, as John King Gamble has pointed out, the liberal use of reservations may encourage participation in lawmaking conventions.[24] Yet Theodor Meron has expressed skepticism regarding reservations to human rights conventions and suggested that they may run counter to the spirit of the treaty.[25] The evidence is inconclusive, but it is certain that reservations on substantive issues will remain an integral part of the treaty process.

An amendment requires a change in the wording of the text and therefore the renegotiation of the treaty. For self-evident reasons most governments hesitate to reopen the negotiating process, and amendments are rare. A noted exception is the treaty (1977) which provided for the transfer of the canal and associated installations from the United States to the Republic of Panama in 1999. The Senate proposed an amendment to the effect that "the United States shall have the primary responsibility to protect and defend the Canal."[26] The government of Panama responded by subjecting the change to a popular vote in the form of a referendum. The voters approved, and ratification followed. The amendment process involves political risk and is therefore not to be recommended.

Ideally proclamation of a treaty should follow within days of its ratification, for it endows the agreement with legal force within the signatory state. In the United States proclamation, like ratification, is a constitutional prerogative of the president. In exceptional circumstances the president may delay proclamation, but such hesitation means that although the United States is bound internationally by a treaty, its terms are not yet enforceable in court. The outcome can be a legal imbroglio. The administration of foreign policy requires the coordinated exercise of presidential authority.

Implementation of a treaty often requires supplementary legislation, for example, the appropriation of the funds needed to fulfill commitments in such fields as arms control. National constitutions may also require the concurrence of both houses of the national legislature. The U.S. Constitution stipulates in Article 4(3) that Congress by joint resolution must approve of any measure calling for the relinquishment of national territory. An international agreement abandoning a claim to territory through, for example, the rectification of a boundary should require a majority in each house of Congress.[27] In 1990, the United States withdrew its claim to Wrangell Island, among other territories in the Arctic Ocean, by concluding a maritime boundary agreement with the Soviet Union.[28] The Senate approved the treaty and the president ratified it, but a careful reading of the Constitution suggests the need for implementing legislation involving both houses of Congress.

---

[24]John King Gamble, "Reservations to Multilateral Treaties: A Macroscopic View of State Practice," *American Journal of International Law* 74 (April 1980): 372, 393.

[25]Theodor Meron, *Human Rights Law-Making in the United Nations: A Critique of Instruments and Process* (New York: Oxford University Press, 1986), p. 80.

[26]United States, Department of State, *Texts of Treaties Relating to the Panama Canal,* Selected Documents no. 6 (September 1977), art. 4, p. 4.

[27]The historical record indicates that this provision has been honored more in the breach than in the observance. For a list of territories abandoned without joint action by both houses, see letter by Ellen C. Collier, Congressional Research Service, to Senator Ernest Gruening of Alaska (April 5, 1960) in United States, Congress, Senate, Committee on Foreign Relations, 86th Cong., 2nd sess., *The Antarctic Treaty: Hearings* (June 14, 1960), 22–23.

[28]Maritime Boundary Agreement (June 1, 1990), reprinted in 29 I.L.M. 941 (1990).

A useful distinction regarding implementation is that between self-fulfilling and declaratory treaties.[29] The former detail specific obligations on the part of the signatory governments and a schedule for carrying them out. The Panama Canal treaty, for example, stipulated that the United States would complete the handover of the Canal Zone by December 1999. In contrast, a declaratory treaty is a statement of intent, and it usually focuses on a norm of international law. The discussion of the Convention Relating to the Status of Refugees (1967), as described in Chapter 6, is a case in point. The convention forbade the forced expulsion (*refoulement*) of a refugee, thereby creating an obligation to grant asylum. Yet the U.S. Supreme Court in *Sale v. the Haitian Centers Council* (1993) took the position that a declaratory commitment requires implementing legislation. As early as 1829, Chief Justice Marshall and later Justice Story suggested a distinction between self-executing treaties of a contractual nature and non-self-executing treaties, which necessitate judicial or congressional interpretation.[30] The determination as to which category covers a particular treaty may be made long after ratification with the result that the other treaty partner is without the benefit of a binding commitment. The underlying principle of treaty law is that of good faith, and each party to an agreement must assume that the other will dutifully fulfill its constitutional requirements. The notion of non-self-executing treaties creates an apparent loophole and may weaken the credibility of the government that resorts to this argument.

EXECUTIVE AGREEMENTS

Treaties constitute only one form of international agreement, and historically they may not be the most significant. In 1817, the United States secured the demilitarization of its frontier with Canada through the Rush–Bagot agreement—an executive understanding not submitted to the Senate. The agreements terminating hostilities in Korea (1953), in Vietnam (1973), and in the Persian Gulf (1991) were executive in nature. Major arms control agreements, such as the Strategic Arms Limitation Talks (1969), were reached outside the treaty process. The political significance of these examples is self-evident, but their standing under international law is not always clear. The Convention on the Law of Treaties (article 7) endows a head of government or his or her diplomatic agent with the authority to conclude an international agreement in any form. Executive authorities in all governments assume that they have an inherent power to reach understandings with their counterparts, and that the efficient administration of foreign policy depends upon the exercise of that power.

The challenge of constitutional democracy is that the operations of government must be transparent. Consultation with the legislative branch is imperative if government is to be truly representative of the people. The opposing argument is that diplomacy requires "secrecy and dispatch."[31] Executive agreements fulfill the practical requirements of

---

[29]The distinction is derived, in part, from Arnold D. McNair, "The Functions and Differing Legal Character of Treaties," B.Y.I.L. 11 (1930): 100–118. McNair divides treaties into four categories: (a) conveyances (territory), (b) contracts (commerce), (c) lawmaking conventions (human rights), and (d) charters (constitutive acts of international organizations).

[30]Jordan J. Paust, "Self-Executing Treaties," *American Journal of International Law* 82 (October 1988): 760, 766–767.

[31]John Jay, *Federalist No. 64* and Alexander Hamilton, *Federalist No. 75* in *The Federalist: A Commentary on the Constitution of the United States, 1787–1788* (New York: Modern Library, 1937 et seq.), 419, 488.

diplomacy, but they also limit the openness of the policy process. The debate in the United States as to the proper role of executive agreements is ongoing. The consensus of opinion is that the president must have the flexibility to conclude agreements essential for the facilitation of foreign policy, but that major political undertakings require congressional scrutiny. In 1972, Congress passed the Case Act, which was an effort to preserve the executive's flexibility and to reassert the role of the legislative branch in the field of foreign policy. The act required that all international agreements other than treaties be transmitted to Congress within sixty days of their conclusion.[32] At the discretion of the president, agreements of a sensitive nature would be sent only to the Senate Committee on Foreign Relations and the House Committee on International Affairs. A subsequent amendment required that oral agreements be committed to writing and forwarded to Congress.[33] The difficulty is that many agencies apart from the Department of State enter into agreements with foreign governments, and that centralized recording of these agreements is a bureaucratic impossibility. The sheer volume of international transactions militates against effective congressional oversight. Nonfulfillment of the Case Act, whether intentionally or by accident, does not alter the binding quality of international agreements. Agreements reached by the executive without the advice and consent of the Senate remain international obligations of the United States.

In addition to treaties and executive agreements, joint resolutions of Congress also constitute a principal means of reaching an international accord. Acts of Congress in 1920 terminated the state of war with Austria and Germany begun three years earlier. Legislative enactment has enabled the United States to join intergovernmental organizations (IGOs), such as the International Bank for Reconstruction and Development (World Bank) and the International Monetary Fund.[34] Starting with the Universal Postal Union in 1874, Elmer Plischke has found that the United States has joined more IGOs by legislative act than by treaties. Often the method is simply an amendment (rider) to the budget resolution providing funds for participation in a particular IGO.[35] As discussed in Chapter 3, subnational authorities within a federation also enter into international compacts with their counterparts in neighboring states. International agreements may take any of four forms: (a) treaties, (b) executive agreements, (c) statutes, or (d) state–province agreements dealing with transboundary problems. The diversity of approaches enhances a government's options in coping with issues of foreign policy, but it also creates ambiguity where certainty is preferable.

TERMINATION OF A TREATY

The Convention on the Law of Treaties places limitations on the circumstances under which a government may terminate an international agreement. Ideally, the states parties to a treaty may voluntarily agree to amend or terminate it, in which case no objection could be raised unless the rights of a third party are involved. For example, China

---

[32]Transmittal of International Agreements (August 22, 1972), 86 Stat. 619.

[33]Lois McHugh, "Congressional Oversight of International Agreements," in Collier, *Treaties and Other International Agreements,* 168, 170–175.

[34]Louis Henkin, *Foreign Affairs and the United States Constitution,* 2nd ed. (New York: Oxford University Press, 1996), p. 215.

[35]Elmer Plischke, *Conduct of American Diplomacy,* 3rd ed. (Princeton: D Van Nostrand, 1967), p. 544.

and Pakistan may agree to terminate the previous boundary treaty and to write a new one delimiting a revised frontier. In this instance the rights of India would be adversely affected, and actions taken without securing Indian concurrence would be subject to challenge. In the aftermath of the proliferation of states following the end of the Cold War, new governments have challenged existing treaties, and old governments have insisted upon their enforcement. The question of treaty termination reflects a basic cleavage in the international system.

Customary and conventional international law recognize seven reasons for declaring a treaty invalid: (a) material breach of obligations, (b) impossibility of fulfillment, (c) fundamental change in circumstances, (d) violation of *jus cogens* (peremptory norms of international law), (e) error or fraud, (f) duress, or (g) commitments contrary to the Charter of the United Nations. To be regarded as material, a breach must be of such a nature as to call into question the validity of the treaty. A failure to meet a debt repayment schedule would not fall into this category, but a unilateral denunciation of a public debt would. A material breach often occurs in conjunction with military pacts,[36] as typified by the congressional resolution denouncing in 1798 the alliance with France. Impossibility of fulfillment is invariably a problem associated with agreements requiring the performance of contractual obligations. An international financial crisis, such as the Asian one of 1997, may affect a government so severely that it must reschedule payment of its public debt. Creditor governments as well as international financial institutions usually demonstrate the flexibility appropriate to the situation. Internal war will disrupt a political system to the extent that the internationally recognized government will place its treaty obligations in abeyance. The customary rule implies that the reason for nonfulfillment be obvious and overwhelming. A policy decision to the effect that upholding the terms of a treaty is burdensome will not suffice. In 1997, the ICJ rendered a judgment regarding the termination of a treaty providing for the collaboration of Slovakia (independent as of January 1, 1993) and Hungary in the construction of a canal with locks. Responding to public pressure, the Hungarian government denounced the project because of its ecological dangers, which were not known when the original agreement was drafted in 1977. In this instance the court acknowledged the legitimacy of the argument of necessity as a reason for terminating a treaty but concluded that the case for Hungary did not satisfy the criteria for invoking this doctrine.[37]

The third ground is a fundamental change in circumstances or *rebus sic stantibus*. While most publicists recognize the validity of this doctrine, it can only be applied in extreme cases.[38] A boundary agreement may not be abrogated, nor may a servitude required for, for example, the demilitarization of a frontier region, be nullified. The convention stipulates that the effect of the change is a radical transformation of the conditions under which the states parties consented to the original agreement. *Debellatio,* or the dismemberment and subjugation of a state, provides a basis for resorting to the argument *rebus sic stantibus,* although the convention recognizes this circumstance but does not prejudge the rights and obligations of a successor state. Throughout the di-

---

[36]Treaty of Alliance (February 6, 1778), 7 Bevans 777. On July 7, 1798, Congress enacted a joint resolution nullifying the treaty.
[37]*Gabčikovo-Nagymaros Project: Judgment* (Hungary v. Slovakia), 25 September 1997, ICJ Reports, reprinted in 37 I.L.M. 168, 182 (1998).
[38]Brownlie, 623–626.

vision of Germany (1949–1990), the Federal Republic of (West) Germany accepted a legal responsibility for acts of the previous regime, but the East German Democratic Republic proclaimed itself as a new state unburdened by the legacy of the past. State succession may well constitute a fundamental change in circumstances.

The violation of *jus cogens* or peremptory norms of international law may create a basis for denouncing a treaty. The convention states in article 64 that the emergence of a new peremptory norm invalidates a treaty, but the convention also adheres to the principle of nonretroactivity; that is, the new rules take effect only when the treaty is in force. The Vienna conference on the law of treaties endeavored to reconcile the invalidation of an existing treaty through the development of a new norm of *jus cogens,* on the one hand, and the ban on retroactive enforcement on the other. The results were inconclusive beyond the assertion by the representative of Chile that *jus cogens* is a "timeless moral concept."[39] The inherent danger in the doctrine is that of instant customary international law. Can a resolution by the General Assembly create a new legal norm? If so, a vote by the Assembly may provide a justification, no matter how transparent, for a government to denounce an inconvenient treaty.[40] The potential linkage between the General Assembly and *jus cogens* has serious ramifications for the law of treaties.

A fifth basis for terminating a treaty is error or even fraud. As discussed in Chapter 11 in conjunction with maps as evidence, an error in a boundary map agreed upon by Spain and the United States in 1819 did not invalidate the treaty, for the U.S. Supreme Court subsequently ruled that the principle of good faith required adherence to the treaty despite the obvious error. In the Global South many boundaries reflect vague compromises between colonial powers, which relied upon incomplete and often misleading maps. Nevertheless customary international law adheres to the premise that historical cartography, once accepted, has probative value. The ICJ upheld this position in a 1962 decision involving a disputed title to a Buddhist temple. Siam claimed the temple site, and Cambodia responded with cartographic evidence based on a French military survey completed in 1907, when the country was a dependency of France. The court accepted the map as definitive because it was regarded as authoritative at the time.[41] Related to error is the problem of fraud, which may involve deliberate misrepresentation or even bribery on the part of a state seeking an agreement. A treaty concluded under these circumstances is invalid.

Duress provides a sixth justification for challenging a treaty. Historical examples of physical coercion to secure assent to a treaty are few.[42] More prevalent is duress in the form of blackmail of a government official. In a broader sense, the Convention on the Law of Treaties condemned the practice of securing consent to a treaty through the use or threat of force. Article 52 of the convention was categorical on this point. During the deliberative conference in Vienna the delegate from Switzerland stated that he would abstain from approving the draft article first because his government ". . . doubted

---

[39]United Nations Conference on the Law of Treaties: Official Records of the Second Session, Vienna, 9 April–22 May 1969 (A/CONF.39/11/Add.1), 122. Hereafter U.N. Law of Treaties Conference.

[40]Mark E. Villiger, *Customary International Law and Treaties* (Dordrecht and Boston: Martinus Nijhoff, 1985), pp. 28–29.

[41]*Case Concerning the Temple of Preah Vihear: Judgment* (Cambodia v. Thailand), 15 June 1962, ICJ Reports 1962, 6, 26.

[42]The Peace of Westphalia included a stipulation to the effect that treaties signed under constraint are invalid. See Articles of the Treaty of Peace, Münster (October 24, 1648), reprinted in 1 Parry 330.

whether the principle set forth in the article was in accordance with the teachings of history and because its adoption might endanger the stability of the entire system of international law." The delegate from the Republic of Cyprus countered that the prohibition on the use of force was *lex lata* (law actually in force) because of the Charter of the United Nations.[43] Ideally the Cypriot norm is attractive, but the Swiss interpretation reflects historical reality. Every treaty of peace bringing to a close an armed conflict is concluded on the basis of military force.[44]

The foregoing discussion leads into the final reason for terminating a treaty, namely that its terms are contrary to the charter, whose article 103 states:

> In the event of a conflict between the obligations of the Members of the United Nations under the present Charter and their obligations under any other international agreement, their obligations under the present Charter shall prevail.

The article raises questions about treaties of guarantee, that is, those instruments by which a third power underwrites the terms of an agreement.[45] In 1960, the Republic of Cyprus achieved its independence on the basis of a tripartite guarantee of the independence and the constitution of the new state. Article 4 stated:

> In the event of a breach of the provisions of the present Treaty, Greece, Turkey, and the United Kingdom undertake to consult together with respect to the representations or measures necessary to ensure observance of those provisions.
>
> In so far as common or concerted action may not prove possible, each of the three guaranteeing Powers reserves the right to take action with the sole aim of re-establishing the state of affairs created by the present Treaty.[46]

The provision authorizes either collective or unilateral intervention by the guarantors to cope with a constitutional crisis, and the terms of the treaty were invoked in 1974. In international law the issue is one of determining whether such a treaty commitment is compatible with the Charter of the United Nations, which commits itself to " ... the principle of the sovereign equality of its members." Intervention is incompatible with the norm of sovereign equality. A treaty of guarantee affording a right of intervention falls within the meaning of article 103, and such treaties as are imposed as a precondition for the independence of new states are open to challenge. The doctrine of *rebus sic stantibus* may well apply. In 1855, Robert Phillimore, a British jurist, noted with regard to a similar guarantee that it " ... is fraught with mischief to the best interests of Public and International Law."[47] Conversely, Lord McNair in his foundation study of treaty law viewed treaties of guarantee as a useful technique of diplomacy, and he endorsed both a collective guarantee on the part of a group of states and an individual guarantee

---

[43]U.N. Law of Treaties Conference, 91.

[44]Ingrid Detter, *The International Legal Order* (Aldershot, U.K.: Dartmouth Publishing Co., 1994), pp. 183–184.

[45]Lauterpacht's Oppenheim, 869.

[46]Treaty of Guarantee (August 16, 1960), 382 U.N.T.S. 3, 6.

[47]Robert Phillimore, *Commentaries upon International Law* (Philadelphia: T. & J. W. Johnson, 1855; reprint, Littleton, Co.: Fred B. Rothman, 1985), II:65.

by one state vis-à-vis another.[48] Similarly, Secretary of State Henry Kissinger included international guarantees in his list of components in a Middle East peace settlement.[49] Notably, treaties of guarantee prove most attractive to the advocates of realpolitik.

THE LANGUAGE PROBLEM

The complexity of treaty law becomes apparent in the process of trying to achieve linguistic equivalency in agreements rendered in more than one language. Traditional diplomacy emphasized reliance upon French and, to a lesser extent, English.[50] Often neither language was that of the states parties. French-language treaties between Russia and China were an example, as were English-language treaties between China and Japan. Since the founding of the United Nations, however, the practice of formulating treaties in the language of each of the signatory governments has become widespread, and the results are often confusing. A case in point is the Four-Power Agreement on Berlin (1971), whose final version appeared in English, French, and Russian with a protocol in German.[51] The agreement specified that the government of the Federal Republic (West Germany) would represent the interests of West Berliners vis-à-vis the international community. The French text translates *interests* as *les intérêts,* meaning the vital interests of the party in question rather than *intéressé* or the self-interest of an individual or group. The distinction between vital interests as opposed to mere self-interest is critical, yet the English word *interest* covers both meanings and introduces a certain ambiguity into the text. The French version is more precise and illustrates the advantage of relying upon French as a language of diplomacy. In the process of negotiation ambiguity may serve a purpose, but confusion as to the meaning of a treaty can only undercut its value.

Even the use of a definite article may be decisive. In 1967, the United Nations Security Council enacted resolution 242 to secure a cessation of hostilities in the Middle East. In its early draft the resolution called upon Israel to withdraw from the territories it had occupied in June of that year. The French version incorporated the definite article and meant that the Israeli withdrawal should be from *all* territories recently occupied. The English version made reference only to territories, thus creating the impression that Israel should relinquish only some of its zone of occupation. Alexei Kosygin, premier of the Soviet Union, appealed for the use of the article, but President Johnson refused.[52] As remarkable as it may seem, the positioning of a definite article can become an issue of superpower diplomacy. The lesson underlines the need for precision in drafting a treaty, for failure to do so may create a basis for future termination of the agreement. *Pacta sunt servanda* will always depend upon the careful use of language.

---

[48]Lord McNair, *The Law of Treaties* (Oxford: Clarendon Press, 1961), p. 239.
[49]U.S. Department of State, Press Release 370B (July 14, 1975) in *Department of State Bulletin* 73 (August 4, 1975): 158.
[50]Manley O. Hudson, "Languages Used in Treaties," *American Journal of International Law* 26 (April 1932): 368–372. Also see J. Hardy, "The Interpretation of Plurilingual Treaties by International Courts and Tribunals," B.Y.I.L. 37 (1961): 72–155.
[51]Quadripartite Agreement on Berlin (September 3, 1971), 24 U.S.T. 283.
[52]Sydney D. Bailey, *The Making of Resolution 242* (Boston: Martinus Nijhoff, 1985), p. 153.

Topics for Discussion

1. Are treaties contracts in the sense of commercial law? Or is the contractual analogy inconsistent with the nature of international politics? Do the vital interests of a state override the dictum of *pacta sunt servanda?*
2. The interpretation of treaties may reflect adherence to either the original intent of the drafters, that is, to the literal text, or to the teleological approach emphasizing the overall goal of the agreement. What are the arguments for and against these two schools of thought?
3. In adhering to a treaty a government may either impose reservations or insist upon amendments. What is the distinction between the two? What diplomatic or legal advantages does each offer?
4. Customary and conventional international law recognizes seven reasons for the termination of a treaty. What are these? Which ones are likely to be relied upon by small as opposed to great powers?

CHAPTER 14

Diplomacy

Through reciprocity international law serves to protect the rights of states and to ensure the performance of their duties. Diplomacy is the means of communication among governments essential for the existence of an international legal order. Nizam al-Mulk (1018–1092), a master of Persian statecraft, wrote:

> It should also be realized that when kings send ambassadors to one another their purpose is not merely the message or the letter which they communicate openly, but secretly they have a hundred other points and objects in view.[1]

The statement captures the essence of diplomacy, for it recognizes that governments send and receive ambassadors to achieve many purposes. Principal among these are representation and negotiation, but an ambassador and the staff of a diplomatic mission also gather information, conduct cultural programs, and provide technical assistance to agencies of the receiving government. Diplomacy is the electrical current which drives the international system. The administration of foreign policy through diplomatic missions requires the protection of international law, for law and diplomacy make possible a stable world order.

THE VIENNA CONVENTION

Customary international law has long recognized the special role of the diplomat. In the European Renaissance, the concept of a *res publica christiana* or Christian commonwealth presupposed orderly relations among governments, and the doctrine of sovereignty embodied in the Peace of Westphalia (1648) recognized the legal equality of states, each state having the right to send and receive diplomats.[2] The first step toward the codification of the law of diplomacy was an annex to the general act of the Congress of Vienna (1815), which set diplomatic ranks and established rules of protocol for the orderly conduct of foreign affairs.[3] The system of congresses and conferences of the Concert of Europe stimulated the further development of the rules of diplomacy, and a United Nations conference on diplomatic privileges and immunities (Vienna, 1961) provided an opportunity to draft a comprehensive lawmaking treaty of universal application.

The resultant Vienna Convention on Diplomatic Relations was an omnibus document drawing together the customary rules of diplomacy into a single statement. Ratifications followed quickly, for all governments realized that the reciprocity of the

---

[1]Nizam al-Mulk, *The Book of Government or Rules for Kings,* trans. Hubert Darke (New Haven: Yale University Press, 1960), p. 98.
[2]Garrett Mattingly, *Renaissance Diplomacy* (London: Jonathan Cape, 1955), p. 295.
[3]Regulations Concerning the Rank and Precedence of Diplomatic Agents (March 19, 1815), cited in 1 Toynbee 575.

convention could only serve their interests. Deserving of particular mention are three principal features of the treaty: (a) consent, (b) immunity, and (c) inviolability. Every state has the right to enter into reciprocal diplomatic relations with another state, as indicated by the constitutional grant of authority to the president as the officer of government who sends and receives ambassadors. The acceptance, however, of a particular ambassador depends upon consent. Specifically, the receiving government issues an *agrément* whereby it indicates that the proposed candidate is an acceptable diplomatic representative in its capital. The reasons for denying an *agrément* may be either political or personal, and they are not subject to challenge. The sending government quietly withdraws the nomination. Ideally bilateral discussions of the *agrément* should take place in an atmosphere of confidentiality so as to avoid embarrassment if a problem should arise. Only after the receiving government has consented should the nomination be announced.

Immunity is a more complex issue than consent. The Vienna Convention includes a broad commitment to the immunity of the diplomat and his or her family from the host country's judicial and administrative procedures, but the practice is somewhat different. The chief of a diplomatic mission may waive the immunity of a member of the embassy staff.[4] The procedure is, however, extraordinary. A more common remedy is for the host government to declare that a named diplomat is no longer welcome (*persona non grata*) and must leave the country within twenty-four hours. Immunity is a sensitive topic, especially when citizens of the receiving state suffer loss of life or serious injury at the hands of a diplomat or a member of his or her family. In such cases the sending government will usually make an offer of compensation. Finally, the matter of exemption from taxation never fails to attract public attention. Large real estate holdings that belong to embassies may not be taxed, and individual diplomats are not required to pay a sales tax. The theory is that the diplomat represents a sovereign authority, which by definition cannot be compelled to pay the taxes imposed by another sovereign. In terms of international law, the matter is symbolic, but municipalities struggling to meet their obligations view the immunity to taxation as an unwarranted burden.

The immunity of diplomats in wartime presents a special problem. The customary practice requires each belligerent power to respect the immunity of the adversary's diplomats and to exchange them through the good offices of a neutral government. For example, at the outset of the war between Japan and the United States, members of the diplomatic missions of both countries were interned and then repatriated.[5] The premises of their respective embassies were sealed and reopened after the resumption of normal diplomatic relations following the conclusion of a treaty of peace in 1951. In 1948, the International Military Tribunal for the Far East concluded its proceedings in Tokyo and sentenced military and civilian officials of the former Japanese government for the commission of war crimes. Among those convicted of conspiracy against the peace was General Hiroshi Ōshima, the wartime Japanese ambassador to Germany.

---

[4]In 1940, British authorities arrested and successfully prosecuted an American diplomat on a charge of espionage while posted at the U.S. embassy in London. A waiver of immunity by the U.S. government preceded the judicial act. See 7 Whiteman, 354–355.
[5]For a description of the internment and exchange of American diplomatic personnel in 1941 in Tokyo, see Charles E. Bohlen, *Witness to History* (New York: W.W. Norton & Co., 1973), p. 115; and Joseph C. Grew, *Ten Years in Japan, 1932–1942* (New York: Simon and Schuster, 1944), p. 533.

The charge against him was the planning and instigating of a war of aggression.[6] Since Ōshima had been acting as his government's chief of mission in Berlin, was his trial and conviction violative of the rule of diplomatic immunity?

The third principle is that of inviolability, which refers to the special legal status of the person of the diplomat, his or her residence, and communications. Again, the theory of sovereignty is the key, for the person or possessions of a diplomat to be subjected to search and seizure would violate the norm of sovereign equality. Inviolability protects against such an offense and thereby guarantees the orderly functioning of diplomacy. The word *extraterritoriality* is not a synonym for inviolability, for the premises of a diplomatic mission remain under the sovereign jurisdiction of the host government even though its administrative and judicial functions are circumscribed. The popularly held notion that the residence and the chancery of the embassy are the territory of the sending state is inaccurate.[7]

ESTABLISHMENT OF A MISSION

The establishment of diplomatic missions in a newly independent state usually follows the admission of that state to the United Nations. Membership in the world organization attests to the legal fact that the criteria for statehood have been met, and that the new government acknowledges its rights and duties under international law. Difficulty arises in the event of civil war and revolution. As noted in Chapter 5, insurgent forces merit recognition in terms of international humanitarian law, and the establishment of a secessionist government over a given territory provides a basis for the limited exercise of diplomatic functions. Recognition being a political rather than a legal act, it can be whatever a government is willing to make of it.

A civil war represents a state of affairs in which a neutral government may find it necessary to put in place diplomatic relations with both sides. The American Civil War is a case in point. At the outbreak of the war in April 1861, the British government had long-established consular officers in the political and commercial centers of the Confederacy, such as Richmond and Charleston. Because lines of communication with the British embassy in Washington were cut, the consuls assumed extended responsibilities needed to cope with the wartime emergency, especially as it involved the protection of British citizens. The consul in Richmond invoked his authority on behalf of a countryman imprisoned on a charge of draft evasion in Mississippi, and the consuls also assumed political functions not usually associated with their office.[8] The U.S. Department of State took a dim view of these activities, as might be expected of any government engaged in a civil war.

The Spanish civil war (1936–1939) presented an analogous problem. At the outset, European powers maintained diplomatic relations with the Republican government in Madrid, which was recognized as the de jure (legal) government of Spain. As the war progressed, however, Great Britain and other governments assigned liaison officers to

---

[6]Carl Boyd, *Hitler's Japanese Confidant* (Lawrence: University of Kansas Press, 1993), p. 177.
[7]Von Glahn, 429, 1 Hyde 740–741; and 1 Lauterpacht's Oppenheim, 417.
[8]Milledge L. Bonham, *The British Consuls in the Confederacy* (New York: Columbia University, 1911), pp. 36, 86–88.

the insurgent fascist authorities, and liaison gradually evolved into de facto diplomatic relations. The end of the war and the dissolution of the Republican government led to the recognition of a fascist regime under General Francisco Franco. The declaratory doctrine of recognition requires the acceptance of a political fact without implying approval or disapproval. In the case of Spain, the United States and the Western European powers followed this doctrine. Conversely, the government of Mexico withheld recognition from the insurgent regime and insisted until the year of Franco's death—1976—that the de jure Spanish government was that of the Republic, whose cabinet was granted asylum in Mexico City.

TERMINATION OF A MISSION

The developments leading to the establishment of a mission are a reflection of those causing its termination. The principal reason for the termination of a mission is *debellatio,* or the subjugation of a state through conquest. In 1935, Italian forces overran Ethiopia with the result that it ceased to be an independent state and became a military dependency of the government in Rome, resulting in the closing of foreign diplomatic missions in Addis Ababa. Similarly, the capitulation of the Japanese government in 1945 led to a closing of its diplomatic missions in neutral countries. In Stockholm, for example, the Swedish foreign ministry took possession of the Japanese embassy and notified the Allies that it had assumed a custodial role for Japanese property. *Debellatio* may not, however, always mean the termination of a government's diplomatic missions. In 1990, following the Iraqi army's occupation of Kuwait, the government in Baghdad declared the neighboring kingdom to be an integral province of Iraq. Acting through the United Nations, the international community denied legitimacy to the Iraqi action, and Kuwaiti diplomatic missions continued to function.

A revolution may also occasion a termination of diplomatic missions although the case is not as clear cut as in the instance of subjugation. In 1959, the revolution led by Fidel Castro succeeded in establishing a new government in Cuba, and after a series of confrontations President Dwight D. Eisenhower severed diplomatic relations. Similarly, the overthrow of the monarchy in Iran and the establishment of an Islamic republic in 1979 resulted in a break in relations. In both the Cuban and the Iranian instances, the government of Switzerland agreed to serve as the "protecting power,"[9] charged with the representation of U.S. interests. In this sense limited contacts continue, but they are the responsibility of a third party. The arrangement falls short of full diplomatic relations, and its continuation over a prolonged period is impractical. In time of war a resort to a third party is essential. During the Second World War in the Pacific, the Swedish minister in Tokyo served as a conduit for Japanese peace overtures to the Anglo-American allies, and the Japanese embassy in Stockholm attempted through the Swedish foreign ministry to find a basis for a dialogue. That the effort proved unproductive does not negate the thesis that during time of war diplomatic contacts between belligerents continue albeit through often informal channels. Starting in 1944, the Swedish minister in Tokyo initiated a successful dialogue aimed at communicating Japanese peace plans to

---

[9]Ernest Satow, *Satow's Guide to Diplomatic Practice,* ed. Lord Gore-Booth (London: Longman, 1979), p. 166.

the Anglo-American allies. The good offices of the Swedish foreign ministry working with the Japanese embassy in Stockholm were indispensable to this effort.[10] A corresponding example was the war in Korea (1950–1953) during which both sides reached an implicit understanding regarding the geographical scope of the conflict. Military action was limited to Korea with the result that targets in neighboring countries were not attacked.[11] In this matter the government of India served as a channel of communication. Even the formal termination of a mission does not lead to a severance of diplomatic communication. In 1981, President Reagan ordered the closing of the People's Bureau of the Socialist People's Libyan Arab Jamahiriya in Washington,[12] whereupon the Libyan diplomats transferred to the United Nations headquarters in New York. Contacts between the two governments continued through their United Nations missions.

THE *HOSTAGE* CASE

The critical test of diplomatic immunity and privileges came with the Iranian revolution. On November 4, 1979, a mass demonstration outside the U.S. embassy in Teheran grew into an assault and eventual takeover of those premises. Fifty-two American diplomatic and consular personnel were taken prisoner and held hostage until January 18, 1981, just two days before the inauguration of President Reagan. The immediate response of President Carter was to order such economic countermeasures as the freezing of Iranian assets in American banks. The United States also turned to the ICJ for relief in the form of provisional measures ordering the immediate release of the hostages. In addressing the ICJ, Attorney General Benjamin Civiletti stated:

> For the first time in modern diplomatic history, a State has not only acquiesced in, but participated in and is seeking political advantage from the illegal seizure and imprisonment of the diplomatic personnel of another State. It even threatens to put these diplomatic personnel on trial. If our international institutions, including this Court, should even appear to condone or tolerate the flagrant violations of customary international law, State practice, and explicit treaty commitments that are involved here, the result will be a serious blow not only to the safety of the American diplomatic persons now in captivity in Tehran, but to the rule of law within the international community.[13]

The speed with which the United States submitted its application for provisional measures brought the counterargument to the effect that the American side had failed to exhaust all the available diplomatic remedies before turning to the ICJ. As a rule, an

---

[10]Gerhard Krebs, "Aussichtslose Sondierung: Japanische Friedensfühler und schwedische Vermittlungsversuche 1944/45" (Hopeless probing: Japanese peace feelers and Swedish attempts at mediation, 1944–1945), *Vierteljahreshefte für Zeitgeschichte* 45 (July 1997): 425–448.

[11]Louis Henkin, *How Nations Behave: Law and Foreign Policy* (New York: Frederick A. Praeger, 1968), p. 39.

[12]Marian Nash, 1 *Cumulative Digest of United States Practice in International Law, 1981–1988* (Washington, D.C.: Government Printing Office, 1993), 1072–1073.

[13]*Case Concerning United States Diplomatic and Consular Staff in Tehran* (United States v. Iran): Pleadings, 29 November 1979, 21.

applicant government is expected to wait sixty days prior to requesting adjudication of a dispute. In the *Hostage* case, the ICJ waived this time limit and allowed the pleadings to begin immediately. As discussed in Chapter 10, the PCIJ determined in a benchmark decision (the *Mavrommatis Concessions,* 1925) that all available remedies, notably bilateral negotiation, should be exhausted prior to turning to the court. The ICJ ruling in the *Hostage* case set a precedent whereby a government could request provisional measures to cope with an emergency. Judge Hermann Mosler (Germany) called for a clarification of the reference in the U.S. application to "hostages . . . and all other United States officials." In response, the agent for the United States pointed outside that consular officers were also being detained, and that the provisional measures should apply equally to these individuals.[14] The ICJ affirmed the protected status of diplomatic and consular personnel by ruling unanimously in favor of the application for the release of the hostages.

CONSULATES

Unlike diplomatic missions, consulates have a limited role, in that their functions are to protect citizens, promote trade, and administer the law of the sending state.[15] The United Nations–sponsored Vienna Convention on Consular Relations stipulates in article 5:

> Consular functions consist in: (a) protecting in the receiving State the interests of the sending State and its nationals, both individuals and bodies corporate, within the limits permitted by international law . . . .[16]

The establishment of consulates usually depends upon bilateral agreements concluded within the framework of the Convention on Consular Relations. The technical term is an *exequatur,* which is a reciprocal arrangement between two governments allowing each to establish a specified number of consulates within each other's territory.[17] Internal war poses a delicate problem because consuls must continue to function in an effort to protect their citizens in a time of crisis, yet the credentials of those operating in territory under the control of insurgents are open to challenge. During the Civil War, British consuls continued to perform their official duties in such southern cities as Charleston and Richmond, for Confederate authorities accepted the *exequaturs* originally issued by the United States. The Confederacy also reserved the right to authorize the establishment of new consular posts and did issue an *exequatur* to a German state for a new consulate in Texas.[18] As indicated in Chapter 5, the political decision to continue the operation of consulates during a civil war may well imply recognition of insurgency or belligerency, an act that the de jure government would deem hostile. Nevertheless, civil strife highlights the need for consular services, and being the only representatives of

---

[14]Ibid., 37.
[15]For an overview of the work of a consul, see William D. Morgan and Charles Stuart Kennedy, *The U.S. Consul at Work* (Westport, CT.: Greenwood Press, 1991).
[16]Convention on Consular Relations (April 24, 1963), 21 U.S.T. 78, 82.
[17]The United States consulate in Jerusalem is an anomaly, in that the *exequatur* was granted in the nineteenth century by the Ottoman Empire.
[18]Bonham, 16.

their government in a disturbed area, consuls must perforce assume the duties of diplomats. Unfortunately the Convention on Consular Relations does not accommodate this state of affairs. The Kosovo crisis (1999) suggests an innovative, but somewhat irregular solution. Yugoslavia severed diplomatic relations with Germany, but continued to operate its General Consulate in Hamburg, which then assumed a diplomatic role. The termination of the Yugoslav mission in Germany was largely symbolic.

While the bilateral nature of agreements establishing consular posts leads to variations in the status of consuls, a generalization to the effect that their privileges and immunities are more limited than those of diplomats is appropriate, the theory being that the consul is an agent rather than a representative of his or her government.[19] In its deliberations leading to the drafting of the Convention on Consular Rights, the International Law Commission (ILC) debated the principle that a consul would enjoy immunity for the performance of all official acts—an expression on whose meaning the members of the ILC could not agree. The members did, however, recommend that consular officials should enjoy immunity from arrest and detention.[20] In practice, a court of the receiving state will decide what is and what is not an official act. In contrast, diplomatic status guarantees immunity from judicial and administrative procedures. The Convention on Consular Relations (article 41) provides limited immunity from arrest, except in the case of grave offenses. Notably, nationals of the receiving state serving as consuls do not possess these immunities.[21] In sum, a consul may claim the protection of the act of state doctrine (Chapter 6), but such protection covers only those acts performed in the interest of the sending state.[22] Motive becomes critical in this instance as well as the act itself. For example, is espionage covered by immunity from detention? Espionage is carried out in the interest of the sending state, but it is hardly an official act as defined by the ILC. The same interpretation applies to subversion against which the receiving state may take legal action.[23]

Civil proceedings against a consul are also subject to the limitations imposed by immunity, but the interpretation varies from that of a diplomat. A summons may not be served on a diplomat, but a consul may be served and required to appear in court. By invoking the principle of official acts before a magistrate, the consul will then be excused from testifying. The burden of proof is on the consul who must establish that personal actions were of a substantive official character. Being more extensive, the immunity of a diplomat precludes the question of proof in a court of law. The fundamental rule regarding a consular official is that the receiving state must not condone any infringement on the honor and dignity of the office.[24] Nevertheless, a consul is accountable for private acts, such as libel or slander, and can lawfully be served a subpoena for actions associated with such offenses.[25]

---

[19]J.-G. Castel, "Exemption from Jurisdiction of Canadian Courts," in 9 *The Canadian Yearbook of International Law* (Vancouver, B.C.: University of British Columbia Press, 1971), p. 176.
[20]United Nations, 1 *Yearbook of the International Law Commission, 1960,* (A/CN.4/Ser.A/1960), 106.
[21]Ibid. (A/CN.4/131), 2 at 15.
[22]B.S. Murty, *The International Law of Diplomacy: The Diplomatic Instrument and World Public Order* (New Haven: New Haven Press for Martinus Nijhoff, 1989), pp. 434–435.
[23]B. Sen, *A Diplomat's Handbook of International Law and Practice,* 3rd ed. (Boston: Martinus Nijhoff, 1988), pp. 292–293.
[24]4 Hackworth 708–710.
[25]7 Whiteman 767, 776.

Inviolability of consular offices covers three points: (a) premises, (b) archives, and (c) communications. The premises of an embassy (both the chancery and the residence) are immune to search and seizure by the authorities of the receiving state. By comparison, inviolability of consular premises is more limited, for they may be subject to search. In an emergency (*force majeure*) such as a fire, local authorities may enter without permission. If necessary, the receiving state may attach property.[26] Finally, while the residence of an ambassador is immune to search, that of a consul is not. The protection afforded an honorary consul, that is, a national of the receiving state on retainer to a foreign government for the performance of consular duties, is even more restricted. The question of premises becomes complex whenever a consulate and a diplomatic mission occupy the same building. In this instance the consular section of the building should be clearly marked so that it is set apart from diplomatic premises. Separate entrances and corridor signs are useful for this purpose. The requirement may appear excessive, but the distinction in degree of inviolability is real and should be reflected in the layout of the offices. The rule of inviolability also protects the consul's archives and communications, as is the case of a diplomat's. In daily activities the consul and the diplomat share many of the same privileges and immunities, but in a legal emergency the control of the receiving state is more extensive over the former.

CONSULAR RELATIONS IN A FEDERATION

The report to Congress by President Harrison (1891) in which he described state and local law enforcement officers as "Federal agents" in the context of international questions is the doctrinal statement covering consular relations in a federal state.[27] The duties imposed by the Convention on Consular Relations are unitary, in that they apply with equal force to officials at all levels of government. The convention requires in article 5 that the responsible consulate be (a) notified and (b) given an opportunity to provide legal counsel in the event that a national of the country in question is arrested and detained on a serious charge. The governing principle is reciprocity, which allows each state to afford protection to its national abroad.

In 1999, the Federal Republic of Germany made application to the ICJ for provisional measures to delay the execution in Arizona of two of its nationals—Karl and Walter LaGrand—who had been convicted on a charge of murder in 1982.[28] With the assistance of German consular officers, the LaGrand brothers instituted a federal appeal based on the argument that authorities in Arizona had failed to comply with the notification requirement stipulated in the Convention on Consular Relations. The prosecution conceded that as early as 1982 it became aware of the nationality of the defendants but contended that they had not asserted their rights under the convention. Nevertheless the prosecution has the duty to advise a defendant of his or her rights, and the doctrine articulated by President Harrison remains valid. The application to the ICJ concluded that the criminal conviction violated international legal obligations accepted by the United States upon ratification of the convention. Accordingly, the United States

---

[26]Murty, 440–441.

[27]See Chapter 3 for the Harrison report and a review of the *Breard* case (1998).

[28]*Case Concerning the Vienna Convention on Consular Relations* (Germany v. United States), Order of 3 March 1999, ICJ Reports 1999, reprinted in 38 I.L.M. 308 (1999).

should provide reparations for the execution of Karl LaGrand, which had already taken place, and order a new trial for Walter LaGrand. The ICJ endorsed the application for provisional measures and issued an order to the effect that the United States should delay the execution. The order was ignored.

Judge Stephen Schwebel (of the United States) did not vote against the court's ruling, but he appended a separate opinion in which he criticized the German government for allegedly delaying its application until shortly before the scheduled date of execution. His opinion stressed that the limits of time gave the United States no opportunity to file a memorial (i.e., a brief) with the ICJ. In fact, the German government had attempted to resolve the matter through bilateral negotiations and then turned to adjudication. The relevant precedent is the decision of the PCIJ in the case of the *Mavrommatis Concessions* (1924), wherein the PCIJ ruled that diplomatic remedies must first be exhausted before judicial proceedings could begin.[29] The refusal of the authorities in Arizona to delay the execution long enough to permit the ICJ to fulfill its role was the root of the problem.

INTERGOVERNMENTAL ORGANIZATIONS

Officials of intergovernmental organizations (IGOs) also enjoy diplomatic privileges and immunities, which include (a) personal immunity, (b) inviolability of premises, (c) financial transactions, including currency matters, and (d) communications.[30] As early as 1920, the Covenant of the League of Nations guaranteed diplomatic status to members and officials of the world organization.[31] The Charter of the United Nations encompasses a commitment to the protection of its accredited diplomats and employees:

> Representatives of the Members of the United Nations and officials of the Organization shall enjoy such privileges and immunities as are necessary for the independent exercise of their functions in connection with the Organization.[32]

A recurrent challenge to the immunity of officials of the United Nations and other IGOs is the frequent demand of member states that their nationals be cleared prior to employment by an international organization. The result is a conflict of interests, for the IGO seeks to protect the supranational character of its personnel process while the government in question insists that its citizens be politically reliable before being declared eligible for appointment. The issue first arose with the totalitarian states belonging to the League of Nations and has continued in the United Nations. The thankless task of finding a compromise invariably falls on the secretary-general, and no satisfactory formula exists for meeting the contradictory requirement between national obligation and supranational loyalty. To fulfill its mission the IGO must protect

---

[29]See Chapter 10.
[30]C. F. Amerasinghe, *Principles of the Institutional Law of International Organizations* (New York: Cambridge University Press, 1996), p. 374.
[31]Covenant, Article 7(4). See F. P. Walters, *A History of the League of Nations* (New York: Oxford University Press, 1952), p. 47.
[32]Charter, Article 105(2).

its officials in the performance of their duties from dismissal or other punitive actions on the part of their national governments.[33]

The Convention on Diplomatic Relations does not define the word *mission* in its discussion of privileges and immunities in article 39. By inference a reasonable definition of a mission might rely upon the performance of recognized diplomatic functions, such as representation, negotiation, and information, rather than recognition of a territorial state. Function instead of statehood would qualify an entity for the title of mission under the convention. Accordingly, the offices of the European Union (formerly European Community) and of the Organization of American States would meet the treaty test of a mission, and in 1978 the U.S. Congress incorporated the expanded definition into legislation.[34] Diplomatic privileges and immunities now apply to regional IGOs as well as to specialized agencies of the United Nations. Bilateral relations with IGOs represent a new dimension in diplomacy, and the relevant international law is in a developmental stage. The framers of the convention thought exclusively in terms of sovereign states, and the expanded application of the convention is indicative of the teleological approach to treaty interpretation, as defined in the preceding chapter. Necessity requires departing from the literal text of the convention to accommodate changed circumstances.

Two multilateral treaties stand out as being of particular importance in assessing the international legal position of international civil servants. The Convention on Privileges and Immunities of the United Nations (1946) followed a year later by a counterpart convention affording the same protection to the specialized agencies of the world organization. The terms of the former convention guarantee officials of the United Nations immunity from legal and administrative processes with regard to acts performed by them in their official capacity. The grant of immunity is extensive, for it covers some 8,000 members of the Secretariat. The secretary-general has the authority to waive immunity, and in the instance of a dispute the parties have agreed to submit to the judgment of the ICJ.[35] Parallel guarantees of immunity and inviolability of premises apply to specialized agencies. Again, immunity from arrest applies only while fulfilling official duties, and referral of disputes to the ICJ is mandatory.[36]

Three points of comparison highlight the distinction between the privileges and immunities of international civil servants and of diplomats.[37] First, the international organization official who is a citizen of the host state possesses only limited privileges and immunities as compared with a diplomat in a receiving state. Second, the international official is under the jurisdiction of neither the country of origin nor the host state, but the diplomat remains, even when posted abroad, a subject of the laws of his or her home country. Finally, the principle of reciprocity which undergirds the Convention on Diplomatic Relations does not apply to an international civil servant. The host government may not invoke the doctrine of *persona non grata* for an employee of an international

---

[33]Robert S. Jordan, "Law of the International Civil Service," in 2 *United Nations Legal Order,* ed. Oscar Schachter and Christopher C. Joyner (New York: Cambridge University Press, 1995), pp. 1072–1073.

[34]Marian Lloyd Nash, *Digest of United States Practice in International Law, 1978* (Washington, D.C.: Government Printing Office, 1980), p. 584.

[35]Convention on Privileges and Immunities of the United Nations (February 13, 1946), 1 U.N.T.S. 15, 24–26.

[36]Convention on the Privileges and Immunities of the Specialized Agencies (November 21, 1947), 33 U.N.T.S. 261.

[37]D. W. Bowett, *The Law of International Institutions,* 4th ed. (London: Stevens & Sons, 1982), p. 345.

organization, for an official of the United Nations or any other public international organization who is accredited to that body and not to a receiving state.

The application of these principles led to the passage of the International Organizations Immunities Act (1945), which grants immunity to United Nations officials while on duty in the United States.[38] The following year, Secretary of State George C. Marshall and United Nations Secretary-General Trygve Lie concluded the Headquarters Agreement, whereby the United Nations agreed to locate in the United States under the condition of territorial inviolability.[39] Initially the application of the dual principles of immunity and inviolability appeared to be foregone conclusions, but a test case soon appeared. At issue was a charge of espionage. A citizen of the Soviet Union working as an official of the United Nations Secretariat endeavored through clandestine means to acquire sensitive information of the U.S. Department of Justice. Exposure led to a demand for his recall and a denial of immunity as an international civil servant. The official petitioned a U.S. district court and argued the protection of diplomatic immunity associated with the United Nations. Predictably, the court found that espionage was not an official act and noted further that, in apparent violation of the Headquarters Agreement, the U.S. Department of State had never concurred in his appointment.[40] Officially the doctrine of *persona non grata* did not apply although the practical outcome was the same.

A more complex case was that involving the Palestine Liberation Organization (PLO) in 1988. The year before, Congress had passed the Anti-Terrorism Act[41] identifying the PLO as a threat to the nation's security. Pursuant to a resolution of the General Assembly[42] the PLO had permanent observer status at the United Nations, meaning that its representative could vote in committee but not in a plenary session. By 1975, the PLO has established the Permanent Observer Mission in New York, only to have it closed thirteen years later on the authority of the Anti-Terrorism Act. The General Assembly requested an advisory opinion from the ICJ concerning the question of whether the closure violated the diplomatic status guaranteed by the Headquarters Agreement. The ICJ quickly concluded that the United States was under an obligation to arbitrate the dispute.[43] The PLO office remained closed, and the United States denied a visa on November 26, 1988, to Yasir Arafat, the PLO chairman, who had been invited to speak to the General Assembly. The General Assembly then adjourned to Geneva to hear Arafat's address. The Middle East peace process eventually obscured the memory of the episodes with the office and the visa, yet the impingement upon the privileges and immunities of the PLO remains an uncertain legacy.[44]

---

[38] International Organizations Immunities Act (December 20, 1945), Statutes at Large 59: 669, 672.

[39] Headquarters Agreement (June 26, 1947), 22 United States Code 1994 §287, Article 3.

[40] *U.S. v. Coplon and Gubitchev*, 88 F. Supp. 915 (1950), 919, 921. V. A. Gubitchev held the diplomatic rank of third secretary of the Ministry of Foreign Affairs.

[41] Anti-Terrorism Act (December 22, 1987), 100 Stat. 1406.

[42] United Nations, General Assembly, Res. 3237, Observer Status for the Palestine Liberation Organization (22 November 1974), reprinted in Dusan J. Djonovich, *United Nations Resolutions,* Series I: *Resolutions Adopted by the General Assembly* (Dobbs Ferry, N.Y.: Oceana Publications, 1984), 15: 254. Hereafter cited as Djonovich.

[43] Applicability of the Obligations to Arbitrate under Section 21 of the United Nations Headquarters Agreement (April 26, 1988): ICJ Reports, reprinted in 27 I.L.M. 803–804 (1988).

[44] In 2000, a White House spokesperson described an airport "pat-down" and a luggage search of North Korean diplomats en route to the United Nations as a misunderstanding. The diplomats protested and returned home. See "North Koreans, Searched at Airport, Skip Visit," *New York Times,* 6 September 2000, A13.

Permanent members of the staff of regional IGOs also possess immunity, as exemplified by a British statute—the International Organizations (Immunities and Privileges) Act of 1950. Carl-Theo Zoernsch, a German national, brought an action against the president of the European Commission of Human Rights alleging negligence and corruption on the part of the commission in the handling of an appeal to that body. Since the serving president was a British subject, the litigation took place in the United Kingdom and was eventually referred to a three-judge panel of the Court of Appeal. Citing the 1950 act, the court concluded:

> In the case of members of the commission, the immunity conferred is in respect of words spoken or written and all acts done by them in their official capacity, the like immunity from legal process "as is accorded to an envoy of a foreign power accredited to Her Majesty."[45]

Notably, a British court applied the concept of diplomatic privileges and immunities to a British citizen because of his official position with a regional international organization. The increase in number and significance of IGOs has enhanced the precedential value of *Zoernsch*.

DUAL ACCREDITATION

For many governments the cost of maintaining both a United Nations delegation and a consulate in New York City is prohibitive. Consequently they may assign consular duties to a diplomat accredited to the United Nations. While the argument of efficiency is self-evident, the arrangement creates an anomalous situation both because the consular and diplomatic roles serve different functions and because accreditation to the United Nations does not automatically entail an *exequatur* to open a consulate. Accordingly, on June 16, 1958, the U.S. Department of State issued a circular to the effect that the United States would no longer countenance the performance of consular duties by a member of a country delegation at the United Nations.[46] In authentic cases of hardship when the Department of State was prepared to make an exception, the policy would lapse.

The Convention on Consular Relations stipulates in article 17, however, that a consular officer may indeed act as a representative of a government participating in an IGO, provided that prior notification of this arrangement is given to the receiving state. The application of this principle enables members of the U.S. Mission to the European Office of the United Nations in Geneva, Switzerland, to perform consular functions with regard, for example, to visas.[47] Formerly the United States maintained a consulate in Geneva, and its closure resulted in the shifting of designated consular responsibilities to diplomats accredited to the United Nations. The same arrangement is, however, ruled out in New York.

A dualistic role is not confined to delegates to the United Nations, for specialized agencies of the organization may also perform limited consular functions, especially in

---

[45] *Zoernsch v. Waldock and Another* (1964), Court of Appeal, reprinted in 8 *British International Law Cases: 1960–1965* (London: Stevens & Sons, 1971), p. 845.

[46] 7 Whiteman 553–554. The Department of State reiterated the admonition in 1982 and 1984. For the text, see Lee, 607–608.

[47] 7 Whiteman 551–553.

relieving the plight of refugees. Beginning with the League of Nations, the practice of asylum developed from the need to provide international protection to those driven from their homelands by war and persecution. Specifically, the League would certify the documents of refugees and assist in their resettlement.[48] In 1950, the General Assembly passed a resolution detailing the duties of the United Nations High Commissioner for Refugees, and the performance of the required protective functions closely parallels consular activity.[49] The growth of interdependence and corresponding extension of IGOs have created new patterns of diplomatic and consular relations, and the traditional answers to questions about immunity and inviolability no longer suffice.

Topics for Discussion

1. What is the international legal principle of reciprocity? How does its application enable governments to establish and maintain organized relations with each other?
2. What were the issues involved in the *Hostage* case? Even though the respondent government did not appear, the ICJ unanimously approved provisional measures. Why?
3. How do consular privileges and immunities differ from those of diplomats? What are the arguments for and against the dual accreditation of a delegate to the United Nations as a consular officer?
4. Under international law the relationship of a permanent staff member of an intergovernmental organization has a special relationship to (a) his or her national government and (b) the host government. Under customary and conventional law, what distinguishes the position of an international civil servant from that of a diplomat who is posted at an embassy?

---

[48]Arrangement Relating to the Legal Status of Russian and Armenian Refugees (June 30, 1928), 89 L.N.T.S. 55.

[49]United Nations, General Assembly, Res. 428, Statute of the Office of the United Nations High Commissioner for Refugees (December 14, 1950), reprinted in Djonovich 3:120–122.

CHAPTER 15

Prospects

Does international law exist? This question opened the discussion and provides a fitting theme for a concluding commentary. International law does exist, but in comparison with municipal law it is imperfect. Efforts at codification through the formulation of multilateral lawmaking conventions as well as the expansion of traditional definitions of concepts such as state responsibility have often proven successful, yet international law confronts challenges which it appears unable to overcome. In 1958, C. Wilfred Jenks proposed a useful solution in the form of an experimental approach by which he meant that international law is an ongoing process capable of assimilating new ideas and expanding its scope. Jenks drew a parallel between the development of international law and the vital life process of metabolism, for both involve the incorporation of new materials and adaptation to new conditions. In this sense the growth of international is indeed metabolic.[1] Jenks's theory merits a test in three issue areas: statehood, human rights, and law-creating structures.

STATEHOOD

Early in its history, the U.S. Supreme Court confronted the complexity of defining statehood in terms of rights and duties of sovereign entities. Justices John Marshall and Joseph Story authored opinions on such questions as recognition, treaty law, citizenship, neutral rights, belligerency, insurgency, and piracy. These issues involved the exercise of state power in the traditional sense that sovereignty is absolute, and that the role of government is to defend its sovereignty. The concepts of sovereignty, independence, and territorial integrity serve to bring key questions into focus, but the application of these abstractions within the modern international system has evolved to give them new meanings.[2] International law must accommodate these changing circumstances.

The changing definition of sovereign immunity is illustrative of the need for new conceptual thinking. In the traditional framework, sovereignty was an abstraction, for it represented absolute and perpetual authority. Indeed the hallmark of the Peace of Westphalia (1648) was the commitment to the independence of the territorial state from external control. The sovereign, whether a monarch or a legislative assembly, enjoyed immunity in the courts of other states, yet under the impact of a global economy that immunity has undergone a transformation. A suit in federal courts for damages sustained as a result of the seizure of property in violation of international law is permissible under the Foreign Sovereign Immunity Act (1976). Exceptions do apply, in that

---

[1]C. Wilfred Jenks, *The Common Law of Mankind* (London: Stevens & Sons, 1958), p. 167.
[2]James A. Caporasso, "Changes in the Westphalian Order: Territory, Public Authority, and Sovereignty," *International Studies Review* 2 (Summer 2000): 4, 9–10.

acts of war lie outside the law. Nevertheless a state is no longer immune in an absolute sense. State responsibility now balances the act-of-state doctrine, and sovereignty no longer provides a cover for whatever a government may wish to do.

The expanding scope of the humanitarian law of war also occasions a rethinking of sovereignty and statehood. In the *Law of War and Peace* (1625), Hugo Grotius recognized the status of noncombatants in war and argued for their protection. The tradition of chivalry supported the belief that violence used as an instrument of policy must be subordinate to necessity. The wanton resort to violence was recognized both as unlawful and, in the long run, impolitic. A massacre of a U.S. army detachment on the Philippine island of Samar in 1901 triggered a reprisal directed against the alleged offending population. General Jacob Smith, the senior commander, ordered the destruction of guerrilla strongholds and specified that the interior of the island be turned into a "howling wilderness." Although the punitive expedition never took place, the order for the indiscriminate use of violence against a civilian population led to the convening of a court martial in 1902. The court found that General Smith's orders exceeded reasonable military requirements, and he was relieved of command and formally admonished.

Secretary of War Elihu Root reviewed the case and concluded:

> General Smith . . . was guilty of intemperate, inconsiderate, and violent expressions, which, if accepted literally, would grossly violate the humane rules governing American armies in the field.[3]

The precedential value of the decision is that it placed upon the sovereign a legal obligation to moderate the use of violence by imposing standards of humanity on the conduct of military operations. The sovereign was no longer free to employ violence in an unrestricted fashion, and international law imposed a restraint on the exercise of state power.

Following the Second World War military tribunals in Europe and East Asia tried civil and military defendants on charges of crimes against humanity. The outcome was the Genocide Convention (1948),[4] which established a norm of state behavior designed to protect ethnic and religious minorities. The United Nations Security Council gave weight to that norm when it created International Criminal Tribunals for the former Yugoslavia (1993) and for Rwanda (1994). The jurisdiction of the former was declared retroactive to January 1, 1991, and the latter to January 1, 1994.[5] Each Tribunal has a prosecutor empowered to issue indictments, and the former president of Serbia, Slobodan Milosevic, was indicted in 1999 on a charge of political, racial, and religious persecution of the Albanians in the province of Kosovo.[6] Although Milosevic was never apprehended, the indictment did challenge his legitimacy and prepare the way for his overthrow in October 2000. The tribunals have advanced the cause of humanitarian law

---

[3]John Bassett Moore, 7 *International Law*, U.S. Department of State (Washington, D.C.: Government Printing Office, 1906), pp. 187–189.

[4]See Chapter 7.

[5]United Nations, Security Council, Resolution 827, Establishing an International Tribunal for the Prosecution of Persons Responsible for Serious Violations of International Humanitarian Law Committed in the Territory of the Former Yugoslavia (May 25, 1993), reprinted in 32 I.L.M. 1203 (1993), and Resolution 955, Establishing the International Tribunal for Rwanda (November 8, 1994), reprinted in 33 I.L.M. 1600 (1994). The U.S. representative voted for both resolutions.

[6]For the text of the indictment, see *Keesing's Record of World Events* 45 (May 1999): 42958–42959.

by making the law apply to both internal and international conflicts. The precedent established in the *Smith* case now covers civil wars. The arbitrary use of violence against one's own citizens qualifies as an international crime as do violations of the law of war in the struggle against a foreign enemy. If one assumes that the state has the right to take a life, international law now circumscribes that right.

To be effective, codification requires institutionalization. Under the auspices of the United Nations delegates of member states convened in Rome in 1998 for the purpose of drafting the constitutive act of the International Criminal Court (ICC). The resulting Rome Statute has not attracted sufficient states parties to be in effect, yet its principles merit consideration. The Statute represents three significant advances over previous war crimes tribunals. First it creates a standing international tribunal with a fixed complement of justices, a prosecutor, and staff. Second, the applicable humanitarian law already exists, notably but not exclusively the Genocide Convention and the four Geneva conventions (1949) sponsored by the International Red Cross/Red Crescent Societies. The question of whether to apply ex post facto law (i.e., law made after the fact) does not arise. Third, the statute provides for an appellate court, which will review verdicts of the trial court. The jurisdiction of the court extends to four categories of cases: (a) genocide as defined under the convention of 1948, (b) crimes against humanity to include murder, extermination, and enslavement, (c) war crimes encompassing the maltreatment of prisoners and the taking of hostages, and (d) aggression as a delict under international law.[7] Of particular importance is the coverage extended by the statute to internal wars and the jurisdiction of the court over those crimes against humanity committed outside of a state of war.

Conspiracy to wage a war of aggression remains undefined, and the tribunal must await further clarification of the law before hearing cases on this offense. The other offenses are well defined with the result that the Statute upholds three key principles of international criminal law. The first is *non bis in idem* (not for the second time), meaning that an individual indicted and tried for a war crime by a national court is not subject to trial a second time by the ICC. The provision applies, however, only if the offense charged at the national level was specifically a war crime rather than, for example, murder. The second is *nullum crimen sine lege* (no crime without law), which requires that defendants be bound over for trial on specific charges under existing humanitarian law. The third is *nulla poena sine lege* (no punishment without law) requiring a fixed sentencing schedule and, above all, banning capital punishment. These three principles serve to fulfill the dual requirements of equal protection and due process. The Statute both contributed to the codification of humanitarian law and established the structures necessary to administer it.

The United States did not sign the Statute, and American critics of the accord abound. Senator Jesse Helms responded as chair of the Committee on Foreign Relations that the ICC would sit in judgment on American vital interests, and he concluded that the United States would never extradite any accused person to the jurisdiction of the court.[8] Reflecting a more moderate point of view, Ruth Wedgwood has urged a

---

[7]Rome Statute of the International Criminal Court (July 17, 1998) reprinted in 37 I.L.M. 1002, 1003–1007 (1998).
[8]Jesse Helms, "Slay This Monster," *Financial Times,* 30 July 1998, 12.

diplomatic effort to improve the Statute so that judicial safeguards will mollify critics. Linking law and policy, she observed that for the United States to play an effective role in world politics it must combine power with legitimacy, which is a lesson as ancient as statecraft.[9] Leadership carries with it responsibility, and the United States would be remiss in allowing an opportunity to create the Court to slip away. Perfection will always elude the drafters of a treaty, especially a complex one on the order of the Rome Statute, and compromise is essential in order to attain the goal of a rule of law.

HUMAN RIGHTS

The notion of modern statehood lacks the iron logic of European political theorists of the seventeenth and eighteenth centuries. Sovereignty is neither absolute nor perpetual. The norms of international law, often interpreted and enforced by the United Nations Security Council, weaken the notion of the impermeable state with the result that sovereignty has become a matter of the performance of given tasks, some of which are assigned to intergovernmental organizations and others are retained by the nation state. The protection of basic human rights is an example. Through the General Assembly and the Commission on Human Rights, the United Nations is able to amass information and pass declaratory resolutions condemning violations of human rights. In 1994 diplomatic pressure exerted by the United Nations finally brought to an end the regime of apartheid in South Africa. The process moves with glacial speed, but it does move. Noncoercive influence may in the long run be more effective than military action. Governments strive for legitimacy, which reflects legal, moral, and political authority.[10] The protection of human rights is the hallmark of normative legitimacy.

Regional organizations may offer a more promising institutional means of upholding international human rights law. The European Court of Human Rights (ECHR)[11] and to a lesser extent the Inter-American Court of Human Rights both offer a judicial response to violations of human rights. As created by the Council of Europe whose members elect its judges, the ECHR receives applications for redress directly from individuals and represents therefore the highest level of appeal for those seeking relief of human rights violations in the states' parties to the European Convention on Human Rights (1950–1998). Although the greatest number of cases heard by the ECHR are appeals from national tribunals, the court also renders decisions in disputes between contracting states. The court functions through screening committees and chambers. Once an appeal has been certified, the case goes to a chamber of seven judges or in cases affecting constitutive treaties to a Grand Chamber of seventeen judges. Of the forty states parties to the European convention, some thirty-six have accepted the optional clause establishing the compulsory jurisdiction of the court.[12]

---

[9]Ruth Wedgwood, "Fiddling in Rome: America and the International Criminal Court," *Foreign Affairs* 77 (November–December 1998): 20–23.

[10]David P. Forsythe, *Human Rights and Peace: International and National Dimensions* (Lincoln: University of Nebraska Press, 1993), pp. 71–73.

[11]The European Court of Human Rights should not be confused with the European Court of Justice. The former is an organ of the Council of Europe and the latter of the European Union.

[12]Compulsory jurisdiction is often a controversial issue, and some governments have attached reservations in the form of time limits or other restrictions to their ratifications.

Two cases are illustrative of the work of the court and its contribution to the development of regional international law. The first concerned the Mediterranean Republic of Cyprus, divided de facto since 1974 between the Greek and Turkish communities. Troops of the Republic of Turkey garrison the Turkish Cypriot northern third of the island, and a United Nations demilitarized zone separates it from the Greek Cypriot south. Nevertheless the international community recognizes a de jure unified state, which is temporarily divided. A Greek Cypriot appealed to the court on the grounds of being denied access to property in the northern area.

Authorities there countered that the lawful government is that of the Turkish Republic of Northern Cyprus (TRNC) proclaimed in 1983 as a separate state, but as yet unrecognized by all but Turkey. The Grand Chamber had to decide if the TRNC was an independent state or an area of the Republic of Cyprus under Turkish military occupation. If the TRNC was a sovereign legal personality, then the applicant's property rights would be subject to local laws. Conversely, if northern Cyprus were a zone of military occupation, the applicant's right of access was unlawfully barred. The court decided by a split vote that northern Cyprus was indeed under a regime of military occupation and, in doing so endorsed the applicant's petition.[13] The case had a far-reaching effect, for the division of a number of European states, especially the Soviet Union and Yugoslavia, has created disputed areas under military control. Chechnya is but one example. In this instance the court rendered a judgment that could affect a number of European states undergoing internal divisions.

The second case also involved the effect of internal conflict on human rights. The applicants were Kurdish citizens of Turkey living in the southeastern region of the republic, where a decades-old struggle for Kurdish nationhood was being waged. Turkish security forces entered their village and in the process of countering insurgency burned their homes. The applicants turned to the court for restitution. The government of Turkey responded that the court lacked jurisdiction because the applicants had not exhausted all local remedies under Turkish law. The Grand Chamber certified the application on its merits after determining that the district prosecutor in Turkey had failed to pursue the matter. Damages for the destroyed homes were awarded.[14]

An unresolved question is whether decisions of the ECHR are binding *erga omnes*. The court's decision in the *Soering* case hinged on the issue of capital punishment, and the ruling made it clear that the court viewed the probable imposition of the death penalty as reason enough to argue against extradition.[15] Governments not subject to the judgment were not bound by it. Similarly the decision in the *Loizidou* case not to grant recognition to the Turkish Republic of Northern Cyprus was not binding on other European states. The court's moral authority may extend beyond the case at hand, but its judgments are specific to the parties concerned.[16] The principal contribution of the European Convention on Human Rights and the court it created is the realization of a collective guarantee of human rights.[17] To that extent, the members of the Council of Europe have set a high

---

[13] *Case of Loizidou v. Turkey* (December 18, 1996), reprinted in 36 I.L.M. 440 (1997).
[14] *Case of Mentes and Others v. Turkey* (November 28, 1997), reprinted in 37 I.L.M. 862 (1998).
[15] See Chapter 7.
[16] D. J. Harris et al., *Law of the European Convention on Human Rights* (London: Butterworths, 1995), p. 648.
[17] Francis G. Jacobs and Robin C. A. White, *The European Convention on Human Rights,* 2nd ed. (New York: Oxford University Press, 1996), p. 6.

standard of communal responsibility for the protection of basic human values. Will other regions follow, or is the European endeavor an isolated experiment?

Latin America is developing regional institutions designed to achieve the European goal of a collective guarantee of human rights. In 1948, the American Declaration of the Rights and Duties of Man issued in conjunction with the Bogotá Charter of the Organization of American States (OAS) enunciated the basic principles of human rights.[18] The declaration was not binding in the sense that it did not create legal obligations, but the U.S. delegate still abstained from signing, thereby setting a precedent for future regional human rights acts. The next step was the conclusion of the American Convention on Human Rights in 1969 embodying obligations that were both absolute and immediate.[19] To achieve implementation the convention designated two new institutions—the Inter-American Commission on Human Rights and the Inter-American Court of Human Rights. They serve separate but complementary purposes. Although the former had functioned in a limited fashion since 1960, it developed into its present form after the adherence of twenty-two states parties gave the convention the force of regional law. The commission may receive complaints from persons, groups, or governments. Inquiry into these matters leads to the presentation of country studies to the OAS, to which the commission also functions as a human rights adviser.[20] The court consists of seven judges elected by the General Assembly of the OAS, and only governments appear before it.[21] Unlike the ECHR, individuals may not petition the Inter-American Court for redress of a human rights violation. Twenty-two governments have adhered to the Inter-American Convention on Human Rights, and twelve have accepted the Court of Human Rights. As was the case in Europe, the progressive protection of human rights follows an incremental course and may be beset with setbacks. Nevertheless, fifty years of effort since the Universal Declaration of Human Rights by the United Nations are beginning to show results.

The Inter-American Court of Human Rights is also empowered to provide advisory opinions, and these have developed into an alternative human rights appeal. In 1997, Mexico turned to the court for an advisory opinion concerning the notification of aliens detained by authorities of their right to consular assistance, as specified under the Convention on Consular Relations (1963).[22] The United States submitted a statement to the effect that the request for an advisory opinion was in reality a complaint stemming from the sometimes failure of local law enforcement officers to abide by the rule of notification. The court rejected this position and delivered an advisory opinion in 1999 to the effect that the convention not only regulated consular relations among governments, but also created a positive human right inherent in the principle of due process. While the Inter-American Convention on Human Rights does not ban the death penalty, the treaty stipulates that the imposition of this punishment requires careful attention to

---

[18]For the text of the American Declaration of the Rights and Duties of Man (April 1948), see Ian Brownlie, *Basic Documents on Human Rights* (New York: Oxford University Press, 1971), pp. 389–395.
[19]American Convention on Human Rights (1969, in force 1978), reprinted in Brownlie, *Basic Documents on Human Rights,* 399–427. For a commentary, see Paul Sieghart, *The International Law of Human Rights* (New York: Oxford University Press, 1971), 57.
[20]Sieghart, 401–407.
[21]Inter-American Court of Human Rights, reprinted in 9 I.L.M. 673.
[22]The *Breard* (Chapter 3) and the *LaGrand* (Chapter 14) cases are relevant.

the rights of the accused, and the Inter-American Court did not fail to emphasize the point that the protection of the defendant's rights depends upon the adherence to procedural standards.[23] The advisory opinion directs attention to a fundamental shift in opinion regarding the nature of international law, namely, a revival of interest in the precepts of natural law. The Austinian tradition of positive law centers on the command relationship of the sovereign to the citizen and often results in the veneration of the state to the exclusion of other values. Conversely, natural law focuses on inherent rights, in this instance the right to life, which are beyond compromise by the sovereign. International tribunals, whether universal or regional, have revived the debate between naturalists and positivists to the benefit of the international community.

A lingering problem in human rights law is enforcement with regard to the political organization of the territory of the state concerned. In the 1950s and 1960s, human rights treaties often included a clause recognizing the internal division of powers of federations and allowing them to adapt the implementation of the agreements to their special constitutional requirements. The Convention on the Status of Refugees (1951) contained a federal clause, which relieved governments of federations of their responsibility for those treaty stipulations falling under the jurisdiction of constituent states or provinces.[24] Federal governments did, however, incur a responsibility to urge the adoption of relevant treaty provisions by subnational authorities. Similarly, in 1992, the U.S. Senate approved the International Covenant on Civil and Political Rights (1966) with the understanding that the treaty would require implementing legislation to be enacted in accordance with the traditions of American federalism.[25] More recent human rights accords, such as those establishing the rights of women and children,[26] identify state responsibility with the national government, irrespective of its internal constitutional arrangements.

LAW-CREATING STRUCTURES

Traditional international law assigned subject status exclusively to a sovereign state. If an individual had a claim for damages against a foreign government, his or her own government had to press the claim. As noted in the discussion of jurisdiction, a general commission organized by the governments of Mexico and the United States investigated and resolved claims for damages brought by the citizens of one state against the government of the other. Through a process best described by Jenks in his metaphor on metabolism, international law has expanded the notion of subject status to include three new legal personalities: intergovernmental organizations, ethnic groups, and in some cases individuals. The widening definition of subject status implies a need to revisit the absolutist concept of sovereignty as it arose from the Peace of Westphalia (1648). State practice remains the basis of international law, but that practice must now take into account international actors previously excluded from the pattern of inter-

---

[23]William J. Aceves, "Case Report: The Right to Information on Consular Assistance in the Framework of the Guarantees of the Due Process of Law," *American Journal of International Law* 94 (July 2000): 555, 558.

[24]Convention Relating to the Status of Refugees (July 28, 1951), 19 U.S.T. 6259, 6279.

[25]U.S. Senate, Committee on Foreign Relations, *Report on the International Covenant on Civil and Political Rights*, 102nd Cong., 2nd sess., 1992, reprinted in 31 I.L.M. 645, 656–657 (1992).

[26]See Chapter 7.

state relations. By analogy the civil rights movement of the 1960s broadened the base of American politics and required adaptation on the part of the political system.

Expanding the domain of international law has created questions with which the established institutions of the international system could not cope. Arms control is illustrative of the point. The Hague Conferences of 1899 and 1907 brought together delegations from Europe, Asia, and the Americas for the purpose of establishing rules of international behavior designed to limit the level of violence in the international system. While certain agreements appear outmoded (e.g., the ban on dropping projectiles from balloons), the principle of subjecting the weapons and tactics of war to the rule of law was established. In 1925, the Geneva Protocol sponsored by the International Committee of the Red Cross banned the first use of asphyxiating gases on the battlefield on the thesis that the indiscriminate use of a weapon of mass destruction was contrary to international humanitarian law. During the Second World War, the tactic of area bombing of civilian centers culminating in the use of nuclear weapons against the cities of Hiroshima and Nagasaki led to renewed attention of the question of whether certain weaponry exceeded the limits of military necessity.

The United Nations serves as a forum within which to focus attention on weapons of mass destruction. At the request of the General Assembly and the World Health Organization, the ICJ prepared an advisory opinion on nuclear weapons in 1996. Mohammed Bedjaoui, the then president of the court, opened the discussion with an opinion founded on the basic principle of humanitarian law condemning the wanton use of military force. Opposed to this precept is the right of survival inherent in every state, which in extreme situations might require a resort to nuclear weapons.[27] The two principles clash, and the ICJ sought to find a synthesis with the result that both sides of the question were displeased. The end of the Cold War engendered the hope that the major powers would make a concerted effort to create a nonnuclear world.[28] The prospects appear dim, especially in view of the nuclear tests conducted by India and Pakistan in 1998. Nevertheless the Comprehensive Test Ban Treaty opened for signature in 1996 shortly after the ICJ's advisory opinion holds out the hope that the spread of nuclear weapons may eventually be halted.[29] Similar efforts designed to spare unoffending civilians the horrors of war are the proposed multilateral ban on antipersonnel mines[30] and the prohibition of chemical weapons.[31] Progress toward arms reduction, if not outright disarmament, is slow but not without hope.

Related to arms control is the complex of issues surrounding the preservation of the environment. International conferences held in Stockholm (1972) and Rio de Janeiro (1996) prepared the way for a series of agreements, the last of which was the Kyoto Protocol (1997). This protocol represented an effort to formulate an international

[27]International Court of Justice: Advisory Opinion on the Legality of the Threat or Use of Nuclear Weapons (July 8, 1996), reprinted in 35 I.L.M. 1345, 1347 (1996).

[28]Max Singer and Aaron Wildavsky, *The Real World Order: Zones of Peace/Zones of Turmoil,* rev. ed. (Chatham, N.J.: Chatham House Publishers, 1996), chapter four.

[29]Comprehensive Nuclear Test-Ban Treaty (September 10, 1996), U.S. Arms Control and Disarmament Agency (Washington, D.C.: Government Printing Office, 1998).

[30]Convention on the Prohibition of the Use, Stockpiling, Production and Transfer of Anti-Personnel Mines and Their Destruction (September 18, 1997), reprinted in 36 I.L.M. 1507 (1997).

[31]Convention on the Prohibition of the Development, Production, Stockpiling and Use of Chemical Weapons and on Their Destruction," (November 30, 1992), U.S. Arms Control and Disarmament Agency (Washington, D.C.: Government Printing Office, 1993).

code of environmental law and thereby accomplish what the law of the sea conference had achieved for the oceans in 1982. In both instances the task was monumental, but persistence had led to the nearly universal adoption of the Convention on the Law of the Sea, which encourages those searching for a solution to such problems as global warming and the depletion of the ozone layer. An international conference system operating under the auspices of the United Nations provides the framework for defining the obligations *erga omnes* essential to international environmental law. The preservation of the environment is a legal duty performed in support of human rights. The right to life is a concomitant of the battle against pollution.[32]

The United Nations Framework Convention on Climate Change (1992) underlined the principle of state responsibility for the preservation of the environment and set differentiated goals for the developed and less developed countries.[33] The convention established a secretariat to administer its standards and stipulated a recourse either to the ICJ or to arbitration in the event of a dispute. The essential elements for an international legal regime were in place, such as normative principles, implementing rules, and a structure capable of administration. Nevertheless, as in the case of the threat or use of nuclear weapons, tension exists between the ideal of sovereign equality and the need to bend to the will of the community. The contrapuntal effect created by the demand for sovereignty as opposed to the global interest in the environment came to the forefront at the United Nations Conference on Environment and Development (Rio de Janeiro, 1992). Deforestation of the Amazon River valley had become an environmental issue, and the conferees formulated the following nonbinding statement of principle:

> States have, in accordance with the Charter of the United Nations and the principles of international law, the sovereign right to exploit their own resources pursuant to their own environmental policies and have the responsibility to ensure that activities within their jurisdiction or control do not cause damage to the environment of other States or areas beyond the limits of national jurisdiction.
>
> * * *
>
> States have the sovereign and inalienable right to utilize, manage and develop their forests in accordance with their development needs and level of socio-economic development and on the basis of national policies. . . .[34]

The statement opens with an appeal to state responsibility through the exercise of restraint in the crosscutting of timber and immediately retreats behind the territorial supremacy of the sovereign state.

The ambiguity in the foregoing statement led to the convening of a consultative meeting in 1995 for the purpose of trying to set environmental standards and a binding

---

[32]W. Paul Gormley, "The Legal Obligation of the International Community to Guarantee a Pure and Decent Environment: The Expansion of Human Rights Norms," *Georgetown International Environmental Law Review* 3 (Summer 1990): 85, 111.

[33]Framework Convention on Climate Change (May 9, 1992), reprinted in 31 I.L.M. 851 (1992).

[34]Statement of Principles for a Global Consensus on the Management, Conservation and Sustainable Development of All Types of Forests (June 13, 1992), United Nations Conference on Environment and Development, reprinted in 31 I.L.M. 882, 883 (1992).

target date for the accomplishment.[35] The resulting Berlin mandate for further development provided a basis for a general conference in Kyoto (1997). The hitherto latent cleavage between the developed and less developed countries became apparent. The Kyoto Protocol required that the industrialized states of Europe, North America, Japan, and Australasia accept specified limits on the annual emissions of greenhouse gases, and that these limits be attained by specific target dates. Less developed countries experiencing rapid industrialization, such as China and India, were exempted. Each state party to the protocol agreed to lower emissions of greenhouse gases by five per cent of the 1990 level within the commitment period 2008 to 2012. The protocol called upon all states parties to take ". . . into account their common but differentiated responsibilities and their specific national and regional development priorities, objectives and circumstances. . . ." in working toward the achievement of the treaty's goals.[36] Australia, Canada, and the United States as well as the European Union raised the issue of parity of obligations, and the protocol failed to find universal acceptance. While most governments support the principle of state responsibility inherent in international environmental law, the stipulation regarding differentiated responsibilities is politically unacceptable. The impasse has yet to be overcome.

A LOOK AHEAD

The origins of modern international law are ancient. In the tradition of Hindu statecraft, Kautilya laid down rules for international agreements and the conduct of diplomatic relations. The Stoics of Athens and Rome provided a philosophical basis for the doctrine of equality which is the underpinning of contemporary human rights law. The metabolic process is slow, indeed often to the point of frustration, and setbacks will occur. Experimentation offers a pragmatic solution to the problem of codification, for progress will vary from subject to subject. In the 1960s, the development of the law of the sea appeared to be at a standstill only to be overcome by the Third United Nations Conference on the Law of the Sea (1973–1982), resulting in a constitution for the oceans. International environmental law is now in the same state, but with persistence it, too, can be moved forward. Overall the record is positive, for multilateral lawmaking conventions now address such problems as the rights and duties of states, human rights, diplomatic and consular relations, and state responsibility. Moreover, the International Court of Justice and regional tribunals, notably the European Court of Human Rights, supply authoritative responses to many issues in international law. Well-defined structures now provide legal answers to questions that in an earlier age would have gone unanswered. That the prospects for international law are good should not, however, distort our vision. Positivism continues to make law the servant of the state in contrast to naturalism which requires the state to adhere to universal legal norms. Challenges in the form of statist ideologies and parochial nationalism will slow the process toward world order, but the forces of interdependence are too strong to be overcome. Governments now recognize the necessity of international law, and this recognition augurs well for the future.

---

[35]Clare Breidenich et al., "The Kyoto Protocol to the United Nations Framework Convention on Climate Change," *American Journal of International Law* 99 (April 1998): 315, 330.

[36]Kyoto Protocol to the Framework Convention on Climate Change (December 10, 1997), reprinted in 37 I.L.M. 32, 36 (1998).

Topics for Discussion

1. Jenks's theory of the metabolism of international law relies upon experimentation as the means of evolving solutions rather than lawmaking conventions that may have the effect of freezing the law and inhibiting change. Are general international conferences designed to codify the law really agents for progress? Or should one look for ad hoc solutions?
2. The impermeability of the state is central to the historical theory of sovereignty. How have intergovernmental organizations (IGOs) brought about a redefinition of sovereignty to mean the fulfillment of functions rather than an absolutist exercise of power?
3. How is the International Covenant on Civil and Political Rights (ICCPR) related to the Kyoto Protocol? Is a halt to environmental degradation a precondition for defending the right to life?
4. In the modern period, constitutional and representative forms of government have taken the lead in the development of international law. Does pluralist democracy necessarily favor the growth of world law, or is an elitist government more effective in furthering this process?

APPENDIX

Research and Writing in International Law

Conducting research in international law poses a challenge not found in the study of municipal law. Guides in electronic and print format enable the researcher to survey quickly the legal history of a statute, yet such guides are unavailable for the study of customary or conventional international law. In this context, one must make a distinction between international law viewed narrowly as the application of American law to foreign situations and the broader view of international law as the rules which govern the relations among states. In the latter sense the study of international law demands patience and persistence, for the available research aids focus only on a single code of municipal law. The internet itself offers an array of new sources, and the dedicated researcher will find exploring the worldwide web a productive exercise. The following five steps identify the checkpoints in the development of a successful paper.

SELECTING A TOPIC

The initial step of selecting a topic is deceptively simple because of the tendency to identify an overly broad theme. A careful honing of the topic is essential. Otherwise the researcher runs the risk of moving in several different directions at once. With the topic in hand, the next step is the formulation of a thesis statement. For example, the establishment balance-of-power system after the Peace of Westphalia (1648) led to the development of modern international law. In this example, the growth of international law is dependent upon the existence of a multipolar international system. The system is the causal variable, whose persistence over time broadens the scope of international law. Does the evolution of international law depend upon a particular type of international system? The relationship between system and law is the thesis statement around which the paper is organized. The topic and thesis statement are a message to the reader and should receive emphasis in the opening passages of the paper.

SURVEY OF THE LITERATURE

The development of the thesis statement requires a survey of the literature to determine what has been written and to identify the gaps in existing research. Following the example of the balance of power and international law, the search would focus on writings on the international system as it relates to international law. Central to this theme is a foundation study by Morton A. Kaplan and Nicholas de B. Katzenbach.[1] The authors relate changes in the international system to step-level changes in international law and thereby demonstrate the covariant relationship between diplomacy and law. The researcher will note that the work centers on European diplomacy and may well

---

[1] Morton A. Kaplan and Nicholas de B. Katzenbach, *The Political Foundations of International Law* (New York: John Wiley, 1961).

ask if the relationship applies to other areas of the world. For example, does the fact that international law plays a major role in the Latin American tradition of diplomacy reflect the existence of a balance of power among the republics of South America? The question is intriguing and deserves attention.

The search will encompass public documents (such as those reprinted in the *International Legal Materials* series published by the American Society of International Law), books, and journal articles. It should not, however, stop with materials in print. The internet offers a wealth of up-to-date information. The American Society of International Law has a website (http://www.asil.org) as do the United Nations and the International Court of Justice. The European Court of Human Rights posts its recent decisions and coming agenda on the web. Regional intergovernmental organizations and foreign embassies also release international legal documents through the World-Wide Web. Materials in print are the starting point, but the careful researcher will turn to the internet for current developments.

RESEARCH SKILLS

General education endows the researcher with special skills, which may be either qualitative or quantitative. The researcher may have a particular interest in Latin America and be willing to read documents in Spanish or Portuguese. A knowledge of French in the study of the International Court of Justice or other tribunals is useful. Secondary literature in a variety of foreign languages will often prove indispensable. The challenge of using foreign-language materials may at first be daunting, but with practice the writer derives the benefit of access to new and stimulating ideas.

The application of quantitative techniques is also rewarding. A groundbreaking study is the investigation by John King Gamble into the types of multilateral treaties most susceptible to reservations imposed by states parties.[2] Using tabular data, Gamble studied the proportion of multilateral treaty commitments to which reservations have been attached. By comparison Frank Horn analyzed the question of reservations from an historical perspective. He used illustrative cases as the basis for generalizations, such as setting the temporal limits within which reservations must be made.[3] Both approaches, the one emphasizing quantitative and the other qualitative data, illuminate the problem. While the dominant paradigm in the study of international law is historical and institutional, the development of new skills will enhance the quality of research.

PRESENTATION OF FINDINGS

The writer's three good and faithful friends are unity, coherence, and emphasis. Unity requires adherence to a well-honed outline. Once presented, the thesis statement should run like a leitmotiv through the paper. Digressions distract the reader and weaken the thrust of the argument. Coherence refers not only to the accurate usage of words and to adherence to the rules of grammar, but also to a style of writing that is unencumbered

---

[2]John King Gamble, "Reservations to Multilateral Treaties: A Macroscopic View of State Practice," 74 *American Journal of International Law* (April 1980): 372.
[3]Frank Horn, *Reservations and Interpretative Declarations to Multilateral Treaties* (Amsterdam and New York: North-Holland, 1988), p. 139.

by needless jargon. In Chapter 1, the German words *realpolitik* and *idealpolitik* were juxtaposed. The former is an established concept in the study of international politics, but the latter may appear as a neologism, that is, a new word qualifying as little more than slang. Nevertheless, idealpolitik is gaining acceptance in the language of diplomacy.[4] The word *ideal* serves as what lexicographers term a "combining form," in that it is often joined with a noun to enhance meaning. For example, one may speak of an ideal type, which is rendered as *idealtyp*. Nevertheless, the writer should take care not to use words outside of their normal meaning, for that defeats the goal of coherence.

Emphasis is the third friend. The reader should never lose sight of the thesis statement, and both the introduction and the conclusion should emphasize the theme of the research. In fact, some authors write the introduction after they have finished the main body of the paper, but the practice is of doubtful value. A carefully crafted introduction leading into a general discussion is invaluable. The conclusions should draw together the various skeins of the research into a meaningful pattern. Highlighting the major points is essential, and while one should avoid redundancy, a limited amount of repetition may be useful.

CONTRIBUTION

Research in international law should make a contribution to the field through one of two ways: either validating or invalidating a theoretical proposition. Again taking the previous example of the balance of power and the development of international law, a case study of European diplomacy from the Congress of Vienna (1815) to the Crimean War (1853–1856) would reveal the workings of a multipolar system that brought about international conventions on such matters as diplomacy, the internationalization of major rivers, the protection of religious minorities, and the ban on the slave trade. The covariant relationship between a stable balance-of-power system and the advance of international law is apparent. Conversely, the bipolarity of the Cold War, which ended with the destruction of the Berlin Wall in 1989, offered little encouragement to the advocates of international law. Is one led to the conclusion that a particular type of international system, either multipolar or bipolar, is a precondition for international law? Such a conclusion would result in other case studies and an enhancement of the field. Research strategy requires a proposal capable of making a useful contribution to the study of international law.

---

[4]For a case in point, see Strobe Talbott, "Democracy and the National Interest," 75 *Foreign Affairs* (November-December 1996): 47. The author writes of a foreign policy rooted in both idealpolitik and realpolitik (p. 49).

GLOSSARY

The definitions provide a contextual rather than a literal translation. Unless otherwise indicated, all expressions are in Latin. Foreign expressions incorporated into standard English do not appear in italics.

a posteriori   A principle derived from observation and experience, as in the case of customary international law.

a priori   A principle based on reason and applied deductively, as in the case of conventional international law.

ab initio   From the beginning. A treaty may be nullified *ab initio*. Cf. *ex nunc, ex tunc.*

agrément   (French) The acceptance by the receiving government of the ambassador nominated by the sending government.

amicus curiae   Literally a friend of the court; often an expert witness.

bellum injustum   An unjust war, implying an act of aggression of one state against another.

bellum justum   A just war, one usually waged in self-defense.

casus foederis   The operative condition leading to the implementation of a treaty of alliance.

corpus separatum   An entity within but not of a state, for example, the Free City of Danzig under the League of Nations (1920–1940).

debellatio   Extinction of an enemy state in war.

de facto   An assessment based on fact rather than legal norms, for example, the recognition of a government de facto.

de jure   An assessment based on the satisfaction of normative legal requirements, for example, the recognition of a government de jure.

erga omnes   Legal obligations toward all, usually with reference to human rights or to the environment.

ex aequo et bono   A judicial decision rendered on the basis of fairness and equity as opposed to a strict interpretation of black letter law.

ex injuria non oritur jus   Law may not always arise from an injury, meaning that an unintended injury may not be imputable to a government, for example, damages resulting from a civil war.

ex nunc   From this point in time onward, usually with reference to the abrogation of a treaty.

ex post facto   A law enacted after the fact, which either makes a given act a crime or increases the penalty for the same. Although generally forbidden, an ex post facto law may be used to rectify human rights offenses committed by a dictatorship.

ex proprio motu   The part of a judicial proceeding that takes place on its own accord; for example, the Rome Statute (1998) incorporates the phrase with reference to the trial of accused war criminals.

ex tunc   From a given date in the past; for example a treaty may be terminated as of the date of signature. The quadripartite Munich Agreement (1938) was declared invalid *ex tunc.*

inter alia   A reference to a particular legal point among others, implying that other issues may also be considered.

jus ad bellum   The law governing the resort to war, implying the argument of self-defense, as compared with *jus in bello* or humanitarian law.

jus cogens   Peremptory norms of international law, a doctrine often associated with the Global South as opposed to the emphasis on treaty law propounded by the Global North.

jus dispositivium   Point of law decided by a court, as compared with *jus cogens.*

jus gentium   Law of the peoples as defined by Roman jurisprudence.

jus in bello   The law of war as applied to the conduct of operations.

jus inter gentes   Law among peoples or the law of nations.

jus naturale   Natural law establishing the equality of rights among individuals.

jus sanguinis   Law of the blood, referring to the acquisition of citizenship based on the nationality of one's parents.

jus soli   Law of the soil or the acquisition of citizenship based on place of birth.

lex ferenda   The law which ought to be.

lex lata   The law which is in being.

mare clausam Enclosed seas over which the coastal sovereign exercises jurisdiction.

mare liberum Freedom of the seas, a doctrine propounded by Hugo Grotius.

non bis in idem A defendant may not be tried twice for the same offense. The Rome Statute precludes trial by the International Criminal Court if a national tribunal has already ruled on the case.

nulla poena sine lege No punishment without law, a doctrine designed to prevent arbitrary sentencing of those convicted of crimes.

nullum crimen sine lege No crime without law, a doctrine designed to bar prosecution based on laws enacted after the fact (i.e., ex post facto laws).

pacta sunt servanda Treaties are to be observed, for they represent binding contracts between states.

persona non grata A declaration by the host government that a diplomatic representative of another government is no longer welcome and must leave the country, usually within 24 hours.

raison d'état (French) or ***Staatsraison*** (German) Reason of state implying that the doctrine of necessity overrides the requirement to obey international law.

rebus sic stantibus A treaty remains valid so long as the conditions under which it was signed continue in effect. The doctrine rejects the contractual view of treaties and allows for unilateral denunciation by a state party.

res communis Territory held in common, for example, Antarctica.

res judicata A matter already resolved by the decision of a court and presumed settled.

res nullius Territory belonging to no one and therefore open to acquisition by a state, for example, a newly formed volcanic island.

status quo ante bellum A determination in a peace agreement that the sovereign jurisdiction of the warring states over territory should remain the same as before the outbreak of hostilities.

thalweg (German) The most navigable channel providing a riparian boundary between two adjacent states.

travaux préparatoires (French) Background documents leading to the conclusion of a treaty and therefore evidence as to the meaning of the terms of the agreement.

uti possidetis As you possess it or the doctrine that territory seized in war may be claimed by the sovereign occupying power.

INDEX